Sporting Colours

Sporting Colours

Sport and Politics in South Africa

Mihir Bose

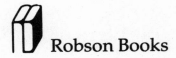

Robson Books

First published in Great Britain in 1994 by Robson Books Ltd, Bolsover House, 5–6 Clipstone Street, London W1P 7EB

British Library Cataloguing in Publication Data
A catalogue record for this title is available from the British Library

Phototypeset by Intype, London
Printed and bound in Great Britain by Hartnolls Ltd, Bodmin, Cornwall

To Chordi, Tapanda and
Anjali for more things than
I care to enumerate.

Contents

Acknowledgements

Books can be conceived in the most unlikely circumstances, but the lunch that led to this book must be the most unusual I have ever had.

In the summer of 1989, Ali Bacher shocked the cricket world by announcing yet another rebel tour. That night I wrote a piece in the *Spectator* which made it very clear that I saw the white South African sports administrator as a threat to organized sport. The boycott of white South Africa has been one of the great issues of our time and ever since the D'Oliveira affair had made me aware of how the white regime in South Africa worked I had no hesitation in supporting the boycott. It amazed me that otherwise rational people, whose company I enjoyed and whose judgement I valued, could not see the stark moral choices the sports boycott presented.

It is much to the credit of the *Spectator* that despite the fact that the tone of the article was much against the line of the paper, the piece was run as I wrote it, although Dominic Lawson, the then deputy editor, suggested that in future when writing against the grain of the paper I should not take such a tough line. However, what I could not have anticipated was the unexpected fallout from the article.

Nick Gordon, the then editor of *You*, the *Mail on Sunday* colour magazine, thought it would be a good idea if I went out to South Africa to examine cricket and interview Bacher. Bacher was due in London and we met for lunch at a hotel in Surrey. Bacher went into lunch thinking Gordon was the editor of the *Spectator*, he still had this notion when I arrived in South Africa a few weeks later to report on Bacher's township programme and the developing opposition to the tour. Although that was five years ago, and the gestation period for this book has been like the birth of an elephant, that marked the true beginnings of this book.

So my first thanks go to Dominic Lawson for commissioning that piece in the *Spectator*. I must also thank Nick Gordon for first opening a window on South African cricket, and Rod Tyler, who wrote some marvellous articles on South Africa for *You*, lent me his wonderful interview with Steve Tshwete which supplemented the one I had done myself.

Since then I have been to South Africa several times and there are a great many people there whose time, help and kindness has made this book possible. First of all Ali Bacher, his wife Shira, and their splendid family. Bacher may not be quite the saint that some people suggest he is, but it's almost impossible to dislike him, his capacity to reach out to people across all sorts of divides is quite legendary.

I have also benefitted from the extensive Bacher network, and to mention them all would be impossible. The lovely Bridget Sprague who, until fairly recently, was Bacher's secretary, Trish Lewis, June Gleason and all the other girls in his office, deserve many thanks for the patient manner and unfailing good cheer with which they dealt with my numerous queries.

The Bacher network also introduced me to three of the most remarkable cricket administrators – Hoosen Ayob, Khawa Majola and Imitiaz Patel. Most countries would be proud to have one, to have all three working for one sport shows how much talent there is not only on the field but off.

Imitiaz, apart from being the Imran Khan lookalike of South Africa (even Bacher's wife Shira speaks of his good looks), is a marvellous host and put me in touch with several of the lost generation of Indian cricketers, in particular 'Uncle Chubb', Yusuf Garda. For a man who has every reason to feel bitter about what apartheid had done, 'Uncle Chubb' proved the most understanding of hosts, devoting much time and effort to help me collect material and meet people who could show me a world beyond the well-documented one of white cricket.

So did another remarkable Afrikaans cricketer, André Odendaal. It is a humbling experience to find that people who have suffered for their beliefs are not only more resilient but also so much more thoughtful and creative than their oppressors. I cannot thank him enough for the insights he provided for me into South African sport. It is a matter of some pride to me that I was instrumental, albeit in a very tangential way, in arranging for Odendaal to meet Bacher for the very first time. These two cannot have followed more different paths, but now that they have arrived at a common path they have much to offer South African cricket.

Much of the research for this book was done during India's historic tour of South Africa and I must thank my old friend Tony Cocklin of British Airways for facilitating my flight to South Africa in club class comfort, no less. I am also grateful to Michael Owen-Smith, Colin Bryden, Peter Robinson and Iqbal Khan for their warm-hearted companionship and for allowing me to plunder their well stocked minds.

Stuart Rock, editor of the *Director*, despite his better judgement, let me write articles on life outside sport and this proved invaluable in judging South African society. Edward Griffiths, then sports editor of the Johannesburg *Sunday Times*, was kind enough to agree to run a guest column from me during the tour: if all sports editors were quite as well balanced, agreeable and even tempered my world would be a much easier place.

My own paper, the *Sunday Times* of Wapping, carried my despatches at some length and I am grateful to successive sports editors for resisting the temptation to mangle them and at times managing to even improve my copy.

I am grateful to Garth Hewitt for proving that it is possible to reach across boundaries of race and culture. I am also indebted to Derek Wyatt, Donald Woods, Tommy Bedford,

Chris Harte, Chris Day, Peter Cooke, Morne du Plessis, Frank Keating, Ian Todd, John Hopkins, Peter Roebuck, Stephen Jones, Chris Lander, Peter Hain, Sam Ramsamy, Dennis Brutus and Graeme Wright.

Jeremy Robson and Louise Dixon, in that excess of optimism that publishers often display, commissioned me to write the book and have been marvellously patient and understanding. As ever, Sue Caincross was a wonderful secretary, and my wife Kalpana bore my long absence with fortitude even if she did make my daughter Indira believe that I had gone to South Africa to get her an elephant. I did get her a toy one, but at times during the birth of this book I have felt it would have been easier to hunt for a real elephant.

Prologue

On the evening of Thursday, 7 November 1991 a group of South Africans gathered at Jan Smuts airport in Johannesburg. It was nearly two years since F. W. de Klerk, the white South African President, had made his dramatic announcement freeing Nelson Mandela and unbanning the African National Congress. But even in this 'new' South Africa the group gathered that evening at the airport's Gate 5 made an incongruous sight: an almost equal balance of whites and blacks travelling on the same plane to the same place. Their destination was so strange that even the pilot, who had often flown de Klerk on international journeys, was unfamiliar with the flight plan. But then, no South African Airways plane had ever flown this route before, let alone to this particular city. Indeed, the country the plane was headed for had been, and still was, one of the fiercest critics of racist South Africa, shunning it for more than five decades.

That country was India. And this specially chartered Boeing 707 was carrying cricket players, officials and supporters to play three one-day international matches in Calcutta, Gwalior and Delhi. All the players and officials were well aware that they were embarking on one of the most powerfully symbolic flights in the history of international sport. Not only had India and South Africa never met in any official competition (except for one tennis match), but for more than 20 years white South Africa had been the great pariah of world sport, the mere possibility of whose participation was sufficient to throw the organization of any inter-

1

national competition into chaos. At least one Olympic Games had been disrupted by the South African question; several sporting tours had been cancelled or emasculated; and for years politicians and sports administrators of many countries had struggled to devise means of keeping their sportsmen happy while resisting the krugerrand-rich blandishments of white South African sporting entrepreneurs.

On the face of it, little had changed. True, the apartheid laws had been removed from the statute books. But South Africa was still ruled by the same white minority Government and Nationalist Party that had imposed apartheid. Its period of continuous power since 1948 had made South Africa even more of an impregnable one-party state than any of the surrounding black countries which the white rulers of South Africa took such delight in disparaging. Negotiations to dismantle white rule, leading ultimately to one man, one vote, had barely started. India would have seemed to be the last cricket-playing country South Africans could visit. It had been one of the first countries to break diplomatic ties with South Africa in 1948, and one of the first to grant recognition to the African National Congress as the legitimate voice of the overwhelming majority of South Africans and to host an ANC office (in Delhi). Although the cricketers would be permitted entry, there was still no question of India granting diplomatic recognition to white South Africa, and none of the South Africans on the plane had visas for India.

Once all this would have been seen as an insurmountable barrier to any sporting contact between South Africa and India (or any other black country). But now the ANC, which had supported the sports boycott so rigorously, was itself opening the doors to sporting contact. It was its advocacy on behalf of South African sport that had made this trip possible. In one of the great turn-arounds of modern sport, white South African sportsmen, shunned for decades, were being welcomed back to the international fold, even to places they had never reached – or wanted to reach – in the years before isolation.

The process, having started after F. W. de Klerk's historic speech to the white parliament on 2 February 1990, had really gathered momentum in the summer of 1991. It had taken two decades of persistent effort to isolate apartheid sport: the barriers came down literally in two days, South Africa's re-admission to the Olympic movement being followed the next day by its re-admission to international cricket. So speedy had been the welcome that, less than three weeks before the chartered 707 left Jan Smuts for Calcutta, South Africa was still not sure if it would be allowed to take part in the 1992 World Cup. This decision was taken only at a special session of the International Cricket Council (ICC) in the United Arab Emirate of Sharjah on 23 October 1991. It was following the Sharjah meeting that South Africa was invited to tour India.

No invitation could have been more unexpected, no sports tour organized in a more impromptu, chaotic fashion. Four days after Sharjah, South African cricket officials arrived in India, partly as a gesture of thanks for India's help in getting South Africa back, partly to get to know the country. The South African party was a neat balance of two black and two white officials, and for the latter India was very much *terra incognita*. However, no sooner had they arrived than they found the Indians facing a crisis of their own. Its neighbour Pakistan, due to send a team to India for a short tour, had abruptly cancelled it because of mounting tension between Hindus and Muslims in India. Just before this, Indians and Pakistanis had played in a tournament in Sharjah which had reignited all the old animosity between their two cricketing boards. The Indians were left contemplating a situation in which they had had no official cricket tour since 1988 (when, ironically, an English tour had been cancelled because the Indians objected to the presence of Graham Gooch and John Emburey, owing to their association with South Africa). The South Africans had been invited as guests of the Indian Cricket Board to watch the matches against Pakistan. Now, with the tour cancelled, South Africa was invited to take over from Pakistan as official tourists. The Indians wanted the South Africans to arrive with their cricket team on 8 November, little more than a week away. Almost any other sports administration would have dismissed such a tour out of hand – the sheer logistics would have seemed impossible. But in Ali Bacher South African cricket had an unusual leader.

A Jew of Lithuanian-Polish extraction, Bacher had been at the centre of white establishment cricket in South Africa for nearly two decades. In 1970 he had been captain of probably the best white South African team ever to take the field. (It had been on the verge of proving this in England, when reaction to South Africa's racist policies finally caught up with its cricketers and the tour was cancelled.) In the following two decades he had turned to cricket administration, and during that time had built a reputation as the 'evil prince' of cricket, the pirate who bribed English, Australian, West Indian and even Sri Lankan cricketers with South African gold to play rebel tours in South Africa. Little more than 18 months before the Indian venture, Bacher's last rebel tour, led by Mike Gatting, the former England captain, had been such a fiasco that it seemed Bacher might not even survive in South African cricket. But he had emerged reinvigorated if not reborn and had used the changed political climate following the release of Mandela to help bring South Africa back to international sport. Bacher has two qualities rare amongst his white South African contemporaries: he is ready to own up to responsibility for past actions – ready to apologize for the racist past of white South African cricket and its many mistakes, something his white colleagues still find it almost impossible to do – and he is a great learner. In a white world which has the arrogance and the certainty of belief that almost four centuries of unchallenged power has given it, Bacher is a break in the mould. He is full of curiosity, is eager to assimilate new experiences, and revels in meeting new situations and challenges. Like a magpie, he hoards information and he loves nothing more than to cultivate new people and situations for the knowledge and information they bring. That, he knows, is the way to acquire power.

His contact with India had brought him into touch with one such 'new' person: Jagmohan Dalmiya, then secretary of the Indian Cricket Board. With his ability to reach out to people, even total strangers, Bacher established instant rapport with Dalmiya – so much so that Dalmiya readily proposed South Africa's readmission to international cricket. But now, as Bacher arrived in India, Dalmiya, in the merry-go-round that is Indian cricket, found himself thrown off the magic wheel. A few months after South Africa had returned to the international fold Dalmiya had lost his post in a stormy annual general meeting of the Indian board. Held in his hometown of Calcutta, it had seen the two camps of Indian cricket – like Indian life, much of Indian cricket is perpetually divided into two camps – competing for positions. The election had witnessed the use of the most dubious tactics, including *goondas* (hired thugs) to intimidate rival cricket officials and supporters. The meeting, held in Calcutta's Taj Hotel, had seen Dalmiya's faction lose out. The victorious faction, led by the board President, Mahadav Rao Scindia (then also a government minister) had offered Dalmiya the option of holding on to his secretary's job, but Dalmiya had refused.

However, Indian cricket has a federal structure and regional cricket bodies wield considerable power. Test matches and internationals, for instance, are bid for, with the regional associations offering the central body central monetary guarantees. Dalmiya could still exercise formidable regional clout, and he now proposed to host a match against South Africa in Calcutta, offering a generous guarantee. Scindia matched this with an offer from his native Gwalior, and a third match was proposed for Delhi.

The deal was done at Scindia's home in Delhi, and it showed how the 'new' South Africa conducted its sporting relations. Over a typical Indian meal the South African cricket officials met not only their Indian counterparts but also the politicians without whose say so there could be no visit. There was Anand Sharma, whose wife was a South African-born Indian and the ruling Congress party's spokes-man on South Africa; also present was the ANC representa-tive in Delhi, whom the Indians treated as the South African ambassador. However keen Dalmiya may have been for the tour, Scindia would not move until he was sure he had ANC support. So, at some point over the tandooris and the nans, the deal was struck. The most curious mix of politics and sport came when the South Africans visited Calcutta. Bacher and his colleagues were taken to meet the local government's Marxist chief minister, Jyoti Basu, in the Writers' Building, originally built by Robert Clive and now a rabbit warren housing Bengal's top ministers and civil servants.

Basu, an unreconstructed Stalinist, came in, took one look at Bacher, and said: 'I want you to play cricket in Calcutta next week.' Then he swept out.

Strictly on cricketing, as distinct from political, grounds the tour made little sense. The Indians were about to embark on a gruelling tour of Australia, their first for six years, followed by the World Cup; the South Africans were only just about to start their season. But this was too good an opportunity to miss, and Bacher knew it would be much more than just a cricket tour. And he particularly relished the circumstances in which it was coming about.

In the years of isolation the antics of the white cricket body, many of them orchestrated by Bacher himself, had convinced many blacks that whites offered concessions on non-racial sport only so that they could break their isolation and resume international contact. It was very important, if this 'new' South Africa was to start off on the right foot, that it did not show too eager an appetite for touring. Indeed, just after South Africa had been re-admitted at Lord's, Bacher had been keen to dampen English speculation as to which country South Africa might first play on their comeback trail. What was important, he kept stressing, was the 'unity process' – which, in South African-speak, means: 'We must not do anything to make our new-found black and brown brothers feel that we are doing all this just to get back into international sport.' And when South Africa did resume international cricket, Bacher knew its first opponents had to be right.

On the evening of South Africa's formal return to the international fold, Bacher had held a small dinner in an Italian restaurant next to the Westbury hotel – the unofficial headquarters of the South Africans in London. The dinner guests consisted of two Englishmen who had long argued the case for white sporting South Africa: John Woodcock, former cricket correspondent of *The Times* and former editor of *Wisden*, and Jack Bannister, once a Warwickshire bowler and now a television commentator. The new friends of South Africa were reflected in the presence of Sunil Gavaskar, who had just returned from his first visit to South Africa (and the first by any Indian Test cricketer).

During the dinner Bacher freely speculated on who South Africa's first opponent might be, and expressed a strong preference for India or some other non-white country. 'Why?' asked Woodcock, quite distressed. 'If you think along such racial lines, then surely you are back in the old thinking.' Bacher, who was deeply grateful to Woodcock for his help to white cricket over the years, disagreed. 'No, no. It is very important. We have never played them. And after 102 years of playing international cricket the new South Africa has to start with them.' Moreover, the abrupt cancellation of Pakistan's Indian tour made the Indians the supplicants and South Africa the 'reluctant' tourists helping out their new-found friends. It also meant reaching out to the Indians of South Africa who, despite having lived in South Africa for 130 years, were still made to feel like aliens and deeply resented the injustices apartheid had heaped on them. So, with this unexpected opportunity, Bacher hoped to kill several birds with one stone, something that pleased him greatly.

In the two and a half years since the extraordinary events

in Calcutta, South African sport has travelled a road that not even its most optimistic supporters could have imagined. Before its isolation white South Africa chose to play sport only with white nations: black nations were not the 'traditional countries' it cared to compete with. So for the first 103 years of its international cricket existence South Africa had never played India, Pakistan or the West Indies. Now, in the space of a few months, it was to do so – and in the process created memorable images. At the Barcelona Olympics – South Africa's first in 30 years – a white South African long-distance runner, Meyer, beaten by the Ethiopian Tulu, ran a lap of honour with her black conquerer. From never having been part of soccer on its own continent, South Africa suddenly became one of the most sought-after rivals on Africa's football fields.

For 20 years sport had been the most potent symbol of the international struggle against apartheid. Now some of the doughtiest campaigners, who had spent their adult lives fighting racist South African sport, were delighted with the prospect of its return to the international scene. Yet even as the Long Bar in the Wanderers and the suites in Ellis Park, homes respectively of South African cricket and rugby, opened up to the anti-apartheid lobby, South African politicians were struggling to create the blueprint for a post-apartheid society. Two and a half years after sporting South Africa was welcomed back in Calcutta, white minority rule in South Africa continued and there was considerable doubt as to whether the country was capable of making a peaceful transition to democracy. While sporting opportunities opened up for an ever-growing proportion of the black and coloured population, Nelson Mandela – honoured by political leaders throughout the world as the authentic voice of South Africa – was still, like 80 per cent of his country's population, being denied the right to vote. Since de Klerk's speech of February 1990, South Africa's sporting teams have played all over the world, but the political situation in South

Africa has been so volatile that more than 10,000 people have been killed.

It is undeniable, however, that the seemingly monolithic rigidity of the social and political scene in South Africa is crumbling. And it is equally clear that sport has been an important trigger of the process of transformation. How did sport acquire such importance? Why had South Africa been singled out for an isolation unique in sporting history? The answers to these questions go to the heart of the South Africa issue, providing an insight to this most abnormal of societies, with its extraordinary mix of sport and politics.

1

The White Game

The importance of sport in South Africa, particularly white South Africa, can hardly be exaggerated. It is an importance that has been recognized by almost everyone in South Africa, from whites chafing at their sporting isolation to politicians fighting apartheid. Nelson Mandela tells the story of how, in the early days of negotiations with F. W. de Klerk the white South African president turned to him and said, 'If the ANC made it possible for All Blacks to come here, then we would really start to change the system.' Since these words were spoken, the formidable New Zealanders have toured South Africa. The country's political problems appear no nearer a solution, but de Klerk's remark illustrates the quite extraordinary significance sport in general, and rugby in particular, has for the white South African nation.

Rugby, according to the writer Richard Dowden, is one of the three cultural activities of the white population, the other two being lying in the sun and eating. White South Africa has always been a tremendous sporting nation. An ideal climate, with blazing hot summers and winters which, to most Europeans, would be considered spring-like, have been exploited by some of the best sporting facilities known to man and the most enthusiastic participants. In the early 1980s it was estimated that one in four of the five million whites belonged to sports clubs; excellent public amenities were backed by a wealth of private sports facilities in clubs, schools and homes. A swimming pool and tennis court were considered so much part of a normal white home that, as early as 1974, a director of the Trust Building Society was complaining that it was 'becoming more and more difficult to satisfy the normal demands of our private clients for private gardens, swimming pool, tennis court, two-car garage, study, games room, carpet and insistence upon "personalized design", etc.'

Peter Hain, the South African-born British MP who led one of the first of many campaigns against apartheid sport, has suggested that the white sporting ethos was a way of making up for the fact that even white South Africa was not a really free society: 'It is almost as if limits on freedom of thought and expression in South Africa force whites to seek self-fulfilment in sporting achievement; and this, coupled with the general sporting interest found in all ex-British colonies, makes for a formidable sports thirst.'

Curiously, this thirst has been quenched by the white nation not in the search for individual sporting glory but in collective sporting endeavour. For all its expenditure of time and money and all its abundance of sporting amenities, white South Africa as a sporting nation has hardly been a world beater. The South African record in Olympic Games is hardly distinguished. It took part in the Olympics for five decades between the Games in London in 1908 and those in Rome in 1960, and in this period South Africa won just 16 gold medals (plus 22 silver and 16 bronze), a haul that puts it far behind many of the black countries whose Olympic participation started long after South Africa's. Unlike Australia, it has never produced any tennis players or swimmers who could challenge and dominate the world in their sport.

White South Africa has produced the odd individual world beater. Gary Player is unquestionably one of the greatest golfers in history, and his predecessor Bobby Locke won four British Opens. Ann Harrison is the only South African swimmer to win a gold in the Olympics, though Karen Muir and Ann Fairlie might have matched her feat if South Africa had not been banned from the games by the time they arrived on the scene.

Indoctrination in the white communal sporting culture starts in the schools. Michael Owen-Smith, son of H. G. O. ('Tubby') Owen-Smith (probably the greatest all-round sportsman white South Africa has produced, honoured both in cricket and rugby), recalls his school in Cape Town where the stress was all on team sports. 'Team sports were important in our set-up. Individual sports were just not emphasized. Lots of schools did not have tennis courts or swimming pools but there were always plenty of grounds for rugby and cricket. If you were good at rugby or cricket, then you were grabbed by it.'

Even in cricket, which among team games provides the greatest scope for individual glory, South African teams, says Owen-Smith, emphasized teamwork 'perhaps because until the 1960s they did not have many great players'. In the 1960s brilliant individual stars did emerge – Graeme and Peter Pollock, Eddie Barlow, Barry Richards, Mike Proctor, Colin Bland – but by then the ethos of the South African approach, with its emphasis on fielding and teamwork, was firmly established.

South Africa's Test match record hardly compares with that of the West Indies, let alone Australia's. In the 81 years from their start in Test cricket at Port Elizabeth on 12 March 1889 to their last Test before isolation on 10 March 1970, also at Port Elizabeth, they won 38 of the 172 matches, losing 77 and drawing 57.

Eight of these 38 victories came in the five glorious years of white cricket between 1965 and 1970. Then they did have a cricket team which was as good as any in the world. They defeated England in England in 1965 (Ali Bacher being a member of the Test side) and Australia twice at home, the 1970 wins coming in all four of the Tests by quite crushing margins. Of course, by its own choice South Africa did not play with half of the cricketing countries – the black and the brown half, including West Indies, Pakistan and India. As Eddie Barlow, one of the stalwarts of the South Africa side, says, 'In those days we did not play international cricket. We just played England, Australia and New Zealand.' So it was almost impossible to judge how good they really were. Would they have beaten the West Indies and India? We shall never know. Clive Lloyd, the most successful captain in the history of Test cricket and leader of the outstanding West Indies cricket teams of the 1970s and 1980s, is not convinced that South Africa would have prevailed against the other countries. Cricket lovers will endlessly debate the proposition, but it can never be resolved.

It was in rugby that the collective approach attained its apotheosis. But in rugby, too, South Africa's start was inauspicious, indeed desperate: on the first British tour in 1891, the visitors lost all 20 of their matches, scoring but a single point and conceding 226. But from the ashes of that defeat came a new white South African rugby ready to take on the world. In 1903 it won its first victory over the British, and for the next 50 years until 1956, when they played New Zealand, the Springboks did not lose a single Test series – one of the longest unbeaten international sequences in sports history. This remains white South Africa's greatest sporting achievement and, not surprisingly, rugby became the white nation's most potent symbol of its sporting prowess. This was the sport which, as the French coach Serge Saulnier told the first-ever French rugby team to tour South Africa in 1958, is a 'religion with temples, high priests and the faithful'.

Rugby, it has been said, is a hooligan's game played by gentlemen, while football is a gentleman's game played by hooligans. Such broad classifications are inherently flawed; but the rugby the South Africans played was very different from the game elsewhere. It was, says Stephen Jones, rugby correspondent of the London *Sunday Times*, 'always more methodical, there was more planning, much more of a communal game. It is more than a national game. There is something in the white South Africans that makes them almost religiously fanatical about their devotion to rugby. Wherever it comes from, it is just inbred in them and it is there for life. I can't describe it. It is just something there, and it is huge'.

This was particularly so after the Second World War when, led by abrasive Dannie Craven, white South African rugby players evolved a new style of play that cut out errors. Henri Garcia says that this technique 'had its basis in a powerful pack of forwards as the main striking force, with the backs as support troops kicking accurately to touch until they had gained enough ground to risk handling movements with comparative impunity'. Garcia believes Craven's methods opened 'a new era in rugby of continuous play: the traditional movement from forwards who, brought back into play by the backs, became crucial attackers'.

By this time South Africa seem to have acquired a monopoly in forwards who were very, very big. Jones says, 'The Afrikaners are just very thick, very big buggers. The reason they were so good was that they were physically bigger than most of us. In the 1950s the average weight of a rugby forward would have been 14 stone; now the average is 16 stone. But in South Africa they were always giants.' Craven's game, feels Jones, 'was totally a percentage game. Not like the Fijians or the Samoans. You would never associate flair with Springbok rugby, only power and percentage. The teams Craven inspired were incredibly dedicated; they established a tradition, and succeeding generations of Springboks did not let down this tradition. They were petrified to lose because it was a great honour to be a Springbok. They had colossal battles with the All Blacks, against whom they would almost rather die than lose.'

There has been much speculation as to why Afrikaners developed this almost mystical identification with rugby. Like cricket, it was a colonial game; it was brought to South Africa in 1862 by Canon George Ogilvie, who had played the game at Winchester College before emigrating to South Africa and becoming director of a diocesan school. Australians took to cricket as John Bull, Jnr out to teach John Bull, Snr a lesson, but for the Boers rugby was different. They had even more reason than the Australians to hate the British, and the memories of their suffering during the Boer War (1899–1902) were still strong through the early part of this century when rugby became the national religion of the Afrikaners. One writer has suggested that the Afrikaners appropriated rugby as their sport because they perceived it as different in kind from football, which had a large black following, and cricket, which was too English. It corresponded to their idea of what the Afrikaner nation was all about. According to Robert Archer and Antoine Bouillon, 'Rugby is a collective sport of combat, which values physical endurance, strength and rapidity. All these belong to its popular origins. At the same time these qualities lent themselves peculiarly well to appropriation by a social elite with aristocratic ideals who were able, in the 19th century, to transform rugby (like boxing) into a school of moral discipline for future leaders. . . . It is a sport ideally suited to "ideological investment", and people conquering barbarism recognized an image of their ideology in its symbols.'

Graeme Wright, a former editor of *Wisden*, believes that rugby's role-based structure encourages Afrikaners to take to it: 'If you think of rugby as being a structured game, as it used to be played until the 1960s and 1970s, each man fitted into a role according to his size or skill, and this locked on to a Boer pre-destined to think that everyone is born to play a role.'

John Morgan, reporting the British Lions tour of 1969, vividly described the way the Afrikaners identified with rugby. He had gone to see Northern Transvaal, probably the most conservative (that is, racist) area of white South Africa, play the Lions: 'I had travelled to the match with a crowd of farmers from a small town called Brits, few of them able to speak English, all of them convinced they were kind to their workers . . . all believing their workers loved them. . . . And until 10 minutes from the end of the match this astonishingly false view of themselves endured. At which point the British Lions took the lead. In 30 years of watching rugby I have never known any experience comparable to the chilling transformation of spirit amongst that multitude. The silence was that of a people witnessing a tragedy rather than the normal disappointment of a home crowd. When the game was lost and over, the crowd did not cheer or groan. Without a word or a sound of any kind, they shuffled out into the dusk and away back to the farm lands and their enchanted dreams and unspoken fears.'

Rugby's attraction for the Afrikaners also lay in the fact that they realized soon enough that it could be an elitist sport. The game had been born in 1823 at Rugby public school when, during a game of soccer, William Webb Ellis suddenly decided to pick up and run with the ball. In England rugby union has remained an amateur and largely middle-class game, played mainly in the public and grammar schools. (Its northern England offshoot, rugby league, a professional, and essentially working-class, game which at its best offers a unique blend of hardness and supreme technical skill, is anathematized by the grandees of rugby union.) In South Africa race replaced class as the dividing factor. But while all white schools played rugby, the Afrikaner schools (as John Horak recalls) played it 'hard and they used to play to win, they were dour about it and they were always rough'. Horak went to an English-speaking white school, where he was taught 'never to play to kill, just to win'.

Cricket, of course, can be just as elitist as rugby. But in South Africa it was the English-speaking whites who safeguarded its purity against not only the blacks but also the Afrikaners. The latter did not really take to cricket in a big way until a decade after the Second World War; and it was only in 1955 that the first Afrikaans book on cricket, *Amper Krieket Kamnpioene* (Almost Champion Cricketers) by Werner Bernard, was published. Before that the Afrikaners saw it as an alien, imperial sport, and members of South African Test sides had, with very few exceptions, impeccable British names.

It was in the 1960s, when South African cricket reached

its zenith, that Afrikaners took to it on a national scale – encouraged no doubt by the fact that Peter van der Merwe was captain. Although he was not an Afrikaner, his name was Afrikaans-sounding and that helped, as did the winning team of Ali Bacher when Australia was vanquished.

Like everything else in South African life, sport was, of course, segregated. Apartheid was to institutionalize it after 1948 in a particularly vicious and evil form, but segregation had been the norm of South African life almost from the moment the whites landed. Marq de Villiers, who has used the history of his own family to write a history of white South Africa, *White Tribe Dreaming*, suggests that the first attempt at segregation came with van Riebeeck, whose arrival at Table Bay in 1652 marks the start of white settlement. Within a short time he had built a 'thick hedge of almonds to enclose the 6,000 acres he considered proper for a refreshment station's needs – South Africa's first futile attempt at segregation'.

Long before the Nationalists came to power in 1948, with their avowed policy of apartheid, segregation was a fact of South African life and, hence, of sports. De Villiers has written: 'Long before 1948, long before Malan finally came to power, the South African statute books were filled with laws that were racially, culturally and linguistically discriminatory. The architects of apartheid weren't inventing a policy from thin air. They changed an accumulation of ad hoc law-making into a system, changed a long series of small acts aimed at petty matters into a comprehensive scheme as radical, as far-reaching, as thorough, as exhaustive and as single-minded as the Bolshevik remaking of Russia – but they didn't invent discrimination, or differentiation. The two northern republics had never accepted non-whites as citizens with any rights; the Cape, though it had a limited non-racial franchise, nevertheless had a pass system and a system of residential segregation, much of it laid down in statutes introduced by the British colonizers that pre-dated the union government of 1910. In Natal the largely English-speaking colony had devised a system virtually as complete as Transvaal's: the Zulus were given no voice at all in the land of their birth.'

So the Nationalists, on assuming office, found a whole raft of policies which could form the basis for their infamous 'separate but equal' development ideas. The Land Act of 1913 had made it impossible for black Africans to acquire land-ownership rights in most parts of the country, the so-called 'white areas'. This, together with the Native Land and Trust Act of 1936, decreed that the majority black population, who outnumbered the whites by four to one, could own a maximum of only 13.7 per cent of the land, although even this maximum has never been permitted in practice.

One of the most notorious laws of the apartheid regime, passed in 1950, prohibited sexual intercourse between whites and non-whites. The title of the act was the Immorality Amendment Act, for it was amending a previous piece of legislation, enacted in 1927, which had made it illegal for whites and Africans to have sex together; in 1950 the ban extended to sex between whites and all non-whites. It was during the debate in the white parliament on what became the 1913 Native Land Act that General Hertzog, founder of the Nationalist party, who had been Minister of Native Affairs, enunciated the principles that were to guide apartheid's rulers. Native Africans would not be allowed to own land in the white man's territory. They would be moved to those parts where there were already large masses of their compatriots. In other words, his plan defined the respective spheres of blacks and whites, and natives would be granted the right to enter European territory only in order to earn a living there.

Even the Group Areas Act, which the writer and politician Alan Paton felt was the greatest sin committed by the white people of South Africa, was built on the 'pegging act' of the late 1940s, passed by the Jan Smuts Government, which put a stop to Indians acquiring any further property in South Africa. The Nationalists were eager to put their own, peculiarly nasty glosses on the racist laws – as in 1957, when the

Minister of Native Affairs was empowered to stop Africans from attending church in a white area.

The other major feature of apartheid legislation was the use of language: an almost Stalinist fondness for twisting the meanings of words so that laws could be interpreted in an infinite variety of ways to suit the Government. White South Africans have been and remain some of the staunchest opponents of communism. To be labelled a communist is to be beyond the pale. Yet historically the tactics the Nationalists have used to maintain white power have all the hallmarks of Soviet communism – the distortions of history, the twisting of facts and, when all else fails, barefaced lying to deny demonstrable historical truth. Orwell's nightmare vision of doublespeak found vivid expression in white South Africa.

Thus the 1959 session of parliament passed the Extension of University Education Act. On the face of it this might have seemed to be a liberal measure to offer higher education to a greater number of people. In fact, it barred non-white students from white universities that had previously been open to them, banishing them to segregated institutions known as tribal colleges. These were established along ethnic lines: colleges for Indians, for Coloureds, for black Africans, and so on. Black Africans were further divided, with separate colleges for Zulus and Sothos. Other examples of doublespeak in the titles of racist legislation were the Indian Representative Act of 1948, which actually abolished the limited Indian representation in Parliament under legislation which in any case had not been enacted; and the Promotion of Bantu Self-Government Act of 1959, which put an end to the derisory, and in any case indirect, representation of Africans. The most hated piece of racist legislation was enacted in 1952. Its title, the Native (Abolition of Passes and Co-ordination of Documents) Act might lead one to expect a welcome loosening of legislative shackles. In fact it required every black African to carry a reference book on him, which had to be produced on demand; failure to do so would lead to the offender being arrested on the spot. For the first time black women as well as men were subject to pass laws. No legislation created more grief or strife than this, and its consequences led inevitably to the Sharpeville massacre.

The use of language is particularly important in understanding apartheid because, right from the beginning, the white man in South Africa appropriated the 'word'. In his highly selective version of history, non-whites just did not exist. In this, too, the whites emulated Soviet communism. Just as Stalin, after Lenin's death, tried to remove all trace of Trotsky's influence and even had his image removed from photographs of the revolution to try to make him a non-person, so almost from the beginning South African whites from all backgrounds refused to see blacks as part of their world. They lived surrounded by blacks, served by them, waited on by them, their material prosperity utterly dependent on black labour. But, for them, blacks were simply not fully paid-up members of the human race.

'Of all the curious experiences in observing South African rugby and talking to its followers,' wrote the journalist John Morgan in 1969, 'none was more astonishing than that none of them raised the question of African or Coloured players. The matter did not appear to exist in their minds. The African and Coloured Rugby Federation might have been in another physical continent, not merely a separate continent of the spirit. Old Springbok players would talk earnestly, even with passion, about the virtues of rugby in uniting the races . . .' – but for them the races were Afrikaner and English, the religions Dutch Reform and Anglican. The blankness with which they responded to the idea that rugby might bring together other races with whites revealed the hopeless naivety of those who insisted that 'tours build bridges'.

Some 30 years before Morgan made these comments the South African writer Joseph Brauer insisted: 'The sports field of South Africa knows neither politics nor racialism; and there is no ghetto, nor will there ever be as long as sanity reigns. When politics clash with sport, the high ideals of sportsmanship are lost. And as long as there is no segregation in South African sport, there will be understanding. The Jewish sportsman will go out and mix with his fellow human beings and between them and him the bonds of fellowship will be woven.'

Brauer was Jewish, and he wrote these lines in 1939, just as Nazi Germany was preparing the final solution for Jews in Europe. It is astonishing that a Jew could, at that moment in history, be so far removed from reality that he could delude himself that in South Africa the overwhelming majority of the population did not even exist.

White sports organizations have always constitutionally barred non-whites from membership. No non-white could be a member of the Durban Surf Club or the Natal Football Association or the Transvaal Cricket Union, though these organizations never had the prefix 'white' in their names. On the other hand, a golf club in Durban that was open to Indians could not be called simply the Durban Golf Club but the Durban Indian Golf Club. The same applied to the Transvaal African Football Association and the Natal Coloured Hockey Association. Other race groups in South Africa had to define themselves in terms of the white man or woman; the supremacy of the whites gave them the power to dictate the agenda. White sports organizations held open championships in golf, athletics and swimming, but the word 'open' applied only to whites.

Between 1895 and 1910 most of these whites-only sports organizations, many with names that falsely proclaimed or implied universality of membership, were admitted to international bodies. The British Empire was then at its height, and racial segregation, far from being unique to South Africa, was the norm. André Odendaal has pointed out that segregation in cricket was practised in almost all the British colonial territories; in Kenya, Nigeria and Ghana, for instance, separate bodies existed for black and white cricketers.

Even in India, the jewel in the imperial crown, the British practised racial segregation, with clubs barring Indians from membership. There was, however, some encouragement for

sports by the British in India, and English teams did play
Indians in various team games. In 1911 a football match
won by a barefoot Indian team against a British regimental
side became a potent symbol of Indian nationalism. Even
clubs that barred Indians would open their doors on special
occasions. The Bombay Gymkhana, for instance, did not
admit Indians, but it hosted the first-ever cricket Test on
Indian soil in 1933. In South Africa there was no such sporting interaction between the races except on very rare
occasions. Then, as Odendaal has written, 'on select Sundays
and festival occasions the paternalistic white hand would
open the door of a club – for instance, Green Point and
Claremont in the Cape – for the backyard cricketers and their
enthusiastic entourages. Then, for a day, there would be play,
and at stumps the doors closed again until some hazy date
in the future.'

The appropriation of the 'word' by the whites meant that
even on the odd occasion when whites played blacks, there
was little inclination to record it. An early *Wisden* referred
to a match between 'Hottentot and Africander [sic] Boers'
in 1854, but declined to give details. The second English
team to visit South Africa, W. W. Read's team of 1891–2,
played a Malay side and defeated them by 10 wickets.
Despite the fact that two of the Malay cricketers did very
well – Krom Hendricks, a fast bowler, took 4 for 50 and L.
Samoodien scored 55 (one of only two batsmen to score a
50 against the Englishmen that season) – neither played for
South Africa. Hendricks, the fastest bowler in the country,
was chosen for South Africa's first tour to England in 1894,
but was omitted as a result of 'the greatest pressure by those
in high authority in the Cape Colony'. In a preview of the
critical comments white cricket would later get, the *Cricketer
Field* in its issue of 31 March 1894 regretted that the South
Africans chose their sides because of the colour of the skin.

There is some debate as to whether any coloured cricketer
played for South Africa before the all-rounder Omar Henry
became the first to play Test cricket for the 'new' South

Africa against India in November 1992. This depends on whether one considers C. B. 'Buck' Llewellyn to be white or coloured. According to Roland Bowen, a cricket historian, he was coloured and was chosen for the 1910–11 tour of Australia, but was obliged to change in the toilet so as to escape the taunts of his white team mates, particularly one Jimmy Sinclair. Brian Crowley has since written that Llewellyn was the product of a white house painter from Pietermaritzburg and a coloured woman from St Helens. Certainly J. M. Kilburn and other observers noticed his dark eyes and dark skin, and there is other evidence to suggest that Llewellyn was of mixed blood. But when in the early 1970s the question of his origins provoked a controversy, his daughter insisted that her father was of pure British descent.

In the 1929 series against South Africa's tourists, England had a non-white player in its Test team: K. S. Duleepsinhji, nephew of the great Ranji, and at this time one of England's finest batsmen. He played in the first Test, made 11 and 1, and was dropped. Although he scored copious runs that season for Sussex, he was not chosen again and was told by the English selectors that the South Africans had objected to his presence. The South African captain denied this, but there were suggestions of South African government pressure. Whatever the truth, Duleep never again played against South Africa – but he remained the only non-white to have played against them until the 'new' South Africa emerged more than 60 years later.

The Duleep episode marked the start of growing white South African interference in other countries' sports. For the next 40 years white South Africa would set an uncompromisingly racist agenda for its international sporting contests, deciding not only who could play for white South Africa but who could *not* play for its opponents. No other country in the history of international sport has been able to exercise such power; no other country has had the impudence to try.

Later, when greater awareness of the brutally repressive

nature of apartheid led to the country's political and cultural isolation, South African whites complained bitterly about what they chose to call double standards and accused countries that refused all sporting contact of using blackmail and introducing politics to sport! It might be wondered who, other than the most blindly fanatical sportsmen or those who subscribed to South Africa's racist policies, such arguments were supposed to convince. The answer is, quite a few of the ruling bodies of sports in other countries. It is significant that the main thrust of South Africa's attempts to thwart an international sports boycott concentrated on rugby and cricket, at both of which she had a formidable reputation. Until the 1970s only seven countries played Test cricket and only eight were a major force in rugby. All these countries, with the exception of two of the rugby octet (France and Argentina), were or had been members of the British Commonwealth. Cricket and rugby are both English in origin and their administration was from the beginning in the utterly reliable hands of a certain kind of Englishman: white, middle-class, educated at one of the better public schools, and imbued with the kind of social and moral values that had enabled England to administer a vast colonial apparatus for more than 100 years. Unlike football or other world sports, neither rugby nor cricket was controlled by an international body. Rugby has since acquired one but it has neither the power nor the influence of FIFA, football's controlling body. Cricket is still painfully trying to reorganize the ICC along FIFA lines; it is less than a year since it appointed a first full-time chief executive.

Although the 1960s saw the change in name of the cricket body from the Imperial Cricket Conference (founded in 1909) to the International Cricket Conference and, later, to the International Cricket Council, it was until late 1993 run as a part-time activity by the MCC. And while the ICC is now acquiring greater powers, cricket at Test level has traditionally been organized on bilateral contacts between countries. Until the World Cup was launched in 1975 the only fixed item in the international calendar was that every eighteen months England played Australia for the Ashes. Apart from that it was a question of any two Test-playing countries deciding when and where they would play each other. Some played each other regularly; others at infrequent intervals. Australia, long dismissive of the quality of New Zealand cricket, did not play its neighbour between 1946 – when the first Test between the countries was played – and the 1970s. India did not play Pakistan between 1960 and 1978 – a period when relations between the two countries were bedevilled by wars and tension. The bilateral basis of contacts produced just the sort of situation made for white South Africa and she soon learnt to exploit it to her advantage and to preserve her ideal of never having any truck with non-whites. When South Africa first made an impact on the Test scene in the early part of this century, there had not been much danger of her having to play non-whites. Duleep apart, there was little chance of a non-white appearing in the English team; and Australia, South Africa's other great opponent, had its own 'white Australia' policy. Its attitude towards the aboriginal Australians was set in the early days of colonization, when the settlers had exterminated thousands of them.

In the late 1920s the situation began to change. In 1928 West Indies made their Test debut in England; India followed in 1932. New Zealand made her Test debut a day before the West Indies. Within two years South Africa had played New Zealand, following her inaugural tour of Australia, but there was no question of her playing the West Indies or India. White South Africa gloried in the fact that she was one of the founders of the Imperial Cricket Conference, but the task of bringing the non-white countries into Test cricket remained the responsibility of England, and specifically that of the MCC, the governing body of cricket in England. In 1929 two MCC sides sailed from England to almost opposite corners of the globe – one to the West Indies, one to New Zealand. On 10 January 1929 a team led by Arthur Gilligan introduced New Zealand to Test cricket at Christchurch. On

11 January a team led by the Hon. F. S. G. Calthorpe led England out against the West Indies at Bridgetown, Barbados.

So from the late 1920s there was one cricket world where all countries were free to play each other irrespective of the colour of skin, and there was white South Africa, who played only England, Australia and New Zealand. This situation continued until isolation and her internal political situation forced white South Africa to change. Then, with an irony that entirely escaped almost all white South African sportsmen, there were loud and long complaints about how the non-white countries were splitting the cricket world, when they had merely been responding to a South African initiative.

Nowhere was the disease of racism more virulent than in South African rugby. The tone was set when, after the First World War, the first South African team toured New Zealand and came up against Maori players. One South African newspaper reporter included this comment in a cable to his paper: 'Bad enough having to play officially designated New Zealand natives but spectacle thousands Europeans frantically cheering on band of Coloured men to defeat members of own race was too much for Springboks who frankly disgusted.'

White South Africa made sure that her players' sensitivities would be affronted no more. In the 1920s New Zealand had the legendary Maori George Nepia, considered by many to be one of the greatest ever rugby players. South Africans objected to his presence in the team. New Zealand gave in, did not choose him for their 1928 tour of South Africa, when he might have won them the series – and Nepia drifted away into rugby league. On the 1937 tour, the second by the Springboks, there was no fixture against the Maoris. In 1949 the All Blacks again visited South Africa and again meekly submitted to white South African dictation about who they could select for their side. The New Zealand Rugby Union announced in August 1948 that, 'much as it regretted it, players to be selected to tour South Africa cannot be other than wholly European'.

It was only in 1960 that rugby-playing New Zealanders began to protest about the exclusion of Maoris. But that year the All Blacks again toured South Africa and the New Zealand selectors once more caved in to South African demands to exclude Maoris. The Labour Prime Minister, supporting the selectors, put forward the view that it would be cruel to send Maoris to a country where they would be discriminated against. Richard Thompson, in his examination of New Zealand's sporting contacts with South Africa, suggests this may have contributed to Labour's election defeat in 1960, as it alienated Maori voters. At this time Graeme Wright was a schoolboy in Timaru, in the South Island of New Zealand: 'There was an island-wide debating competition amongst schools. The topic was whether or not an All Black team should go to South Africa in 1960 without Maori players. I had to defend the argument that a side should go to South Africa and I found that very difficult to do because basically there was no moral ground. The only argument one could use was that it was polite, rather like if you were invited to a black-tie function, one wore a black tie because that was the done thing. There was also a precedent in that previously New Zealand had agreed to South Africa's wishes. My opponent was a blonde girl who had all the arguments, the emotion and the looks!'

The All Blacks were given a state reception as they left from South Africa; and, at another after their return, one speaker felt able to praise them for 'the great work you have done in the cause of Commonwealth trust and friendship'. It was then announced that for future tours to South Africa Maoris would be selected on merit. But would they be allowed through Customs and Immigration at Jan Smuts airport?

The answer was unequivocal and it came from the highest authority. On 4 September 1965, in a speech at Loskop Dam, Prime Minister Hendrik Verwoerd, the architect of apartheid, declared: 'When we are the guests of another country we have to behave according to their tradition. We will play there in the exact way it has been arranged by New Zealand. Like we subject ourselves to their customs, we expect that when other countries visit us, they will respect ours of mixed teams.'

Three days later the Afrikaner newspaper *Die Transvaaler* commented in an editorial: 'It must be ascribed to one particular factor that the whole race has hitherto maintained itself in the Southern part of Africa. The fact that there has been no miscegenation was because there was no social mixing between whites and non-whites. Social mixing leads inexorably to miscegenation . . . it is today the social aim of the Communist. . . . In South Africa the races do not mix on the sports field. If they mix first on the sports field, then the road to other forms of social mixing is wide open. . . . With an eye to upholding the white race and its civilization not one single compromise can be entered into – not even when it comes to a visiting rugby team.'

This is as clear an assertion of sporting apartheid policy as one could wish for. It was made in the middle of the 'Swinging Sixties', when racial and other social and psychological barriers were coming down all over the world. Even in the Deep South of the United States racial segregation – which in any case was never legally entrenched on the scale of apartheid in South Africa – was slowly being eliminated. The great freedom riders had travelled through the South awakening America to the evil within. President Lyndon Johnson's civil rights legislation outlawed discrimination and ensured that blacks could register to vote. In the Deep South blacks had long since had the vote, although gerrymandering and intimidation often denied them the chance to exercise it. But in South Africa blacks never had the vote.

Die Transvaaler's conviction that the presence of a single Maori among the visiting All-Blacks would undermine the racial purity of white South Africa was no doubt grounded in paranoia. Equally striking was the ease with which white

politicians deluded themselves on matters of race. Soon after
that editorial was published, the Minister of the Interior Jan
de Klerk (father of F. W. de Klerk) said: 'I want to emphasize
that it is wrong to assert that this is political interference in
a purely sporting matter. The Government was elected to
oppose the various forms of integration, including social
integration. It had to see the national policy was respected
in the field of sport as in all other spheres.' So the government's racist policies could not be described as political;
they were simply part of the 'customs and traditions' of the
country. However, any attempt to change that policy was
not merely political but part of a gigantic communist conspiracy. It says much for the level of political debate in South
Africa, and of the calibre of its white politicians, that few at
the time questioned the ramshackle intellectual basis of de
Klerk's speech. Indeed the argument was supported by a
majority of white South Africans for the next two decades,
as South Africa sought to maintain apartheid in sport.

In 1965 a Springbok team had toured New Zealand, and
Graeme Wright had been given a glimpse into white South
African racist thinking: 'I had a friend who was a photog-
rapher. His girl friend was a part Maori girl, very pretty but
dark. He took her to a reception for the South African
players. Many of them came up to her and treated her like
a tart. Now, she was a good looking girl, but my friend got
the distinct impression they treated her like this because she
was Coloured. None of the other ladies there – who were
white – were so treated. I was just shocked and disgusted.'

As it happened, Verwoerd's speech finally made the New
Zealand rugby worm turn, and Prime Minister Holyoake
refused to accept what he rightly saw as dictation by white
South Africa and an attempt to discriminate between New
Zealand citizens. Verwoerd made a cheap debating point
by suggesting that New Zealand itself perpetuated racial
differences: 'If they are one nation why refer to Maoris at
all?' But New Zealand had had enough. Holyoake said '. . . it
appears that the South African Prime Minister is trying to

dictate the composition of the New Zealand team and is
asking New Zealand to suspend its racial policy for South
Africa's sake'. For the first time, a South African rugby tour
was abandoned.

Verwoerd's was, of course, not only a major Government
intervention: it brought two prime ministers into direct conflict. It showed that under pressure from the international
community white South African politicians were having to
come into the sporting arena to uphold apartheid in sport.
In the half century before this, when nobody questioned
white South Africa's right to dictate the sporting agenda –
or even to act as a super-selector for its opponents – there
was little need for the Government to do so. The white
sporting bodies did it themselves. Apartheid in sport was not
so much imposed by law as maintained by custom and the
natural inclinations of the white sportsmen and their administrators. White sports administrators saw segregation in
sport as the natural order in South Africa. So in 1955, when
the Bloemfontein City Council banned black spectators from
its new stadium, preventing them from watching the British
Lions play South Africa, the white rugby authorities supported the ban. The municipal authorities felt the presence
of blacks 'would cause friction' – and the rugby authorities
knew that if the blacks were allowed in they would cheer
the Lions.

Interestingly, there has never been any law in South Africa
that banned inter-racial sport: in all the multifarious apartheid legislation there was no enactment which specifically
prohibited matches between different races or even racially
mixed teams. There was, in fact, no need for such prohib-
itions: the provisions of laws such as the Group Areas Act
and the liquor laws could be used to stop multi-racial sports.
It was only in 1973 that the Government issued Proclamation
No. R 228, an amendment to the Group Areas Act, which
had the power to stop multi-racial matches. This amendment
was a response to the activities of the multi-racial Aurora
Club playing cricket in Natal – though no prosecution was

ever brought against the club. And in the only case ever tested in the courts the judge held that no law prevented multi-racial sport.

In October 1963 Lincoln City Football Club, a multi-racial club in Durban, played a match in an Indian area. This violated the Group Areas Act (or seemed to do so), and two whites, five coloureds and two Indian footballers of Lincoln City were taken to court. The charge was they had illegally 'occupied' property zoned for Indians. But the judge ruled in their favour, holding that the act was intended to prohibit individuals spontaneously coming together to play, not a properly constituted team. In any case, they had not stayed on after the match to have drinks together. In the white South African world, playing a multi-racial match was bad enough, but players having a drink afterwards opened themselves to the accusation that, however briefly, they regarded each other as equals.

The ruling was important because it showed that, *pace* the assertions of white administrators, mixed sport was not illegal. But it also made the task of those seeking to defeat apartheid sport all the more difficult. They had to take on all the apartheid laws of the country. Laws like the Group Areas Act, the Liquor Act and a host of others so regulated life that it made it impossible for sport to be either organized or played in ways normal to most countries.

In later years, as international pressure on South Africa grew, white sports administrators, at last proclaiming their opposition to apartheid, blamed everything on the Nationalist government, insisting they were helpless against politicians who would not allow them to cross the racial divide. In short, they offered the plea that they were only carrying out orders. (The verdict of history might have favoured them more if they had carried out such orders with less ruthless fervour and efficiency.) The Government, in turn, took expensive advertisements in Western papers, claiming that there were no laws relating to sport, that sports bodies were autonomous and that these bodies liked to organize along separate lines in accordance with the 'traditions and customs' of South Africa. The hypocrisy was transparent to most sophisticated readers, but the doublespeak was useful at times in fooling the more gullible, especially when it was backed up (as in Britain) by the assertions of some UK politicians and businessmen with 'interests' in South Africa.

White sports administrators often enough made it clear that they saw demands for mixed teams and mixed trials as something of a temporary expedient. In 1962, when there was much debate about merit selection in athletics, the Western Transvaal Amateur Athletic Association had issued a statement saying, 'It is not necessary to send combined teams. . . . We are looking for trouble if we go against the policy of the Government. . . . Recreation for the non-whites does not depend on competition with the whites. When the Bantustans are developed they will get all the competition they want.'

It was only when the white regime felt it was under pressure from international sport that ministers intervened to revise policy. The first Government statement on sport came only in 1956, more than half a century after South Africa had started participating in international sports. That year marked the first in which white sports organizations suffered a series of defeats across a wide front. Several black sports bodies, including South African Cricket Board of Control and the South African Weightlifting and Body-Building Federation, applied to international sports organizations for membership. They were peremptorily brushed aside, but the International Table Tennis Federation recognized the non-white South African Table Tennis Board. Originally the international federation had been prepared to recognize both the white and the non-white bodies, but during a tour by the Israeli table tennis team, non-whites were banned even as spectators by the white South African table tennis organization and, for the international body, this was the last straw. A relatively recently formed international body, it had few of the cobwebs of the other sporting bodies and was run by an enlightened president, Ivor Montagu. It became the first international sports organization to recognize the sporting nature of white South Africa. Others would follow – but not for some years yet.

It was in 1956, in response to all this and to the fact that, for the first time, non-whites in South Africa had formed a body to campaign against apartheid sport, that Dr T. E. Dönges, Minister of the Interior, made a statement. He formally confirmed that whites and blacks must organize their sports separately; that there could be no mixed sport within the borders of the country; that no mixed teams could come from abroad; and that international teams competing in South Africa against white South African teams must be all-white. If non-white organizations wanted international recognition they could do so only through white bodies, and any attempt by non-white bodies to challenge white South Africa's sporting links would be deemed 'subversive'. Within months the South African police would raid the Johannesburg offices of the Transvaal Indian Congress and triumphantly produce a letter that charged the South African Olympic Council with being discriminatory. The letter was later used as evidence during the Johannesburg 'treason' trial of 1956.

The one concession made by Dönges was that, at least in South Africa, non-white sportsmen could compete against non-whites from overseas. (In the early 1950s Jake N'Tuli had not been allowed to box for South Africa or even against overseas opponents in South Africa. He left for Britain and became British flyweight champion in 1952 and the British Empire flyweight champion in 1953.) Such was the nature of South African society that Dönges's mealy-mouthed concession was hailed as a major breakthrough. It was nothing of the kind, and Dönges's mendacity became apparent when, over the next few years, a boxer and a non-white table tennis team were denied passports and an Egyptian table tennis team was denied entry. All had been invited to engage in perfectly legal sports events against non-whites.

Sometimes, despite the welter of apartheid law, and the

fact that the facilities for whites and non-whites were hugely unbalanced in favour of the whites, the odd non-white sportsman was able to prove he could be as good, or even better, than the whites. In January 1962 Sewsunker 'Papwa' Sewgolum won the Natal Open Golf Championship. However, under the Group Areas Act he could not enter the clubhouse at Durban Country Club to receive the prize and was forced to accept it outdoors in the pouring rain. Not all Indians like 'Papwa' were banned from the clubhouse – but the ones inside were waiters serving food and drinks. The South African Broadcasting Corporation refused to report the result. A spokesman explained: 'We do not broadcast multi-racial sport.' Sewgolum had success abroad (he won the Dutch Open three times) and he would win the Natal Open again in 1965; but in South Africa he always had to fight to take part. In January 1961 the South African Golf Union had delayed its decision on his entry long enough to keep him out of the Natal Open. But in March of that year he was allowed to play in the South African Open after ministerial permission had been sought. However, the minister refused to allow Sewgolum to use the practice ground or the clubhouse facilities. Other non-white golfers had decided to leave South Africa rather than put up with the humiliation. Sewgolum chose to fight. And the picture of him receiving the trophy outdoors in the rain said more about apartheid sport than any number of words.

His victory was followed in 1965 by another change in the Group Areas Act, although it was not entirely directed at him. In its previous form the Act had made black 'occupation' of a white area illegal for a wide variety of purposes. However, the words used in the act referred to 'any public cinema'. Bioscopes, as cinemas were known in South Africa, had long been segregated. Now Proclamation R 26 replaced 'any public cinema' with the words 'any place of public entertainment'. If Sewgolum wanted to play golf and did so on a course intended for whites he could now be said to be illegally occupying a white area of entertainment. He was effectively banned from competing in major golf events in South Africa.

The amendment had been brought in because many overseas artists visiting South Africa insisted on performing before multi-racial audiences. They would now be required to sign a declaration saying they would not do so. And when, in December 1964, the singer Dusty Springfield refused to sign, she was thrown out of the country.

Later ministerial statements clarified how the proclamation would work. If separate seating, entrances and toilet facilities were provided at public entertainments, non-whites could attend provincial and international events provided they did not disturb whites. What exactly was meant by 'disturb' was never made clear. In any case, black South Africans could not attend any event below provincial level. In Newlands stadium non-whites were allowed to enter but the Government ordered a six-foot high wire fence to be erected to separate them from whites. As Adrian Guelke has said, 'Proclamation R 26 of 1965 stands out as the pinnacle of petty apartheid.'

At this time in the mid-1960s the campaign to isolate white South Africa from international sport was still to get into its stride. The first of the protests that were later to become common were staged in 1964. That year a Davis Cup match in Norway saw 50 arrests after protestors stormed the court; the Test wicket at Wellington was damaged during the cricket tour of New Zealand; and a bowls tour of Britain was constantly disrupted. The Lord Provost of Glasgow refused to hold the customary civic luncheon for the visiting Springboks; there were demonstrations in Cardiff; and a match in Dublin was cancelled. South Africa's white football governing body, which had been suspended in 1956 and later reinstated by the FIFA executive, was suspended once more in 1963 by the FIFA congress.

The white sporting bodies, aware that they were coming under pressure, began to make the first of a series of compromises. Football provides a case study of how the white body reacted to the threat to its international affiliation. Football had generally been seen as a black sport in South Africa, very popular with the emerging black working class employed in the mines and the cities. The white working classes also played the game. Before the Second World War Boskburg, a small town a few miles east of Johannesburg which became infamous in the later 1980s for voting to reinstate petty apartheid – segregation of parks, toilets, and so on – contributed no less than nine players to English and Scottish professional soccer. Given that the population there was less than 20,000 white inhabitants, this was quite remarkable. However, soccer made no impact on what was considered polite white society, and newspapers catering for a largely white readership hardly ever reported the game. In the late 1920s the best soccer teams had been Indian. A team had toured India and in 1933 the Indians came to South Africa. The first professional league, formed only in 1959, was a black initiative. This developed from the SA Soccer Federation, which had brought together all the black racial federations and was soon to become fully non-racial.

The official white body retaliated by setting up its own all-white league. It also allowed the South African Bantu Football Association, which represented black footballers, to affiliate to it and soon gave it a seat and a vote on the executive. B. P. Morola, the Bantu FA president, was made a member of the white body's delegation to FIFA's conference during the World Cup in Chile in 1962 in order to plead for the white organization. The representatives of the non-racial SA Soccer Federation were refused passports by the South African government, so they were unable to plead their case.

The main objection to the official white body was that it was practising a highly paternalistic form of multi-racialism. Each race group – Indian, Coloured, Bantu (as the Africans were then known) – would have their own body, and the white organization would co-ordinate all their activities as an overlord. There were even to be inter-racial matches – but the Government objected to this after only one match had been played and the scheme was abandoned. At the same time the white body set about trying to strangle the non-racial black soccer organization. It successfully appealed to the municipal authorities responsible for the grounds. Since at that time every football ground in South Africa was owned and administered by the municipalities, this had a devastating effect. The non-racial body found it could not play; its clubs faced bankruptcy; and a series of non-racial matches that were to be held in protest had to be cancelled because the police removed the goalposts.

Although the FIFA had suspended the white body in January 1963 it had also decided to send a commission to look at the situation on the ground. Before it arrived the white body hurriedly created a new Indian football federation and a new Coloured association, both of which sought affiliation with the white organization. By the time the FIFA enquiry team, led by Sir Stanley Rous, had arrived, the non-racial body was virtually defunct. It had lost grounds and supporters, and its secretary, George Singh, was a banned person. The Rous enquiry, after 10 days of lavish feasts and cocktail parties, came to the conclusion that the suspension should be lifted. It seemed that the white body's tactics had worked. Vivian Granger, the manager of the white national football league, who had declared 'total war' on the non-racial soccer clubs, hailed this as a 'defeat for communism'. South Africans, he said, 'were obliged to practise apartheid in sport because it is the policy of the Government and traditional, but we must ensure in future that it is Christian apartheid'.

In the end, as we have seen, the tactics of the white body did not prevail and the FIFA congress overruled its executive. But throughout the later 1960s and early 1970s the white body tried to destroy its non-racial counterpart, and it came within an ace of doing so. Its tactics were typical of the ways white bodies reacted to pressure both from within and without. As Robert Archer and Antoine Bouillon observed, 'Initially the white federation gave way to foreign pressure; it was then brought short by the Government when it made

concessions which began to weaken apartheid, and proceeded, as the gap widened between the demands of apartheid and those of the international authorities, to concoct
increasingly bizarre and implausible negotiating positions.'
At one stage, in trying to avert an FIFA suspension, the white
body had proposed that South Africa would enter a black
team for the 1966 World Cup, a white team for the 1970
event, and so on. Such absurdities were not confined to
soccer. In 1963 a so-called multi-racial team of amateur
boxers left South Africa for a tour of America. Five whites
and three non-whites were chosen. The whites flew in one
plane, the non-whites in another. The South African press
was not allowed to photograph them as a group. And since
government ministers had said often enough that non-whites
could not qualify for the Springbok colours, none of the
boxers were awarded them. Once they left South Africa,
however, the group travelled and lived together, apparently
without coming to serious harm. A few months later 10
South African athletes toured Britain, but being black they
were not allowed to wear the Springbok emblem. Bennet
Makgamathe set a new South African record in his event,
but this did not mean he would be selected for the Olympics
team.

For white South African sport officials, merit selections
were a nightmare. In 1962 the white Amateur Athletic Union
had sent what was described as a team selected on merit to
compete in Mozambique, then still under Portuguese rule.
The team consisted only of white runners, although two
black athletes had run their heats faster than the whites
selected instead of them. When Matt Mare, head of the white
athletics union, was asked why Humphrey Khosi, whose
time was 0.1 seconds faster than the white man selected, was
not chosen, he uttered the immortal words: '0.1 second
does not really count.'

Merit selection for South African sportsmen hoping to
compete in the 1964 Olympic Games in Tokyo triggered
even more extraordinary behaviour by the white adminis-

trators. The International Olympic Committee was threatening to ban South Africa from the Games. The white South African Olympic Games Association proposed that blacks would be selected on merit for the Olympic team – but not in direct competition with whites, as this would contravene government policy. But what, it was asked, if the separate trials produced identical results? The white body replied that tests would be carried out in a medical laboratory to determine which athlete was 'better': 'By the use of objective tests of physiological and psychological capacity we hope to help with the final assessment of material available for selection in 1964. . . . Thus should a situation arise in which two sportsmen of like ability vie for the final place available in our athletics or cycling teams, this laboratory will be able to recommend which of the two performers should be selected.'

White South Africa had its sympathizers within the IOC, but this was too much even for them and South Africa was eventually excluded from the Tokyo games – the first it had missed since it started participating in 1908. The decision to ban South Africa was arrived at only after several meetings at which she was offered many 'last chances', but these served only to demonstrate how tenaciously South Africa could fight to maintain her international sporting position on her own terms.

It also showed the great differences in the attitude to South Africa of world organizations governing sports such as table tennis, football, cricket and rugby. In rugby South Africa's membership of the international body was never suspended or even seriously questioned. In cricket, there was the most curious and very cricket-like decision which illustrated the link between white South African cricket administrators and the MCC.

South Africa's cricket status had come into doubt not because of any sporting pressure but because of political change initiated by white South Africa itself. In May 1961 South Africa had voted to become a republic and left the Commonwealth. This meant that it should lose its member-

ship of the Imperial Cricket Conference. South Africa, represented by R. E. Foster-Bowley, President of the SA Cricket
Association, asked that the rules be changed so that she
could continue to be a member. India, Pakistan and the West
Indies voted against this, while South Africa had the white
votes of England, Australia and New Zealand to support
her. Thus the ICC was deadlocked, and the decision was
deferred. In other words, the ICC swept the problem under
the table.

The Pakistan board argued that unless South Africa was
prepared to play matches entirely on equal terms with Pakistan, India and the West Indies, other countries should not
play Test matches with South Africa. In other words, the
division in cricket created by South Africa should be ended.
True, this argument had morality and logic on its side, but
for the white South Africans it was a monstrous demand.
They denounced it as political, and C. O. Medworth, a
leading white sports journalist of the time, observed: 'The
Indian, Pakistan and West Indies delegates, who must know
precisely what the position is as it concerns South African
cricketers, have every opportunity of not allowing politics to
encroach on the noble game of cricket. By depriving South
Africa of her status on the ICC, it is the players who are
suffering, not those who frame the laws of the country . . .
there is precious little chance for some time to come of South
Africa changing her views on the playing of mixed sport.
That is a Government decree and there it must remain. There
is absolutely nothing that cricketers and cricket legislators
can do about it, try as they would. Springbok teams would
only too gladly visit the West Indies, India and Pakistan – if
they would have us. But the trouble is that we could not
reciprocate without causing our guests some embarrassment
on the social side and in the matter of accommodation.'

As far as her friends in England, Australia and New Zealand were concerned, South Africa's policy towards the black
Commonwealth cricketers could be ignored. Playing cricket
with South Africa meant keeping the options open, 'building

bridges'. But as Derek Wyatt, who played rugby for England, was to ask, 'How long is this bridge?' England had been playing cricket with white South Africa since 1889; there were ties of friendship, blood and traditional culture, not to mention business associations. White South Africa was a wonderful place for whites, and the English cricket administrators saw no reason why this should change. On the other hand, the West Indies were just emerging as a major Test-playing country, while neither India or Pakistan were considered good enough to merit full-scale Test series, and England had traditionally sent a 'B' team, shorn of its best players, on tour there. In any case, a tour to the sub-continent was something to dread – all that squalor, the suspect food, the undrinkable water; whereas a tour to South Africa was a wonderful six-month holiday with sun, sand, lovely weather, wonderful food, beautiful women, and of course the pleasure of playing against 'our' kind of chaps.

So, although South Africa was out of the ICC, England, Australia and New Zealand continued to play Test matches with her. And despite the fact that they were meant to be unofficial, at some stage – nobody quite knows when – they were made official. It is doubtful if a formal decision on this was ever taken by the ICC. England, Australia and New Zealand just treated the Tests as official and carried on as if nothing had changed. Initially the Tests against New Zealand in the South African summer of 1961–2 were deemed to be unofficial and were played over four rather than five days; but both countries refused to accept that these were not full internationals. Australia announced that the 1963–4 tour by South Africa would also have full international status. R. E. Foster-Bowley submitted the South African board's view that 'matches between fully representative sides belonging to two countries constitute an international contest in the fullest sense of the word'. After the series was over, the ICC, in July 1962, agreed that there was nothing to prevent matches played in South Africa being called Tests, though these were not recognized as official. But they were nonetheless treated as such and remained so.

If this seems to be a fairly typical example of the way entrenched and unaccountable authorities of any kind deal with difficult issues by saying something but meaning something else, it must be remembered that in the 1960s more people were willing to believe that protesting about apartheid in sports – in other words, bringing politics into sport – was frightfully bad form. The obvious truth was that South Africa had brought politics, in the form of brutally repressive race laws, into sport. In 1960 even the newspaper editor Donald Woods, who would later be forced to flee South Africa because of his anti-apartheid views, upbraided demonstrators outside Lord's who were protesting against the visit of the South African team: 'They are sportsmen, not politicians.' At that time Woods, by his own admission, was a racist who, in his student days, had argued that blacks should be kept segregated. Later he was mortified when he heard that Jackie McGlew, the South African captain on the 1960 tour, had joined the Nationalist party and had stood for Parliament. 'That,' he writes, 'was the start of my disillusion with the doctrine of "keeping politics separate from sport" – a lunatic view in retrospect, since sport is part of life, and all life is connected with politics.'

For more than 12 years after the Nationalists had come to power in 1948, South Africa had continued to be a member of the Commonwealth. Just as in cricket it did not play the black and brown countries even though the governing bodies of all Test-playing countries met once a year at Lord's, so politically it had no relations with the black nations of the Commonwealth although once a year the leaders of this co-called family, with the Queen at its head, forgathered for a conference. Then the South African prime minister would consent to sit next to the Indian prime minister. Indeed in 1948 Dr Daniel Malan, just elected as the first Nationalist Prime Minister, supported the Indian premier Jawaharlal Nehru in his contention that the Commonwealth would have to be modified if the emerging brown and black countries were to belong to it. India had originally wanted to leave the Commonwealth which, before Indian independence in 1947, was really an association of the white dominions of Australia, New Zealand, Canada and South Africa. The British government pressed Nehru to keep India in the Commonwealth, which led to the evolution of the form of association in which the new republics remained members without accepting the British monarch as their head of state.

It was only in 1960, following the massacre of Sharpeville, that the South African issue became a Commonwealth problem. South Africa, for the first time, found that the ex-colonial Asian and African countries would no longer tolerate her membership of the Commonwealth. Hendrik Verwoerd, unwilling to face rebuff, withdrew, declaring South Africa a republic in May 1961.

The spirit of the times was reflected within South Africa as well. In 1960, at the end of a two-year trial on patently trumped up charges, Nelson Mandela would tell the court:

'I would say, "Yes, let us talk", and the Government would say, "We think the Europeans at present are not ready for the type of Government where there might be domination by non-Europeans. We think we should give you 60 seats – the African population to elect 60 Africans to represent them in Parliament. We will leave the matter now for five years and we will review it at the end of five years." In my view, that would be a victory. . . . I'd say we should accept it, but, of course, I would not abandon my demands for the extension of universal suffrage to all Africans. That's how I see it, my lords. Then at the end of the five-year period we will have discussions and the Government says, "We will give you again 40 more seats." I might say, "That's quite sufficient, let's accept it", and still demand that the franchise be extended, but for the agreed period we should suspend civil disobedience.' This a far cry from the one man, one vote idea that would inspire the anti-apartheid movement from the 1970s onwards. Indeed, Mandela's proposals seem nowadays to have been unduly modest. Yet so dangerous was Mandela thought to be that he was moved to the notorious Robben Island penal colony, north of Cape Town, and branded as a dangerous subversive.

Graeme Wright thinks we need to look at the changes in the world political situation to appreciate why it was only in the late 1960s that South Africa and its racist policies became an important international issue. 'I always feel, as far as the major powers were concerned – that is, the Western Alliance – that we need to look at when the Simonstown naval base at the Cape of Good Hope lost its strategic importance.' The base was an ideal place for maintaining and refuelling warships moving between the Atlantic and Indian oceans. And as long as NATO submarines, especially, had a vital need for the base, it was strategically unthinkable that South Africa could be on the 'wrong' side, or even neutral, in the Cold War. With the development in the late 1950s of the nuclear submarine which could sail submerged for months at a time, Simonstown lost much of its strategic importance, and for that reason alone the West could afford to give in to pressure from some of the African countries who were opposed to South Africa. This pressure was in any case growing steadily because the industrialized world needed to trade and have good relations with newly independent black Africa. By the time the Biafran war had finished in 1970, Africa had emerged from its colonial past and consisted of independent countries that had to be courted as trading partners. One way of courting them was to proclaim opposition to South Africa.

The South African journalist Alister Sparks, once editor of the *Rand Daily Mail*, has written in *The Mind of South Africa* that 'There is a strange chemistry by which the world from time to time reaches a consensus on some great moral issue such as this [racism].' Slavery had been practised for millennia without any of the great religions or great philosophers denouncing it. Neither Christ, nor Muhammad, nor

Saint Augustine or Thomas Aquinas, even Luther and Calvin found anything wrong with it. Then suddenly at the end of the eighteenth century it became anathema. So it was with South Africa and racism. Its time to be the pariah of the world had come.

2

The White Ambulance and the
Black Patient

On 13 May 1946 Oscar State, Secretary of the British Amateur Weightlifters' Association, wrote a letter in reply to an appeal by black weightlifters of South Africa, asking for his support in their campaign to gain recognition from their white counterparts. State replied, regretting that the Central Council could not bring any pressure on the South African Weightlifting Federation to force them to recognize their black counterparts: 'Their rules, as with all national sporting associations in South Africa, will not permit mixed contests between white and coloured athletes. This is also a condition of the South African Olympic Council. Therefore, no coloured man could be chosen to represent South Africa in the international contests. For these reasons we cannot support your claim against the South African Weightlifting Federation.'

We move forward some 16 years to 15 February 1962 and the lounge of the Marine Hotel at Summerstrand, along the seafront at Port Elizabeth. Gordon Leggat, manager of the New Zealand cricket team touring South Africa, was meeting a man called Dennis Brutus. Although the world had changed a great deal since 1946, white South African sport and the attitude of the international community towards its racist nature had changed little. Indeed, Leggat's response to Brutus's extremely modest appeal was a mixture of arrogance and rudeness that, appalling as it may seem to us now, was quite characteristic of its time. Brutus was later to produce a remarkably accurate recollection of the meeting – so accurate, indeed, that Leggat accused him of secretly tape-recording it. It provides a chilling insight into a certain kind of sports official, who, 30 years ago, was by no means confined to South Africa.

Port Elizabeth was Brutus's home town, but the hotel where Leggat was staying was for whites only. Brutus, a Coloured man (as South Africans of mixed race are known) could not just walk in there. 'I was able to call in advance and ask to see him, and when I got there I explained that I had an arrangement to see him.' He was allowed into the hotel foyer. Almost immediately Leggat took Brutus to task for daring to write to the New Zealand board suggesting they should not tour South Africa. The letter had been posted from Christchurch in New Zealand, and Leggat said: 'We do not like the idea of receiving correspondence from your body posted, by registered mail from Christchurch, by someone whom I know personally and who knows little about cricket.'

Brutus explained that the letter had been posted from New Zealand because if it had been sent from South Africa it might have been stopped. Leggat responded: 'It might well have been stopped – I don't know. But it caused resentment in New Zealand to receive the letter in that way.'

Then Leggat explained why New Zealand had to tour white South Africa: 'You asked us not to come unless we were assured by the South African Cricket Association that it would select teams from all the players. Now a team that is invited can never tell the hosts whom to select: you just can't do it.' This was from a New Zealand official whose rugby authorities had, for almost 40 years, willingly agreed not to include Maoris in teams playing against the Springboks in New Zealand.

But, protested Brutus, the Kiwis were playing international matches. Shouldn't they make sure the teams they played were representative of the country they claimed to represent? But Leggat, seizing on the confusion caused by the ICC's failure to determine South Africa's status, insisted that strictly speaking no Test matches were to be played. He then trotted out the old argument: 'Whose cause would be advanced by not coming? You would only be depriving yourself of any good. You would be punishing players who are not allowed, through no fault of their own, to play non-whites. I believe that, among the cricketers, the majority are opposed to the present State policy, but they have no hope of changing it – not at present.'

This ran contrary to everything Brutus knew to be true. Legally, as we have seen, nothing prevented whites and non-whites from playing together. The white cricketers had the vote, so they could use it to express their disapproval of government policy. But most of them, even if they did not follow Jackie McGlew by joining the Nationalists and standing for Parliament, mouthed the standard 'I am opposed to apartheid' line but when the chips were down dutifully voted for it. Before the ICC meeting in July 1961 Brutus had approached Arthur Coy, president of the white cricket body, and Algy Frames, its secretary. Would they be prepared to admit non-whites to their body? Frames replied that the matter had been considered, and now it was closed.

Brutus's request seems so moderate to us today. All he wanted was a statement by the white sportsmen that they were willing to play non-whites. 'If all the white sportsmen in the country stated that there was danger of their losing international recognition and they insisted there should be fair play, I believe they would get away with it – because they are also the electorate and their votes decide the policy of the country.'

But for Leggat, ever ready to see the good side of white South Africa and unable to see any merit in the non-white case, this was impossible. Even when Brutus told him how he had often been refused a passport to present the non-racial case abroad, Leggat was unmoved. And when Brutus pressed him to do something at the ICC about the all-white cricket body, Leggat simply said that was for the ICC to decide.

Joined by Murray Chapple, vice-captain of the touring party, Leggat then took Brutus to task for appealing to non-whites not to attend the tourists' matches: 'I notice there has been no material support from the non-whites. They have not attended our matches. The tour is going to show a loss; we are losing money on it. And there have been very few non-whites.'

'Particularly in Johannesburg,' put in Chapple. 'There was only a handful of non-whites. At Umzinto I do not think there were more than two Indians – and they were gatekeepers. . . . Support from the non-whites has been very poor and we are going to show a loss on this tour.' For both New Zealanders, a profit-making tour was of far more importance than the fact that they and their fellow country-men were aiding and abetting racism. As Leggat said, Bru-tus's behaviour was no way to earn the gratitude of the New Zealand board. 'I can tell you we are losing on the tour and this is one of the things that will not endear you to people in New Zealand.'

In later years Leggat became a power in New Zealand and a top administrator in the country's cricket. His attitude and behaviour in this encounter with Brutus found an echo over the years in many other sports administrators in the white Commonwealth, who thought (or pretended to think) that a boycott of South African sport would do no good and, despite all the evidence, continued to argue that white South Africa would not change under international pressure, and that it was necessary to 'build bridges'. But few could match Leggat's mixture of arrogance, condescension and eagerness to see nothing but good in the whites and the worst in the blacks.

Brutus had an education and cultural background similar to that of many men of his race. He had studied in segregated schools in Port Elizabeth and then gone to Fort Hare, the most famous black college in southern Africa. Robert

Mugabe, now president of Zimbabwe, had been there and recalls playing tennis with Brutus; so, for a short time, was Nelson Mandela and, later, Krish Mackerdhuj, the current President of South African cricket. Brutus, who majored in English and psychology and gained a diploma in education, played rugby and soccer, did some cross-country running and was quite a good left-arm medium-fast bowler. It was while watching the high jumping of Seretse Khama, whose marriage in 1948 to the English girl Ruth would so shock white South Africa, that Brutus became aware of racial discrimination in sports. Khama jumped higher than any other South African athlete, white or black, but he never could make, or even be considered for, the Olympic team. Then a friend told Brutus, 'Did you know the Olympic Charter forbids racial discrimination or any discrimination on the basis of race, colour, religion or politics?' Brutus, with characteristic thoroughness, looked up the charter and discovered this to be true. He returned to segregated life in Port Elizabeth and slowly began his campaign of protest against white sport's blatant disregard of the Olympic Charter.

Initially he had some success. He helped organize the boycott of the white table tennis body and the recognition of the non-white one. This was a forerunner of other non-racial sports bodies applying for recognition. The non-white South African Cricket Board of Control got nowhere, but the application by the weightlifting and body-building organization made some impression on Avery Brundage, then president of the International Olympic Committee (IOC). He thought that the problem of South Africa might come on the agenda of the IOC. And the non-white cycling organization forced the white body to offer help, the first offer of such assistance.

Brutus, encouraged by this, attempted in 1955 to form the Co-ordinating Committee for International Relations in Sport, a sort of clearing house for non-racial bodies to apply to the international organizations. Even to organize a meeting in apartheid South Africa took some doing. Most halls and hotels were for whites only, and it was only through some Muslim friends that Brutus hired the hall at the Muslim Education Institute in Port Elizabeth's Kempson Road. About a dozen non-white sports administrators attended the meeting, but because of their timidity, the Co-ordinating Committee never really got off the ground.

Three years later, however, in October 1958, a much more substantial group of 50 met for two days in the non-white Milner Hotel in East London. Inevitably, members of the Special Branch came along and tried to force their way into the meeting. Brutus and his friends barred the way and closed the door on them. One of the Special Branch officers said, 'We will get a warrant to come in.' Brutus replied, 'Go ahead and do that. Until you do, you can't come in.' They did not get a warrant; instead, they tried to smuggle in a black member of the Special Branch as a sports administrator, but he was spotted. Then, apparently rebuffed, they left and did not come back for the second day's meeting. The South African Sports Association (SASA) was launched – the first non-white body to challenge the dominant white set-up.

Its first conference was held in January 1959 at Durban in a hotel in the Indian area. Alan Paton addressed it, defining the purpose of the organization as one of trying to 'co-ordinate non-white sport, to advance the cause of sport and the standards of sport among non-white sportsmen, and to see that they and their organizations receive proper recognition here and abroad and to do so on a non-racial basis'.

Within two months there was a project dear to Brutus's heart. One of the objects of his movement was to put a stop to matches along racial lines – whites against whites or even a white team against a black one – where the criterion for team selection was solely the colour of each player's skin. In 1956, for the very first time, a non-white cricket team had toured South Africa. In the history of non-white cricket in South Africa that tour by the Kenyan Asians was a seminal event. The non-white South Africans won the first two Tests, and the third was drawn. The series marked the emergence of Basil D'Oliveira, who led the South Africans. The Kenyans, impressed, invited the South Africans to tour their country and, for the first time, a truly non-white cricket team, representing all races except the whites, left South Africa: it proved another triumph, the tourists winning 13 of the 16 matches.

The non-white cricket administrators were much enthused by this. For much of the 1950s they had tried to bring about tours by India and Pakistan. They felt that, if the home players performed well against such opposition, the non-white body might be admitted to the ICC. In 1959 they thought they had an even better opportunity when Frank Worrell agreed to bring over a strong West Indian side, including Gary Sobers, Rohan Kanhai, Everton Weekes, Conrad Hunte, Sonny Ramadhin and Alf Valentine.

It was this tour, Brutus decided, that would be the first target of the SASA, in spite of the fact that the West Indian stars were heroes to non-white sportsmen in South Africa. Such a tour, he argued, would endorse apartheid since it would entail, however unintentionally, tacit acceptance of the separation of people by race. The politicians agreed with SASA, almost all shades of black political opinion in South Africa appealing to Worrell not to come; even Learie Constantine joined in. Curiously, one man who supported the tour was C. L. R. James, the doyen of West Indian cricket writers. After many years in the United States, he had returned to the West Indies, and he responded to a letter by Constantine published in *The Nation*, the Trinidad newspaper. He was as opposed to apartheid as Constantine but he argued that the tour would help defeat it:

'The argument is that, by accepting the conditions, you accept apartheid. Do the Africans who live under apartheid thereby accept it? If the Africans play West Indians under apartheid conditions, do the Africans accept apartheid? I cannot see that at all. I once spent six months in the USA organizing a strike of sharecroppers. I was kicked around as usual, eating in the kitchens when I travelled, sitting in the rear seats of buses, etc. Did I "accept" segregation? Did I happen to strengthen it? The facts are that I did exactly the opposite. The sharecroppers whom I worked with had a larger objective. . . . For my part, I want to see an African making a century in the first Test, and bowling Sobers and Kanhai for 0 in the same over (despite the fact that I admire these two more than any living cricketer except Worrell). It will be in a good cause. It will hit the headlines in Pakistan, in England, in Australia, in the West Indies, and in South Africa, too.'

James was a Trotskyite thinker with vast political experience. His *Beyond a Boundary* is a classic of cricket literature, perhaps the first book to appreciate the wider political and social considerations that underpin the game. Yet *à propos* of the Worrell tour he was advancing arguments about maintaining contact – the old 'building bridges' nonsense – that could have been made by a white official. To some extent, perhaps, James was seduced by the fact that had the tour taken place, a black man, Worrell, would have captained the West Indies for the first time. However, the fact that even a sophisticated political thinker such as James could fail to appreciate that methods of fighting apartheid sport called for different tactics than those involved in the Popular Front (that had preoccupied pre-war Left-wing political thought in Europe and with which James drew an analogy in an article supporting the tour), showed that South Africa and its apartheid policy had still not fully engaged the attention or stirred the conscience of the world outside. Sharpeville was soon to correct that.

Sharpeville marks the great divide in modern South African history. Before Sharpeville, and despite apartheid having been the law of the land for more than a decade, South Africa, if it existed in world consciousness, still had some of the glow created over 30 years by the work of Jan Smuts on the world stage. All this was destroyed by Sharpeville, where on Monday, 21 March 1960, several thousand black Africans gathered at the police station of this small town outside Johannesburg to protest about the hated pass laws. They had come without passes – the documents they had to carry or face arrest – and they were offering themselves for arrest. Unarmed, peaceful if noisy, this was a protest in the great tradition of the non-violent campaigns Gandhi had launched so successfully against the British in India. But facing them were not British soldiers but young Afrikaners, men brought up on tales of black danger, of the half naked black man jumping into a white farmhouse and impaling a white infant on his assegai. For all the passivity of the crowd and the fact that they were unarmed, the police, without orders and quite unprovoked, opened fire and killed 69, wounding 178. Many of them were shot in the back trying to flee the murderous bullets. The atrocity made headlines around the world, and South Africa would never be the same again.

Alan Paton has written that 'the effect of Sharpeville on the outside world was immense'. In 18 months 240 million Rand flowed out of the country, and for the first time the international community began to take critical notice of South Africa. Smuts may have played a leading part in the creation of the UN. Now the Security Council for the first time voted 9–0 for a resolution condemning South Africa. Shamefully, if not to any great surprise, Britain abstained in the vote, as did France.

Sport, too, was affected and for the first time organizations were formed to protest about South Africa's participation in international sport. In England a body called the Campaign Against Race Discrimination in Sport came out in opposition to the 1960 South African cricket tour, and the Rev. David Sheppard, one of England's leading batsmen, said he would not play against the tourists. But his was an isolated position. Despite Sharpeville, most people in England probably agreed with *The Times* editorial which, welcoming the cricket team to the country, said Englishmen must understand the conditions white South Africans lived in and should be kind to them as they were England's 'old friends'.

South Africa also took part in the Rome Olympics, Brutus finding it almost impossible to get his case heard abroad. His home, along with that of other SASA leaders, was raided by the police. Documents such as a petition to the New Zealand Prime Minister on the rugby tour and a letter to David Sheppard about the cricket tour were deemed subversive, threatening the very existence of white South Africa – an interesting example of how the white regime saw the nascent non-racial sports movement. Brutus was very keen to go to Rome to present his case, but he was denied a passport. However the non-racial case was heard, Rev. Michael Scott going from England along with Nelson Mahono, a former member of the Pan-African Congress, then living in Ghana.

The main battleground was, obviously, going to be the Olympic Games. Brutus had himself chosen this battleground for – as he would later tell Leggat at the Marine Hotel meeting – the principal target of SASA was the Olympic Games 'because of the number of codes of sport involved and because a breakthrough here would result in a major breakthrough in most codes of sport'.

On the face of it this offered promising ground. The Olympic Charter outlawed racial discrimination and even the Nazi Olympics of 1936 had shown how the success of one black man, Jesse Owens, could rattle Adolf Hitler. The problem for Brutus was the quite extraordinary hold white South Africa had over international sport.

At this stage, in the early 1960s, the International Olympic Committee had only two delegates from Africa. Both of them were white, both having the Christian name Reg; one was Reg Alexander from Kenya and the other was Reg Honey from South Africa.

On 15 January 1961 Honey came to address the SASA conference at the Patider Hall in Fordsburg, a suburb of Johannesburg. After lecturing the delegates about the spirit of the Olympic Charter and how it made no distinction of race, colour or creed, Honey told them that he had assured the IOC that if a 'non-European' was good enough to represent South Africa he undoubtedly would do so. Before the meeting SASA had passed a resolution asking the IOC to expel South Africa from the Olympic Games. Honey, not surprisingly, thought this was not a good idea. But he was a reasonable man, a fair man, he had discussed the position with the National Olympic Committee, and the white bodies affiliated to the NOC were willing to offer something to their non-white sporting colleagues. The offer was this:

1. The representatives of the non-racial body on the national body must be white.
2. The total votes of the non-white *national* body would be equal to that of one white *provincial* body.
3. Trials and championships must be staged separately (which, of course, would make it impossible to ensure that conditions were equal and fair).
4. The existing state of affairs with the white and non-racial bodies functioning under widely different conditions would be preserved.

For most of the SASA delegates this seemed to merely preserve the discriminatory status which they had been fighting against. But not for Reg Honey. He was 'agreeably surprised' at what he saw as a generous concession by the white bodies. His worry was about the 'non-European' bodies who were still not willing to affiliate to the white bodies. Yes, he realized, 'our affiliates and officials are insisting upon your representation being a European'. But this, 'I say, you must accept. It will at least give your candidates an opportunity. . . . The non-European should give in even if he only has his foot in the door.'

But even when the non-white bodies had accepted subservient affiliation it did them little good. Athletes were forced to accept a white representative and their selection trials were held four or five weeks before the European trials in a totally different city – Durban – instead of the European venue of Cape Town. The classic case was that of weightlifting. The white trials were held at Bloemfontein, capital of the Orange Free State in the heart of Afrikanerdom. The black trials were held in Cape Town. The non-whites invited a certain Mr Healey, who was chairman of the white body, to act as one of their judges at the non-racial trial. Precious

MacKenzie took part in the featherweight division and Mr Healey was quite satisfied that his lifting was correct and that he made a certain total. In the whites only trial at Bloemfontein the white weightlifter Gaffley failed to equal MacKenzie's total and indeed failed to record any total whatsoever. But when it came for selection for the 1960 Olympics at Rome it was Gaffley who went, not MacKenzie. However, for Honey, what the non-whites were asking would only be possible in an 'ideal state of affairs'. The fact that in the United States blacks and whites could compete together was for him 'the perfect state of affairs' – but that was impossible in South Africa.

Astonishingly, despite the crude racism that Honey was spouting, the meeting in Patider Hall was quite cordial. Brutus thanked Honey for his courtesy and at the end of it all the president of SASA, G. K. Rangasami, said it was his 'pleasure to move a vote of thanks to Mr Honey'. Honey, playing the part of the big white chief to the end, responded by saying he appreciated the non-whites' points 'a little more fully' and that he would put them to his colleagues at the IOC.

While he was doing so the white South African Government acted. In 1961 Dennis Brutus was banned under the Suppression of Communism Act, which meant a person would be violating the law if he or she met more than one other person in any place – be it a public one or in the privacy of their own home. Brutus's ban was intended to stop him presenting the non-white case to the Olympic Committee.

The IOC was to meet in Moscow in 1962 and just before it met the Government issued another ruling: all invitations to overseas teams must be approved by it before they were sent out. Jan de Klerk made it very clear that the Government policy was that no mixed teams should take part in sport inside or outside the country. After that, Honey felt there was little point in attending the IOC meeting. And in Moscow Avery Brundage confirmed that Honey's promises had not been fulfilled. But even then the IOC was full of understanding for the white South African position. Only five members voted for immediate suspension and it was decided to give the white body another chance: until October 1963. By then the IOC hoped the South Africans would have eliminated racism in sports.

The white South Africans should have celebrated this victory but *Die Transvaaler* spoke for many when it said the decision 'confirmed what has been happening on the South African sports field for the past five years – that international sport has lost its value. It has now become a battlefield where political differences must be settled.' And Matt Mare of the South African Amateur Athletic Union, the man who had felt that 0.1 second did not really count when judging performances on the track, was sure that this decision of the IOC was 'a political trick against the South African Government'.

The white South Africans' victory in Moscow forced the non-whites to reorganize. SASA had served its purpose. In August 1962 SASA announced it had launched a plan to form a non-racial Olympic body which would apply to represent South Africa on the IOC in place of the existing white one. On 7 October in Durban a decision was taken to form the South African Non-Racial Olympic Committee (SANROC) and in June 1963 SANROC was officially launched. For the third time in five years the non-whites had formed a body to try to combat racism in sport and at last they had come up with an organization which would outlive apartheid in sport.

One man who couldn't attend SANROC's launch was Dennis Brutus himself. He was now not only a banned person but had been jailed for violating his banning orders. It had come about the previous month, in May 1963, when Brutus attempted to meet Robert Basliger, a Swiss journalist who had come to Johannesburg to do a story on racism in sport. The meeting was meant to be held at the white Olympic body's offices but no sooner had Brutus arrived, than so did the police. Many of the SANROC officials felt that the whole thing had been the work of Frank Braun who had just taken

over as head of the white Olympic body. A former boxer,
with cauliflower ears, he had for long been head of the white
South African Boxing Association. Braun will figure more
prominently in our story. One indication of the kind of man
he was can be gauged from a remark he made when inter-
viewed by *Sports Illustrated* in June 1968. Asked about all-
white teams, Braun said, 'Some sports the African is not
suited for. In swimming the water closes their pores and they
cannot get rid of carbon-dioxide, so they tire quickly.'

The police had come from an office next to Braun's but
Braun denied that he had anything to do with tipping them
off. 'When I arrived I found Brutus was there. It was illegal
for him to speak to a meeting this large, and I told him so.
I said "Dennis, you know that you cannot speak to this
meeting. Will you please leave?" Harris [John Harris who
was now head of SANROC] said that Brutus was there only
to introduce us all, since he knew everyone. But I could have
done the same thing. I knew everyone there. But before
anything else could take place, the Special Forces came in,
arrested Brutus and took him away for breaking the law. I
have been accused of having tipped them off, but that
would have served no purpose. I think myself that Harris
tipped off the Special Forces simply to create a disturbance
and a martyr.'

Worse was to follow. Brutus was very keen to present the
case against white South Africa, at the IOC meeting in Baden
Baden in October. This meant escaping from his house arrest.
Under the terms of his house arrest he had to report to the
police and was allowed out of the small house on Park Road
in Johannesburg's Fordsburg area for a couple of hours for
that purpose. A young friend of his, an Indian South African
called Ibrahim, mentioned that he might be able to help him
make his getaway to Swaziland. Ibrahim's father had a shop
along the Swaziland border and had noticed that on Sunday
afternoons the white South African border guards, after a
good meal, were very casual in checking papers. Often they

would just wave people through. Brutus decided it was worth
a try and one day, towards the end of July, he made his bid.

'I had to go to the police station in Fordsburg and sign
the register. But that day, instead of coming back home I
went to join Ibrahim and a couple of other friends. They
had organized a Volkswagen combi, a sort of station wagon,
and the four of us, the driver, his wife, Ibrahim and I started
off for the Swaziland border. It was a drive of about four
hours and sure enough when we arrived there we found the
guards dozing and they waved us through. I had a place to
stay, the house of Jordon Ngubane, who had fled from South
Africa some time before. Swaziland then was a British Protec-
torate and I thought that since I had been born in Rhodesia
[he had left when he was a small child] I would be entitled
to British protection. I felt the British would be sympathetic.
But they said I could only stay a month and at the end of it
I would have to leave. My immediate thought was of taking
a flight out of Swaziland. I found a pilot of a small four
seater plane and he was willing to fly me to Botswana. I paid
him 500 Rands and booked the plane. But just before he
was due to fly me he had flown out a couple of South African
activists and received a threat from the South African Air
Force. They told him that if he used his plane again for such
a purpose then the South African Air Force would shoot it
out of the sky. So he refunded my money. Soon after, I had
dinner with a black doctor in Swaziland, a Dr Sibi. He
offered to drive me to Mozambique's capital, Lourenço Mar-
ques (now Maputo), from where I could take a flight to the
IOC meeting. George Singh, an Indian businessman and a
man who played a big part in the reorganization of non-racial
soccer, had got me a plane ticket and Robin Farquharson had
obtained a Rhodesian passport for me. Something I was
entitled to. Both of these were delivered to me in Swaziland.
Everything seemed fine. What I didn't know was that Sibi
was a South African agent. He was being paid to hand me
over to the South Africans. And no sooner did we cross the
Swaziland border into Mozambique at a place called Goba

than we were arrested by the PIDE (Portuguese Secret Police).'

Sibi returned to Swaziland, where some years later he became a high official in the Swazi government. A photocopy of the cheque he banked in his account for betraying Brutus was later printed in the papers. Brutus was taken to the Villa Algarve and for three days was interrogated by the PIDE.

'They told me that they had a secret arrangement with the South Africans. The South Africans caught the people they wanted and they caught the ones the South Africans wanted. They treated me very gingerly and I remember how very hesitantly they opened my Pelikan pen, thinking there might be a bomb in it. They did not torture me but there was heavy interrogation and I decided to go on hunger strike unless I saw a lawyer. I had committed no crime and I demanded legal assistance. After three days they promised to take me to the Swaziland border. I half believed them.'

But the PIDE took Brutus not to Goba but to a place called Komatipoort, on the South African frontier with Mozambique. Brutus realized the trick only when, as he got out of the car, he was confronted on that dusty border road by the two Special Branch men who had arrested him in Frank Braun's offices: Helsburg, the grey-haired, older, almost fatherly figure, and his young assistant, Kleingeld, whose name meant 'small change' and who was determined to give Brutus no change whatsoever. He threatened to rugby tackle Brutus should he try to escape. The next day, after a night in Komatipoort jail, he was remanded in custody by a magistrate. What struck Brutus was that there was no publicity, there was nobody in the courtroom. He feared the worst: he might be spirited away into a white South African prison while the outside world did not even know he was arrested and his friends would assume he was on his way to the IOC meeting. If the world was not alerted the white South African authorities would be able to do virtually what they liked with him.

Helsburg and Kleingeld, both armed, bundled him into the

back seat of a car and headed for Johannesburg. One of them drove, the other sat with Brutus, handcuffed to him. At about five they arrived in Johannesburg and stopped at McLean Square [now known as John Vorster Square] opposite the city's main police station:

'They instructed me to remove my suitcase and take it to the station. Although it was not heavy I carried it as if it was, half crouching, and when I got to the pavement I dropped it and began to run. I was gambling on being recaptured. I thought that Kleingeld would rugby tackle me and bring me back, but that it would be a public capture. We were in the middle of Johannesburg and it was the rush hour so people would notice, the media would notice and my kidnapping would no longer remain a secret. I really didn't think they would shoot. . . . But what I didn't know was that Helsburg had won a gold medal for markmanship. If I had known that I would have thought twice about it.'

Brutus's run took him past four blocks. He saw a bus and tried to clamber on to it. As he did so Kleingeld tried to pull him off and then the conductor kicked him and he fell back. Recovering quickly he started running again. That is when Helsburg shot him, point blank, in the back:

'At first I didn't feel anything, it was like someone had punched me in the back. Then I noticed a stain on my chest and it was spreading rapidly. What had happened was that the bullet had gone through my back and come out of the other side, it is what is called a through and through wound. I knew if I kept running I would bleed to death.'

Brutus collapsed opposite 44 Main Street, the imposing headquarters of Anglo-America, white South Africa's most powerful company and the symbol of white economic prosperity. As Helsburg came up, Brutus said, 'I have been shot.' Helsburg replied, 'I know, I shot you.' He then asked Brutus to walk back to the prison but Brutus could only lie there bleeding.

'As I lay on the pavement I could see 44 Main Street, the

office of Anglo-America. Someone from the office, I believe,
rang asking for an ambulance.'

An ambulance arrived soon enough. The stretcher was
brought out and the stretcher bearers approached Brutus.
Then the awful reality of white South Africa struck. The
ambulance, called by the man from the Anglo-America building, was a 'white' one. Brutus was a non-white. There was
no way he could be put on that stretcher, or travel in that
ambulance. It drove away and Brutus was left there to bleed.

'I thought I was going to bleed to death. I had put a
handkerchief on my chest to plug the hole. Then I felt my
back and found there was a pool of blood there. Obviously
I had more than one wound. And I could have bled to death.
By now lots of passers-by had gathered round, although
Helsburg shooed them away and kept them at bay.'

Eventually a non-white ambulance arrived and he was
taken to Coronation Hospital in the non-white area of
Coronationville. Uniformed and Special Branch policemen
accompanied him on the journey, their notebooks and pencils
poised as they asked Brutus questions about his contacts.
Even after arriving at the hospital the drama did not stop.
Some members of the Indian Youth Congress planned to
rescue him. Brutus was on a second floor ward and they
planned to come and spirit him away in a coffin. With police
microphones hidden under his bed, Brutus did not feel safe
to talk but gave a carnation to his brother as a signal that
he was agreeable to be rescued:

'But at six o'clock on the evening they were going to rescue
me the police shift changed – six uniformed policemen were
guarding me, and one of the policemen told me that they
had been issued with live ammunition, that if there was any
attempt to escape they would shoot me and that an armoured
car was patrolling the grounds of the hospital. So that evening, when the nurse came to check my temperature, I took
a pen and wrote in the palm of her hand: "call it off". Even
without all this I do not know how the rescue would have
worked. I was attached to two drips; glucose in my left arm,

blood in the right arm – I had lost a lot of blood – and I was on a respirator because one of my lungs had collapsed.'

Brutus was not kept long at the hospital. He was soon taken to the Fort, a major prison in Johannesburg, after the doctor had falsely certified that Brutus's 22 stitches had been removed. Brutus now waited in jail for his trial knowing it would probably land him on Robben Island. With Brutus out of the way, John Harris tried to get to Baden Baden but he, too, was arrested. However, he managed to smuggle out a tape-recording stating SANROC's position to the IOC.

It was Frank Braun who went to Baden Baden, taking along J. R. Rathebe, who was described as a Bantu boxing official. South African blacks scratched their heads on hearing Rathebe was in Baden Baden because few had heard of him, even those who followed boxing avidly. Harris's description of him as a 'smoke screen' seemed appropriate. Much of the talking at the meeting was done by Braun, who promised that if necessary trials would be held outside South Africa in order to finalize a team for the Olympics. However, there was nothing he could do about apartheid; this was an internal matter which did not concern the IOC.

The fact that there were no mixed trials caused concern but the white Olympic Committee was given yet another chance. It was told that it should make a firm declaration of its acceptance of the spirit of the Olympic Code and by 31 December 1963 must get a change in policy from the Government regarding 'racial discrimination in sport and competition in its country'.

If this did not happen, warned the IOC, 'the South African National Olympic Committee would be debarred from entering its teams in the Olympic Games'. However, even this mild resolution was too much for 20 Olympic nations who, as die-hard friends of white South Africa, voted against it.

Nonetheless, the white sporting bodies recognized they had to do something to keep their hold on the Olympic Games. Before Baden Baden the white South African Cycling Federation had announced that it would seek closer ties with non-white cyclists and even send qualified non-white cyclists overseas. Now the white weightlifting selectors offered to allow Precious MacKenzie to represent South Africa, and even wear the coveted Springbok colours (he would be the first non-white to be awarded the colours) in the World Championships in Stockholm. But there was one condition. MacKenzie belonged to the weightlifting body that was part of the non-racial National Federation. He would have to leave that body and join the puppet non-white body which had affiliated to the white national body. Sportsmen do not often find it easy to refuse the chance of glory for the sake of principle, but MacKenzie did and in a memorable statement said: 'The National Weightlifting Association want me to join them now so that they can gain official recognition with the world body and say they have no apartheid. But I don't swing so easily. Why do they want me in such a hurry now? Is it because pressure is being applied because of their racial policy?'

The next IOC meeting was in Innsbruck in January 1964. Despite pressure from the African and Asian delegates who wanted to suspend South Africa immediately, the IOC was still prepared to give the white South Africans some more time. At Baden Baden white South Africa had been given until 31 December 1963 to mend its ways; at Innsbruck it was given until August 1964. It seemed that there was still a chance that South Africa might take part in the 1964 Olympics.

In March and April of that year the first South African Games were held. Inevitably there were separate events for whites and non-whites. The white one was held first in March and the non-white one in late April running into May. They were meant to be pre-Olympic tests on which a provisional list of the South African team for the 1964 Olympics would be based. This, for the first time, included some non-whites. But SAONGA (the South African Olympic Committee having become the South African Olympic and National Games Association) still could not say that it publicly dissociated itself from the policy of segregation in sport. And unless it did so the IOC could not invite it to Tokyo. In any case, selecting a mixed team on the basis of separate trials was a farce. Interior Minister Jan de Klerk soon made it clear that non-whites would never represent South Africa in international competition and in July, when the Afrikaans paper *Dagreek* asked the Government what would have happened if SAONGA had attempted to send one team to the Olympics, it was told that two teams would have had to go to the Olympics: white athletes representing white South Africa and non-whites representing non-white South Africa. The two teams would have had to travel separately, could not have competed in the same events, and could not have worn the same uniform. After this there was no hope of South Africa taking part at Tokyo. It was the first time since South Africa had started participating in international sport that it had paid a price for its racial policy.

Not that SANROC could long celebrate this triumph. Within weeks its South African existence had virtually come to an end. In July John Harris was arrested for the bombing of a Johannesburg railway station in which a woman was killed and 15 people injured. This event had nothing to do with sport or SANROC. Harris was a member of the Liberal Party and, as Alan Paton was to write in his memoirs, was 'a highly intelligent and a highly unbalanced man'. The Government had broken an organization called the African Resistance Movement which had been planning a campaign of sabotage and violence against Government installations. Harris, disturbed by the nationwide arrest of members of the ARM, decided to take up the cause. All he succeeded in doing was to endanger both the South African Liberal Party and the whole movement for non-racial sport.

Had Harris's bombing stunt come earlier it is possible that white South Africa might still have taken part in the Tokyo Olympics, as the IOC might well have been persuaded that the non-racial movement was totally discredited. Harris, despite being declared legally insane by an eminent private psychiatrist (two Government psychiatrists opposed this view) was held responsible and sentenced to death. He went to the gallows singing 'We shall overcome'. While Harris was on trial his wife had taken shelter with Walter and Adelain Hain, also members of the Liberal Party. Walter Hain had hoped to give the funeral oration, but he was a banned person and on the night before the police refused to let him speak. His 15-year-old son Peter took his place: the eulogy at Harris's grave would mark his political awakening. Harris's death signalled the end of SANROC in South Africa, but within a few years the campaign against apartheid in sport would find a formidable new champion in Peter Hain.

News of South Africa's exclusion from the Tokyo Olympics came as Brutus was serving an 18-month jail sentence on Robben Island. He had been taken there in chains and, like all those who went through the ghastly prison, Brutus had at first been badly beaten.

'We were made to carry stones to build a wall round the island. We would carry them up a sloping beach and the guards kept insisting there were not enough stones in the wheelbarrow. They would then load the wheelbarrow so heavily you could hardly move it and they would beat you for not being able to move it. I was in such a bad shape that the guards sold my shoes, thinking I would never need them.'

Brutus eventually lodged a complaint which resulted in solitary confinement, the only compensation for which was that his fellow 'solitaries' were the greats of South African politics: Nelson Mandela, Walter Sisulu and Ahmed Katharada (in whose house in Johannesburg Brutus had hidden when under house arrest).

The other compensation came with the news from Innsbruck that South Africa would not be invited to the Tokyo Olympics. There being no radio or newspapers it was some time before Brutus heard it on the bush telegraph. A prisoner, who had recently been jailed, arrived on Robben Island and gave them the news.

'It gave us great satisfaction. The cheering in the quadrangle at Robben Island, where we were breaking stones, must have deafened the guards.' But for some time this was to remain an isolated shout of joy – the world of sports was hardly deafened and white South African sporting authorities were far from worried. In February 1966, Colonel Vissier, a leader of the South African Amateur Athletics Union, said 'We are one of the strongest bodies in the country and the time has come for us to say how we feel on this point. We must make it clear that there can be no deviating from Government policy.'

Vissier not only knew his white constituency: he was sure of his international friends. The International Amateur Athletics Federation was led by Harold Abrahams, the legendary British runner. Two months after Vissier's statement Abrahams said, 'I do not believe South Africa is in danger of being expelled [from the IAAF]. What would such a move achieve? The Olympic body forbids the practice of segregation. The IAAF does not.' When the IAAF annual meeting took place in Budapest, Vissier and Abrahams were supported by the membership. Sierra Leone's motion to exclude South Africa was comprehensively defeated. At Budapest the IAAF had adopted a weighted voting system that gave the 37 predominantly white nations 244 votes and the 99 predominantly non-white nations only 195 votes. Such a voting system also prevailed in the International Tennis Federation, where the major tennis-playing nations, nearly all white, controlled a vast majority of votes and ensured that the old ties of friendship and warmth which had always existed with white South Africa would continue.

One international sports body which had one member, one vote, and had been a persistent thorn in the side of white South Africa, was that governing soccer. Despite the influence of the egregious Stanley Rous, yet another of white South Africa's sporting friends, it had been one of the first international bodies to suspend South Africa. After that, despite moves to lift the suspension, white South Africa never really got back. The reason was that the Football Federation had complete equality in voting, much to the chagrin of Dave Marais, president of South Africa's white soccer body.

'The tragedy,' he asserted, 'is that most of the important countries are sympathetic. But there is such a large block of African countries when it comes to one man, one vote, we don't have a chance of reversing the decision. I think there should be a qualifying vote. It is absurd for each little country to have the same voting power as countries like England and Italy.'

In December 1966, representatives of 32 black African countries gathered in Bamako, Mali, to form the Supreme Council for Sport in Africa. Its basic purpose was to coordinate and promote sport throughout Africa; but Dennis Brutus, who was at the conference, believes that one of the driving forces was to isolate South Africa and its sporting structure. This was the theme of the major resolution passed at the conference.

Black Africa had already flexed its sporting muscles. The 1963 IOC meeting in Baden Baden was originally due to be held in Nairobi but the then Kenyan Minister of Home Affairs, Oginga Odinga, insisted that the representatives from South African sport be multi-racial, which led to the IOC switching to Baden Baden. Three years on there was an even greater realization in Black Africa about the role of sport. Soon after the Supreme Council's formation, South Africans were invited to the Uganda International Tennis Tournament. The Kampala newspaper *The People* condemned it and underlined how black South Africa now saw sports: 'There is a field in which Africa does not need to plead, cajole or threaten other powers to take action against apartheid; we can act decisively ourselves . . . the South Africans do not consider it minor.'

Just as the white South Africans had felt that the arrival of a New Zealand rugby team with Maoris in it would threaten their way of life, so Uganda now argued that having white South African tennis players would threaten the anticolonial stance of the Organization of African Unity, which had called for a total sports ban on South Africa.

Ten days after the editorial John Vorster, who had taken over as South Africa's Prime Minister following the assassination of Verwoerd in 1966, laid out what was hailed as a new sporting policy for South Africa. It was a characteristic Vorster speech: a mixture of lies, half-truths and new wrinkles on old policies. Vorster began his speech by saying politics should not be mixed with sports, the irony of which clearly escaped him. Then he made it clear that there could be no mixed sport between whites and non-whites in South Africa. His explanation was simple and brutal. 'We do not apply that as a criterion because our policy has nothing to do with proficiency or lack of proficiency. If any person, locally or abroad, adopts the attitude that he will enter into relations with us only if we are prepared to jettison the separate practising of sport prevailing among our own people in South Africa, then I want to make it quite clear that, no matter how important those sports relations are in my view, I am not prepared to pay that price. On that score, I want no misunderstanding whatsoever. . . . In respect of this principle we are not prepared to compromise, we are not prepared to negotiate and we are not prepared to make any concessions.' As far as the Olympic Games were concerned, being a unique event in which only one team from any one country was allowed to take part, then, 'If there were any of our Coloured or Bantu who were good enough to compete there, and whose standard of proficiency was such that they could take part in it, we would make it possible for them to take part . . . because the Olympic Games lays it down as an absolute condition, the people who are then selected will take part as one contingent under the South African flag. . . .'

Vorster's speech was hailed as a great breakthrough by white South Africa, Alan Paton's being one of the few dissenting voices. Many in the IOC were impressed with Vorster's speech, backed by the statements that were now pouring out of Frank Braun.

In May 1967 the IOC met in Tehran and Braun announced that there would be one team to represent all South Africans, the team would travel together, live together, wear the same uniform, and march under an integrated team flag. Whites and non-whites would also compete against each other in the Games and an equal number of whites and non-whites, under Braun's chairmanship, would select the participants. He had to admit that integrated and mixed sports or even mixed trials would not take place in South Africa but, articulating the line favoured by white sports officials, he pleaded with the IOC to accept these concessions. If he went back empty handed then these concessions would be immediately rescinded. Even Dennis Brutus was surprised by Braun's speech. 'My first reaction on reading the concessions was that they were really quite spectacular. Compared to South Africa's previous position they represented a real advance.'

He had a suspicion that Braun was actually promising more than he could deliver but he was aware that these 'concessions' would make it difficult to keep South Africa out of the 1968 Mexico Olympics.

And so, for a time, it proved to be. Fourteen African delegates led by Nigeria and supported by the Russian Communist bloc proposed that South Africa be immediately expelled from the Olympic Movement. But the IOC decided not to make any decision on South Africa until a further meeting in Grenoble in February in 1968. Meanwhile it would send a fact-finding commission to visit South Africa and report at the Grenoble meeting. If this was half a victory for SANROC then the IOC did slap it down on an initiative of Reg Alexander, the white delegate from Kenya and an old friend of South Africa. It approved a resolution which ruled that the IOC would not communicate with SANROC as long as it used the word Olympic in its name.

The fact-finding commission of the IOC was a neat illustration of the way world sports administrators still saw South Africa. It consisted of Lord Killanin, Reg Alexander and Sir Ade Ademola, Chief Justice of Nigeria. Of the three Ademola was the only black and shortly before the commission arrived Braun announced that for the duration of the visit apartheid would be suspended. Ademola would live and travel with Killanin and Alexander. But once in South Africa this hardly mattered because most social functions, including meals, were held in private; when Ademola met Frank Warring, the South African Minister of Sport, for lunch in Pretoria, no photographers were allowed. Just three weeks before the commission arrived Warring had warned outsiders not to interfere with South Africa's internal politics and that mixed sport could lead to racial friction. Ademola was certainly not interested in increasing that friction. There was a classic moment shortly after his arrival which illustrated his approach to South Africa.

A bus was taking the IOC delegation to Atteridgeville, a black township near Pretoria. It pulled up in front of a suburban cafe and Ademola got out and marched purposefully towards the pavement. The press travelling in accompanying cars waited for the dramatic encounter between the white cafe owner and Sir Ade Ademola. But then just as it looked as if he was about to enter the cafe, he veered and entered the chemist shop next door. Confrontation with petty apartheid had been averted. Ademola was later to reprimand non-whites for always seeking Government and city council help: 'Why don't you go ahead and do something yourself?' he asked a group of Indian sports administrators in Durban. 'When we want stadiums and other facilities in Nigeria, we charge an entrance fee ... surely there are enough Indians in Natal to provide finance?' But when the Indians explained that under the Group Areas Act they were about to lose the lease they had, Ademola declined to comment.

SANROC tried to present the other side. Dennis Brutus, allowed to leave South Africa, had along with Chris de Broglio reorganized SANROC in exile in London. The IOC Commission on its return to Lausanne met Brutus. But Brutus got the distinct feeling that 'they weren't impressed and that they had already made up their minds'. Indeed they had. The report, when it emerged in February 1968, condemned SANROC for being a body that was not representative of non-whites in South Africa and whose methods 'are a source of embarrassment to the majority in South Africa for whom it claims to speak'. The Commission was more inclined to accept the non-whites it had met in South Africa. At Grenoble the IOC decided to have a postal vote of its 70 members and SANROC feared the worst. In a private document it noted: 'The real danger of this is that the Socialist countries will have a fairly free hand because they will not have (a) control over their members' votes and (b) there will be no real way for accounting how the vote went. . . . All we have on our side are the uncertain votes of some friends.' The 'uncertain' friends turned out to number no more than 27. They were the only ones to vote against the resolution agreeing to allow South Africa to take part in the Mexico Olympics.

The resolution showed international sports administrators were still unable or unwilling to grasp the true criminality of apartheid. The first line of the resolution noted the IOC's grave concern that 'racially discriminatory internal policies of the South African Government prevent the NOC (National Olympic Committee) of the country from achieving fully the aims of the IOC and the Fundamental Principle 1 of the Olympic Code.' This meant that, contrary to IOC's own rules, the white South African Committee was not completely independent of Government. Nevertheless the IOC deluded itself into believing that SAONGA had done enough to deserve some encouragement, and the IOC President Avery Brundage felt that the Olympic movement had done more for non-whites in South Africa than anybody else.

White South Africa was cockahoop. Braun could not praise Ademola enough, who, he said, 'fought for us like a hero'. Honey praised South Africa's old friends, and Vorster was 'glad for the sake of our young sportsmen and athletes since they can again take part in the Olympic Games, which

it is their right and privilege to do'. Vorster, it seemed, had
not only changed Verwoerd's policy but also won increasing
support for his own Nationalist party. Reports coming back
from the white constituencies indicated that they were ready
to support his 'outward-looking policies'. The London *Daily
Telegraph* sang the old tune of building bridges and the *New
York Times* thought that South Africa had made revolutionary concessions.

It was the Secretary General of the Ethiopian Sports Federation, Y. Tessema, who asked the critical question: 'What
happens after the Games? Each athlete will return to South
Africa and join his segregated club. What has the IOC
achieved if the status quo is maintained in South Africa after
the Mexican Games?'

Ethiopia was one of the first nations to announce that it
would withdraw from the Games if South Africa took part.
Algeria and others followed. Braun dismissed the African
boycott as a giant bluff, 'like a lot of spoiled kids. They may
form their own Afro-Asian Games instead of competing at
the Olympics. That should restore the old prestige of the
Games.'

But this was 1968. Braun and his white South African
compatriots were not operating in the cosy world they had
so long inhabited. In America the Black Power movement
had begun to flex its muscles in the Olympic arena and
Dennis Brutus had already allied SANROC to this. Within a
month of the Grenoble decision more than 30 countries had
indicated they would boycott the Mexico Games. Everything
now depended on the Soviet Union. On 7 March the
National Olympic Committee of the the Soviet Union
announced that the IOC must convene an emergency session
to decide on South Africa. If it did not do so, the Soviet
Union would have to reconsider the question of participating
in the Games. Whether the Soviet Union would ultimately
have withdrawn or not is debatable.

Brutus feels the lure of potential gold medals in Mexico

would probably have persuaded the Soviets to go to the Olympics.

The IOC executive was due to meet at Lausanne on 20 and 21 April, and the weeks preceding it were full of action: claims, counter-claims and the slow but definite indication that white South Africa was backing away from the promises it had made in order to get the invitation in the first place. Soon after the Grenoble decision Braun had warned that the Olympic team would not have very many non-whites but that he was certain that there would be quite a few for the 1972 Games. For this 'new' South Africa there was to be a new badge for the Olympic team, the redesign forced by white pressure.

The IOC meeting was a furious one. The IOC executive itself would call it a 'harsh discussion', at the end of which it came to the unanimous opinion that 'it would be most unwise for a South African team to participate in the Games of the XIX Olympiad. Therefore the Executive strongly recommends that you endorse this unanimous proposal to withdraw the invitation to these Games.' Forty-seven voted for, 16 against with 8 abstentions. Brundage observed ruefully: 'We seem to live in an age when violence and turbulence are the order of the day – though of course we are concerned with the safety of the participants and the dignity of the Games.'

In America he was under attack for being anti-semitic and anti-black. The Montecido Country Club he owned in Santa Barbara, California, did not allow Jewish or black members, and just before the vote Brundage's Chicago hotel was sacked by blacks while he was in it. Clearly, he feared racial violence in Mexico and for many of the IOC members the possibility that South Africa's presence might spark riots or violence was a real worry.

White South Africa condemned the IOC proposal. Honey called it 'illegal and immoral' and Vorster felt that, if this was how world events were going to be arranged, 'we are back in the jungle. Then it will no longer be necessary to arrange Olympic Games, but rather to have tree climbing events.' There were abortive moves to circumvent the ban so that outstanding athletes like the swimmer Karen Muir, the middle-distance runner Humphrey Khosi and the sprinter Paul Nash could, somehow, take part. They were a forerunner of white South Africa's attempts, several years later, to get round the boycott.

But hurt as white South Africa was it still could not believe that this exclusion was anything other than temporary. The white electorate was certain that apartheid was the policy to follow. The 1966 general election had provided Verwoerd with a landslide victory and, what was even more significant, for the first time a record number of English-speaking South Africans – the ones the 'bridge-builders' in Britain and elsewhere claimed were against apartheid – had voted for the Nationalist party.

Perhaps this overconfidence explained why within months white South Africa would dig its own sporting grave. This time there would be no escape. It had taken the brutally harassed anti-apartheid forces a long time to organize, but between 1968 and 1970 it would win some spectacular victories from which white sporting South Africa would never recover.

3

The Tide Turns

In 1963 Arthur Coy, then president of the white cricket body, had airily dismissed Dennis Brutus's threat to persuade the MCC to take action against it. 'Go ahead and try,' he said. The secretary, Algy Frames, based at the Wanderers Club in Johannesburg, showed an even more patronising white face. Frames told Brutus that he knew from British intelligence that if the South Africans included blacks there would be riots in England. Five years later, however, England selected a black for her own Test side – a black who, moreover, had had to come to England to play top-class cricket because he could not do so for white South Africa. Now the question was: would white South Africa accept him as a member of the England touring side?

This has come to be known as the D'Oliveira Affair and, as with Kennedy's assassination, almost everybody in South Africa can recall where they were when John Vorster made the announcement that finally sealed the fate of white sporting South Africa.

Basil D'Oliveira himself was the ultimate proponent of the 'don't bring politics into sports' philosophy. He evidently never appreciated the struggle being waged on his behalf. In his autobiography, written in 1980, he would say that the 1959 tour by Frank Worrell's team had been cancelled 'for no apparent reason'. However, in 1968 he became, perhaps despite himself, a great symbol in the struggle against apartheid sport. It was now eight years since D'Oliveira, unable to play a reasonable standard of cricket in South Africa, had left for England. His first steps in England were largely due to John Arlott, one of English cricket's most far-sighted writers. On his only visit to South Africa Arlott, asked to specify his race, had written: 'human'. In England D'Oliveira proved that, despite the dreadful conditions in which he had learnt his cricket, or the fact that he had played all of it on matting wickets – when turf was the norm in good-class cricket around the world – he could adjust, and even aspire to play in the highest company. In 1966 he made his debut for England against the West Indies and soon became a regular member of the England team.

His success came at a time when non-white cricketers in South Africa felt there were at least another half a dozen 'Dollys' who, if given the chance, could do just as well. Krish Reddy, a historian of non-white cricket, has written that the 1950s and 1960s were the golden age of black cricket when, apart from D'Oliveira, there was a host of cricketers who might have played for a South African team representing all the races. There were all-rounders in the D'Oliveira mould such as Gesant 'Tiny' Abed, Cecil Abrahams, John Neethling, Basil Waterwich and Walter Stephens; batsmen like Chong Meyer, 'Shorty' Docrat, Ahmed Deedat, 'Lam' Raziet, Basil Witten, Armien Variawa, Hassiem Abrahams, Marlie Barnes and Abbas Dinath; bowlers like Ben Malamba, George Langs, Owen Williams, Essop Jeewa, Eric Petersen, Mohammed Garda, Alec Bell, 'Goofy' Timol, Doolie Rubidge, Edmund Ntikinca and Sam Ntshekisa. And Sallie 'Lobo' Ahmed was, in the view of many experts, a better wicket-keeper than anyone in the white ranks.

It is impossible to say how good these cricketers might have become or whether, given the chance, they would have played at the highest level. Some of them, like 'Tiny' Abed and Cecil Abrahams, did go abroad to play, but they never really made it in the way D'Oliveira did. However, D'Oliveira's success meant that many non-whites could claim that he was merely the tip of an iceberg of non-white talent. Non-whites felt that if D'Oliveira toured South Africa as an

English player, they would be redeemed: now at last their white compatriots and the outside world would believe them when they spoke of the injustices of apartheid. White South Africa, however, could just as easily conjure lurid images of non-whites in their segregated stands 'rioting' in support of D'Oliveira as he took the field with England.

England was to tour South Africa in the winter of 1968–69, and for almost two years before that there had been intense speculation as to whether D'Oliveira would be allowed into the country. In January 1967, Denis Howell, then Minister of Sport in the Labour Government, had told the Commons that the tour would be cancelled if he was not allowed in. White South Africans produced contradictory responses with Piet Le Roux, the Minister of the Interior, suggesting D'Oliveira would not be welcome, but Vorster seemingly keeping the door open. He certainly gave Sir Alec Douglas-Home, the shadow Foreign Secretary, that impression when the latter met Vorster during a visit to South Africa. But Lord Cobham, like Home a former President of the MCC, got exactly the opposite impression from Vorster.

Clearly Vorster was under some pressure. After succeeding Verwoerd he had been trying to change the image of the Afrikaner leader from a humourless, grim *volksleier* (people's leader), to borrow Donald Woods's description, to someone more human or at least capable of assembling his craggy features into the suggestion of a smile. He had even been photographed playing golf. Donald Woods, who was then editor of the East London *Daily Dispatch* and met Vorster often, believes Vorster might have been prepared to accept D'Oliveira if the MCC had not messed up the selection.

If Woods is right, Vorster is not as much the villain of the piece as he has been painted out to be, and much of the blame for what happened rests with white South African cricket officials, who displayed a remarkable mixture of arrogance and lack of moral courage, and the MCC, which either bungled the whole affair or, more likely, could not bring itself to face up to the reality that was apartheid sport.

The mood of white cricketing South Africa was revealed shortly before Vorster made his fateful announcement. Woods, speaking at a public banquet in East London attended by South African Test cricketers, suggested that the cricketers should speak out in favour of non-racial cricket. That caused an uproar. Some shouted, 'Don't drag politics into sport', and a couple of cricketers were said to have walked out.

Woods pointed out that politicians had already dragged politics into sport and that if the cricketers did not support merit selection it would weaken Vorster's position in his party over the D'Oliveira issue. It could even result in South Africa's isolation from international sport. After his speech he was approached by Trevor Goddard, the South African cricket captain, who said, 'I agree with a lot that you said, but we cannot speak out. We are in a difficult position.'

'No,' said Woods, 'you are not in a difficult position. You're in a very safe position. You are national heroes and you won't be thrown into jail if you speak up.'

Five years earlier, prior to the tour of Australia and New Zealand, Goddard had been advised by Verwoerd on how to handle questions about apartheid and sport. Now, as Woods pressed him, he moved away in embarrassment, mumbling, '. . . very difficult position'.

How Goddard, who later became a born-again Christian, squared all this with his conscience, is not known. But he was hardly alone: almost all white cricketers preferred the soft option of appeasing apartheid, while claiming the moral high ground and obeying the law of the land. The fact is that at this stage white cricketers had no understanding of, or even feeling for, non-white cricket. Most of them did not believe D'Oliveira was that good, and some of them even said so.

Whites and blacks very occasionally played each other at cricket but Krish Reddy, the non-white cricket historian, can only record two of any importance: on New Year's Day in 1944 when a South African Indian XI played a Transvaal

Cricket Union XI in aid of the Bengal Famine Relief Fund; and then in April 1961 when Johnny Waite, a white South African Test captain, led a team against S. A. Hague's combined black Transvaal team which, much to the surprise of Waite and his players, beat them by 20 runs. Ali Bacher, then 17 years old, played in the match. It was on a Sunday and for the whites it meant travelling to an unfamiliar part of Johannesburg: the Natalspruit Indian sports ground. Unlike the lush green carpets they were used to playing on, this was a sand ground on which a mat had been laid. Also unlike white grounds with proper changing rooms, here there was a temporary changing room. There was no bar and no fraternization with the opposition and at the end of the match, recalls Bacher, '. . . we went our way. The following day nobody wondered why we didn't play like this all the time. We didn't ask, do they have any facilities, do they have any money or sponsorship? If I regret one attitude of my life in the '60s it is this. I used to vote for the Progressive party (opposed to apartheid) but I still played in front of segregated crowds in Newlands and Wanderers with the blacks sitting in cages in the hottest part of the ground. I just didn't think about it. That was the terrible thing. That really was the sad part of our cricket.'

Between 1961 and when the D'Oliveira affair erupted, all contact just ceased.

Not that there were no whites of goodwill. D'Oliveira, seeking to raise money to come to England, had received some white support, including that of Tubby Owen-Smith. But whites did not see any need to play with non-whites: they were just not part of their world.

In England the MCC saw things in much the same way. They eagerly accepted Home's advice that the moral issue was none of Britain's business. Home was certain, or claimed to be certain, that to break off cricketing relations with South Africa would have no effect on her attitude to apartheid. In his political youth Home had been a supporter of Neville Chamberlain and his appeasement of Hitler. As Chamberlain's Parliamentary Private Secretary he had stood next to him when he had waved his infamous 'piece of paper' on his return from Munich. Home's attitude towards white South Africa contained the same lack of moral vision. Somehow, through some vague and never defined process, white South Africans were to be persuaded to change their apartheid policies.

This, of course, was the classic 'bridge-building' view. In 80 years of Test cricket with white South Africa, the MCC had shown no inclination to build bridges to black cricket. English writers such as A. A. Thomson had eulogized white South African cricketers for their warmth and their 'colour' (but not in the sense we are talking about). A South African tour was always popular with English cricketers. Many of them, complaining of endless winter tours, missed out on visits to the Indian subcontinent but never to South Africa. John Arlott had been an early and courageous protester and E. W. Swanton, a conservative journalist writing for the arch-conservative *Daily Telegraph* of London, was so sickened by the sight of black spectators in cages that he did not return to South Africa for almost 30 years. Yet even such a truly sensitive English writer as Alan Ross, while aware of apartheid and very critical of it, could be curiously blind to apartheid in sport. His *Cape Summer and The Australians in England*, a marvellously evocative book about South Africa observed while following England's tour in 1956–57, had almost nothing to say about the realities of South African cricket.

One of the earliest players to evince disgust at the treatment of blacks in South Africa was, perhaps surprisingly, Jim Laker, the great England off-spinner. In *Over To Me* he provided one of the most direct and unvarnished reactions to South Africa that any English cricketer has ever given. He had toured there in 1956–57 and this had given him a glimpse of black-white relations. Once, while being driven by his team-mate Alan Oakman, a black man on a cycle rushed out of a side street and was run over. Crowds immediately gathered – but they were more interested in getting the players' autographs. A policeman who arrived on the scene suggested that the black man must have been drunk, and asked a neighbour of the victim, 'You live near this nigger – he's always drunk, isn't he?' Laker recounts that 'slowly, fearfully, the black head nodded'.

On the next England trip to South Africa in 1964–65 another cricketer, Mike Brearley, broke away from the insular shackles of his cricketing colleagues to try to explore the reality of South Africa. He did it so well that Denis Compton, whose defence of white South African sport became increasingly notorious and fantasy-ridden over the years, could hardly contain himself. He would later tell Frank Keating how disturbed he was about Brearley. Why? asked Keating, assuming that he was worried about the fact that Brearley hadn't scored many runs on the tour or perhaps that he hadn't kept wicket very well. No, said Compton, Brearley didn't understand the 'ambassadorship' of touring. The youngster kept reading histories of South Africa and going off in taxis to see what was happening in the townships. That was no way to be a sporting tourist, was it? Brearley has vivid recollections of the tour:

'We arrived in Salisbury [Rhodesia] . . . and I remember the anger of the local whites when they heard that Harold Wilson's Labour party had just won the [1964] election. Rhodesia under Ian Smith was about to declare UDI and there was extreme hostility towards us because Labour was opposed to UDI. I remember a local white smashing a glass down in front of us, venting his anger. I had just come out of Cambridge and I knew nothing about anything. But I did become friendly with an Indian waiter in Johannesburg and he took me to his house on Christmas Eve. I found it a very strange experience, the women hardly appeared, it was a small house and they had no curtains, all of which gave it a very strange feeling. I was also friendly with Ray White, who had played for Cambridge. His sister was extremely liberal and married to Ernie Wentzel, who had been in prison under the 90-day Law. We had Christmas lunch there – Geoff Boycott, myself and a few others – and during the lunch Jill Wentzel went round the table asking us each to raise a toast to a particular place. I think Geoff Boycott raised it to Fitzwilliam, and when it came to Jill she said 'Johannesburg Central Jail' where John Harris was under sentence and would soon be executed. Some of the cricketers were aware of South African realities. I remember talking about South Africa to Geoff Boycott on our way out there and he said that he was not sure that he could control himself if he saw any black man being physically ill-treated.'

Through the summer of 1968, as England battled Australia on the field, English cricket officials wrestled with the D'Oliveira question. He was selected for the first Test but despite being England's top scorer in the match – 87 not out – was dropped from the next one at Lord's and not chosen for the next two Tests. At Lord's, one senior official had the impudence to tell him he would solve a lot of problems if he made himself unavailable for England but available for South Africa – a suggestion which showed how official cricket minds were working.

Just before the final Test at the Oval, a South African businessman, Tiene Oosthuizen, UK Managing Director of Carreras Tobacco Company, of which Rothmans was a subsidiary, offered D'Oliveira £4,000 a year for 10 years if he agreed to go to South Africa to coach coloured cricketers and make himself immediately unavailable for the tour. He was to work for the South African Foundation, a supposedly independent organization but in fact set up to promote apartheid. A few days later, more by chance than anything, D'Oliveira was selected for the final Test. Mr Oosthuizen vanished and the die was cast. In the Test, with England requiring a win to draw the series, D'Oliveira made 158, and then on the final afternoon took a crucial wicket to break a stubborn stand, opening the door for Underwood to bowl Australia out.

The next day the MCC selectors, representing the cream

of English cricket – Alec Bedser, Peter May, Doug Insole, Don Kenyon and Leslie Ames – with Colin Cowdrey, Arthur Gilligan (President of the MCC) and Gubby Allen in attendance, selected the team.

To their eternal shame they omitted D'Oliveira. Donald Woods believes that, had they chosen D'Oliveira, Vorster might have allowed him in. For the first time the reality of playing cricket with apartheid South Africa forced itself on English consciousness. Lord's was deluged with messages with the great majority of them opposed to D'Oliveira's omission. Among those in favour was a mock telegram of support, signed 'Adolf Hitler'. Former Test captain David Sheppard, now the Bishop of Liverpool, called an extraordinary meeting of the MCC proposing motions expressing lack of confidence in the committee and asking that there be no further cricket contact unless South Africa showed progress in racial matters on sport. Sheppard won the argument but lost the vote, with three quarters of the MCC members against him. D'Oliveira was now engaged by the *News of the World* to report the tour matches. Five days later the swing bowler Tom Cartwright, nursing an injury, dropped out of the tour party, and now the MCC, having already applied liberal quantities of egg to its face, contrived to shoot itself in the foot. It replaced Cartwright with D'Oliveira whose omission it had previously justified on the grounds that his bowling was not suited to South African conditions.

The news broke just as Vorster was speaking to the Orange Free State congress of the National Party, quite the most right-wing gathering in the country. Vorster declared:

'We are not prepared to accept a team thrust upon us by people whose interests are not the game but to gain certain political objectives which they do not even attempt to hide. The team as constituted now is not the team of the MCC but the team of the Anti-Apartheid Movement, the team of SANROC, and the team of Bishop Reeves.'

The MCC reacted by refusing to accept Vorster's diktat; and despite the efforts of Arthur Coy and Jack Cheetham, now President of the white South African cricket body, both of whom flew out to England to try and rescue the tour, it was doomed.

Even now, however, few people thought this was the end of England's cricket relations with South Africa or that the 'bridge-building' campaign could not be sustained. Ali Bacher, then practising as a doctor, heard the news at his hospital. 'I was disappointed, but the next day I felt another tour would come along.' Within months the Springboks were due to come on a rugby tour of England, and in 1970 their cricketers were scheduled. After the debacle over the Mexico Games, white South Africa accepted that, in areas where Third World countries had the vote, sporting relations would be difficult. But with its 'traditional' friends like England and Australia it saw no reason for any disruption. The D'Oliveira affair, it felt, was just a hiccough.

In fact it was to prove the turn of the tide in the fight against apartheid sport. Vorster had once explained to Woods why he frequently gave him interviews despite his known anti-apartheid views. He did so, he said, because he wanted to know what the real enemy was thinking. He was surrounded by *ja-broers* (yes-men) who told him what they thought he wanted to hear. Now white sporting South Africa, having heard only what their friends in the West told them, were suddenly struck by an enemy they never knew existed.

Interestingly, the enemy was marshalled by one of their own – a white driven into exile by apartheid. We last met Peter Hain delivering the eulogy for John Harris. Two years after that he and his family left South Africa for exile in London. Now 19 and one of the leading Young Liberals – then the most radical young political group in the country – he set about organizing a campaign. It was intended to stop the 1970 South African cricket tour of England planned for 1970 and that was the name given to the campaign: Stop the Seventy Tour (STST). In the summer of 1969 Wilfred Isaacs brought a cricket team over, as he had done every year since 1963, while in the winter of 1969 the white rugby team arrived. STST started its campaign against these tours, and also included action against a Davis Cup match involving South Africa in Bristol in the summer of 1969.

The side actions soon took centre stage, particularly Hain's campaign against the white rugby team. Few gave the campaign much chance of success. But Hain mobilized at least 50,000 people to demonstrate against the white South Africans, and as Hugo Young, then political editor of London's *The Sunday Times*, recalled in 1973, it 'was the most successful pressure-group action in recent British political history . . . it is hard to think of a single large political campaign which has had anything like so immediate an impact.'

Coming at the end of the 1960s, a decade of unprecedented youth radicalism which had almost unseated Charles de Gaulle in France and led to a worldwide revulsion against American policy in Vietnam, it tapped a rich source of youth activism which the white South Africans just could not comprehend. Hain and his campaign were pitted against the clean-cut white young men of South Africa who had scant knowledge of, or even interest in, the world outside the white enclaves of their homeland. They had come from a country which claimed to be a defender of Western civilization but which (as Trevor Huddleston pointed out more than a decade ago) had in truth cut itself off from the Western world.

In the month leading up to Vorster's decision to ban D'Oliveira, the white parliament had passed the Prohibition of Improper Interference Bill which was designed to prevent any political contact between different race groups. There were also amendments to other pillars of apartheid. The Population Registration Act, for instance, would stop what the minister Le Roux called 'a form of insidious integration which is beginning to assume alarming proportions' owing to the fact that some white people were ready to give evidence that they were prepared to accept some non-white persons as white. Such cases inevitably arose out of the complex system of racial classification that people were subjected to under the act. Then there was the Prohibition of Mixed

Marriages Amendment Bill, which stated that a marriage
contracted abroad between a male South African and a
woman of a different race would not be recognised in South
Africa. This bill had been prompted by the marriage of
Breyten Breytenbach, a white South African author living in
Paris with his Vietnamese wife. Breytenbach had also been
refused a visa to visit his parents in South Africa.

Against such a background, Hain's campaign was a case
of men against boys: the white South Africans stood no
chance. From the moment they arrived at Heathrow, Dawie
de Villiers' rugby team faced protesters, not merely political-
placard wavers but demonstrators willing to invade rugby
pitches and disrupt the games. Demonstrators would rush
onto the pitch, sitting down on the grass or chaining themselves to the uprights or cross bars, scatter drawing pins on
the field of play and even throw smoke bombs. The Springbok players were targeted in the hotels, where alarms would
be set off, phone calls made late at night, or noisy marches
organized outside on the night before the match. Nothing
like this had ever been seen in relation to a sports tour and
de Villiers' men just did not know what to do. They fulfilled
their programme but lost heavily and were obviously relieved
to go home. De Villiers came back to England three years
later to testify in a private prosecution against Hain which
received a lot of support from whites in South Africa. On
his return home he stood for parliament for the Nationalists
and later, as ambassador to Britain, he became one of the
most prominent apologists for the regime. His most memorable, and revealing, comment defending the non-selection of
blacks was that blacks had become interested in white sports
only 10 years before, in flagrant denial of the fact that they
had been playing most sports for more than a century.

Despite Hain's success, English cricket felt no fear that
there would be any disruption to relations with South Africa.
The 1970 tour looked all set and *Wisden* had an article
on 'The Ups and Downs of the Springboks' by Michael

Melford. Melford made no mention of any non-white cricket nor gave any hint that South African cricket was segregated.

The Cricket Council, the body that had taken over the running of cricket from the MCC, were just as sanguine and refused to alter plans for the 1970 tour. They proceeded as if nothing had changed, although it was obvious that a cricket match could be much more easily disrupted than rugby. In a single night in January 1970 a dozen cricket grounds were damaged. The authorities ordered 300 reels of barbed wire to exclude saboteurs, and estimates of the cost of protecting a three-day match ranged from £7,000 to £18,000. As the season approached, the Cricket Council announced that the tour would consist of only 12 matches; but it still persisted in ignoring the advice being given to it by prominent leaders, including Prime Minister Harold Wilson. Many were worried about the effect the tour would have on race relations in Britain.

On 14 May, after a noisy House of Commons debate, James Callaghan, the Home Secretary, summoned the Council to the Home Office and asked them to 'uninvite' the South Africans. Four days later the English cricket establishment considered this advice but refused to accept it. However, it did manage to say that future tours would have to have teams selected on an inter-racial basis. As opposition to the tour continued, Callaghan summoned the Council to the Home Office again and asked them to withdraw their invitation 'on grounds of broad public policy'. The Council, with bad grace and making it clear that they were being dictated to by government, gave in.

Ninety years of Test contact between white South Africa and England had finally come to an end and, as the *New Statesman* commented, during this period South Africa's 'racial ideas have made more headway with us than ours with them'. Some indication of this was provided when, in response to the West Indian campaign against apartheid cricket and a warning by its spokesman that a white cricket tour might jeopardize relations with the West Indies, Peter

Tombs, leader of the Anti-Demonstration Association said, 'These West Indians come to this country as guests and they had a bloody cheek to say the least. They are in Britain on sufferance and must behave themselves. We are becoming so overwhelmed by the colour question in this country that we are allowing these people to dictate to us.' Change 'West Indians' to blacks, Bantus or Kaffirs and you could be hearing the voice of a typical white South African – or of a member of the British National Party or any other neo-fascist faction of the loony right in Britain.

The cricket tour had been called off on 22 May 1970. Less than a week before that South Africa had become the first country to be expelled from the Olympic Games.

White South Africa had fought hard to prevent this. After the rebuff at Mexico it had sought to improve its image by staging an Olympics of its own. However, this was to be a very special white South African version: one games for whites and another for blacks.

The white games were held in 1969, the black games only in 1970, and then almost as an afterthought. Invitations to the white games were for white athletes, not only the South African ones but also those from overseas. The French sprinter, Roger Bambruck, was not invited: he happened, as one newspaper put it, to be 'dusky'.

The games, far from improving South Africa's international image, muddied it still further and dealt a severe blow to its hopes of staying in the Olympics. At its meeting in Warsaw in July 1969 the IOC originally had no plans to take a major decision on South Africa but the whites-only games of 1969 began to change the picture. Lord Killanin warned that Warsaw would not just be about whether South Africa would participate in the 1972 Munich Olympics but whether it could even stay within the movement.

At Warsaw, however – as so often – the issue was fudged and the final decision was put off until a further IOC meeting in Amsterdam in May 1970. The trouble was the IOC's voting structure favoured white South Africa's traditional allies. Membership of the IOC, according to Baron de Coubertin, its founder, was an aristocracy and this, effectively, meant a white aristocracy. Those with long athletic traditions – the Western white countries – were more heavily represented on the IOC. Although the 1960s had seen most of the African and Asian countries enter the Olympic movement, by 1970 they still had only one third of the votes in the IOC. For while many of the white nations had two or more IOC representatives, many of the black nations had none.

A survey conducted by Richard Lapchick in the spring of 1970 to determine how the national Olympic committees felt about South Africa's participation in the 1968 Olympics showed that while 98% of the non-white nations opposed it, 68% of the whites favoured it, including all the Western white countries. The white countries that did not favour it were part of the Soviet bloc. Malawi was the only black country to want South Africa. Even Sweden and other Scandinavian countries, who would so strongly oppose apartheid in later years, wanted South Africa to participate.

Not surprisingly, white South Africa approached Amsterdam with great confidence. All it feared was another exclusion: from the 1972 Munich Games. Did this confidence perhaps mislead Frank Braun? In the past his IOC performances had, to put it generously, been two-faced. At meetings he promised change, knowing that once he was back in South Africa things could remain as they were; and, if he were questioned about it, half-truths and lies could always confuse the issue. But at Amsterdam he made a speech that could not have been more provocative: a mixture of bluster, threat and warnings of horrible things that would visit the Olympic movement if it continued in this fashion.

It is impossible to say what, apart from stupidity, made Braun adopt such an aggressive stance. Lapchick suggests he may have thought South Africa would be suspended anyway, so he might at least win some brownie points with his Government. But the tactics misfired. He aggravated even the friends of South Africa and South Africa was expelled.

Even now the vote was hardly overwhelming: 35 favoured expulsion, 28 did not and 8 could not make up their minds. Today this seems astonishing, but in 1970 the anti-apartheid movement could not have cared how close the vote was: it still represented a great victory.

Braun's failure at Amsterdam may also have indicated the sheer confusion in white South Africa as it tried to cope with what looked like a relentless onslaught on its cherished sporting institutions. This confusion was most evident in tennis. Here was a sport where white South Africa should have felt most secure. Basil Reay, the Secretary of the International Lawn Tennis Federation, had been one of those friends that white South Africa cherished. In 1966, when South Africa's expulsion had been discussed – the motion was rejected – Reay had said that one couldn't expect the white South African tennis body to change the country's laws.

By 1969 things were more difficult but still Reay was confident. He visited South Africa and tried to get the non-racial body to affiliate to the white body. He admitted the offer was not attractive or in accordance with international law, but it would have meant protection for the white body. The South African Government allowed an Iranian Davis Cup team to play in the country giving them 'honorary white' status. This was one of the great absurdities of apartheid. Under this ruling the Japanese swimming team could be honorary whites but not Japanese jockeys. Japanese businessmen were also honorary whites but not Chinese: there was a fair number of Chinese living in South Africa, but Japan was important for trade. However, when the Iranians, having become honorary whites, wanted to play against a non-white team, the white tennis body refused. Despite this, Reay returned from South Africa giving the white body a very favourable report, and when the ILTF meeting came to discuss the issue Reay ensured South Africa retained membership. If South Africa were to be expelled, he said, it would be a 'tragedy for South African tennis and world sport'.

However, there was nothing even Reay could do about the Arthur Ashe saga. Ashe had overcome segregation in the United States to become the first great black player to emerge in modern international tennis. Just before the ILTF meeting in 1969 Ashe had announced he had been refused a visa to play in the South African championships. This should have stirred the ILTF. Here was a championship held by a ILTF member country refusing the citizen of another country the right to participate. Reay did not think this was a 'tragedy'. But Ashe would not give up. Later that year he applied again and his application to play in the championships was accepted by the white body. Ashe had signed a statement saying he would not make political statements about South Africa. This did not endear Ashe to black militants in the United States who thought, as Ashe put it, that he was 'nuts' for wanting to go to South Africa. A series of high level South African-US Government contacts followed – some in Pretoria others in Washington, and one in Paris where Ashe met the American Secretary of State Rogers, who told the South Africans he had a personal interest in the issue.

Despite this, Vorster's cabinet unanimously rejected his application. An articulate black sportsman who had definite views on South Africa was too dangerous. However, the Government made it clear that Ashe would be welcome if he came as part of the Davis Cup team. This was not quite as illogical as it seems; that way, white South Africa hoped to stay in the Davis Cup. Refusing Ashe as an individual at most affected the South African Open championships. In the event, a special meeting of the ITLF called by the Americans led to South Africa being excluded, although only temporarily.

That decision was reached in March 1970. Two weeks later, with that gallumphing footwork that has long distinguished white South Africa's diplomacy, a 13-year-old Chinese girl was stopped by the South African security branch from playing in an East London white school tennis tournament. The ILTF now excluded the South African Open as one of its grand prix tournaments.

Some of the Vorster government's decisions were taken with an eye to the South African elections. Vorster had inaugurated what was called the 'outward looking' policies. Much of the policy met with approval except the bit about sports and the admission of Maoris. Dr Albert Hertzog, already sacked from the cabinet, painted a lurid picture of the corruption that would follow if Afrikaner girls danced with Maori players. Hertzog's opposition did not amount to much. He was warmly applauded at the Transvaal Nationalist party congress in September 1969 – but the votes were with Vorster. However, Vorster was sufficiently rattled to bring the election forward from 1971 to April 1970. While white South Africa battled to stay in the Olympics and minimize the damage caused by the Ashe affair, Vorster campaigned. His theme included a reference to sports and, attempting to steal Hertzog's thunder, he warned his Afrikaner audience that South Africa's exclusion from international sport was all part of a well-laid Communist plot to control the world. Not many in the IOC, even South Africa's friends, thought a vote for expulsion meant surrendering control of the Cape sea route to the reds, but this is how Vorster told the story in the veldt, and it helped to return his party to power.

Nonetheless, Vorster knew he had to have a new sports policy. The old one was in tatters and for the first time in white South African sporting history, some of the white officials themselves were making noises suggesting they wanted changes. All the years of bridge-building had changed nothing, now a few months of isolation was causing the most astonishing changes. Jack Cheetham, trying to save the 1970 cricket tour, had said he had instructed the selectors to choose the team on merit – which, if true, would have been remarkable; it was, however, merely one more addition to the mountain of lies that South Africa's white sports officials routinely spouted on behalf of apartheid. Leading sports adminis-

trators and officials had condemned the refusal to grant
Ashe a visa. And three days after the 1970 cricket tour was
cancelled, Dennis Gamsy, a white cricketer, wrote a front-
page editorial in the Rand *Daily Mail* calling for a national
sports conference – a call that was echoed by Alf Chambers
of the white tennis body. Peter Pollock, an English-speaking
white who had always opposed apartheid, had initially condemned the UK demonstrators as 'Communist inspired'.
Three weeks later he appears to have recognized that, Communist or not, they had made an impact, and he asked
sportsmen to call for multi-racial sport and for the Government to help in that.

There can be little doubt that isolation and cancellation of
tours galvanized sportsmen, and particularly cricketers, into
showing a political courage they had never shown before. In
April 1971, with a tour to Australia coming up, the white
cricket body wanted to include two black cricketers. This
was the worst kind of tokenism, but in the South African
context it was a major advance. The Government rejected it.
The news broke on the first afternoon of a match between
Transvaal, the Currie Cup champions, and the rest of South
Africa in Newlands. Intended as a trial, it now became the
focus of a remarkable protest. That evening Peter and
Graeme Pollock, Barry Richards, Mike Proctor and Dennis
Lindsay met and thought of refusing to play as a sign of
protest. After much discussion an alternative plan was
worked out. The next day, after one ball was bowled, the
players all trooped off the field and issued a statement saying
that they supported the inclusion of non-whites 'on the tour
of Australia if good enough, and furthermore subscribe to
merit being the only criterion on the cricket field'. Then they
returned to continue the game.

In the mythology of white cricket this has gone down as
an act of great moral courage; certainly, given the shameful
timidity of most white sportsmen in South Africa, it was a
remarkable statement. Just two years earlier, Gary Player,
a long-standing supporter of apartheid, had finally come out

in support of 'Papwa' Sewgolum's right to play in major events in South Africa. But then two days later, faced by a backlash, he had hastily changed his mind, saying, 'The Government of South Africa, rightly or wrongly, has decided on a policy of separate development. This is the law, and whether one is white, black, brown or green, one had to obey it', and then further undermining his ethical credentials by advancing the view that apartheid, after all, was intended 'for the betterment of all races'. As Steve Mokone, an exiled black athlete commented: 'Player thinks all blacks are happy because the only black he speaks to is his maid.' In a world which equated dissent with treason and Communist conspiracy, the cricketers' protest kicked up a storm; but as Donald Woods remarked, it was too little, too late. The 1971 cricket tour of Australia could not be saved. White South Africa had at last produced a quite brilliant team -- they had beaten the Australians 4–0 at home in 1970 – but after years of dictating to the world who they would play with, the world had taken away their ball. Or at least cricket had.

Like Britain, the Australians had had a taste of what a sports tour of South Africa might mean. The 1971 rugby tour of the country faced protests on a scale even greater than the one in Britain and, apart from New Zealand rugby, which was still keen to maintain links, white sporting South Africa appeared to be isolated.

It was against this background that on 22 April 1971 Vorster launched his 'multi-national' sports policy. South Africa was divided into four nations – whites, Coloureds, Indians and Africans. They could, under certain circumstances and in certain sports, play against each other inside the country – but not at club level, or provincial level, or even at national level. (Nobody even discussed schools level since the foundations of apartheid rested on the fact that young black and young white boys could not meet on equal terms on a school playground.)

What the so-called different nations could do was to play against each other at international level, provided the tournament had non-South African competitors. And a country which had traditional sporting ties with white South Africa could send a mixed team and this could play separate matches against blacks or Indians or Coloureds in, say, cricket or rugby. Only a white South African steeped in the imbecile logic of apartheid could have come up with such a tortuous policy. What the international community wanted was normal mixed sport where people of whatever race took part, as they did all over the rest of the world. Vorster offered a unique South African solution: a wonderfully abnormal sporting solution for an abnormal society.

with Sellschop, which developed after this match, merely led to the latter being ostracized by his white neighbours.

'Jasmat would often visit me with his family, along with some other Indian friends of his. The sight of so many Indians arriving in that white neighbourhood was unusual. Our kids used to play with our neighbour's kids, but after that they wouldn't let their children play with us.'

Following his match with Drysdale the white tennis body tried to recruit Jasmat, provided he resigned from the non-racial organization. Jasmat refused, and some time after this left to play tennis in England, as he had often done in the past. In England he continued to make his views known about apartheid sport and, learning that the Special Branch were interested in his date of return, he decided to stay abroad and become an exile.

Even under Vorster's multi-national policy such a match could not have taken place without the presence of foreigners. In any case Jasmat, who was from Indian stock, would have been in the odd position that as a tennis player he was supposed to belong to the 'Indian nation'. Yet no such nation existed and, as Vorster was promoting this supposedly 'outward-looking' sports policy, his ministers were telling Indians that there were too many Indian traders. If they did not turn to some other way of making a living, the Government might have to stop giving them licences, so preventing the growth of Indian business.

As multi-nationalism was coming into sport, so were the Bantustans, the so-called independent homelands, each to be peopled by a different African 'nation' supposedly corresponding to the different African tribal groups. The process began with Transkei's 'independence' in October 1976. In terms of the logic of Vorster's own multi-national sports policy, since he had decreed there was one black 'sporting nation', there should have been one black nation. But that would have defeated the purpose of creating Bantustans, which was to fragment the black majority and, hopefully, undermine the anti-apartheid argument that a minority of whites held power over the majority blacks.

If this indicated how tortuous the 'multi-national' sports policy was, it reflected its origins. It had come via the Broderbond (Brotherhood), the powerful, secretive Afrikaner group to which almost all the governing elite belonged. The Broders, as they were commonly known, had been heavily involved in the politics that had preceded Vorster's 1971 announcement of the 'multi-national' policy. A committee of Broderbond, chaired by Dr Andries Treurnicht (already known as 'Dr No' and later to become the symbol of white conservative opposition to change in South Africa), had been given the task of formulating the sports policy.

It drew up the guidelines that formed the basis for Vorster's speech of 11 April 1971. At one stage it had appeared that the Broderbond would actually take over the running of sports in South Africa, and a report in the *Sunday Tribune* of 12 September 1971 claimed that 'the Government is seriously considering a secret Broderbond master plan to establish a Sports Council, which will become the virtual dictator of all South African sport'. Nothing came of this, although many of South Africa's leading sports administrators were members of the Broderbond.

The absurdity of the multi-national sports policy was brought home by the South African Games of 1973. Hailed as a major breakthrough by the South African establishment, the event featured 800 South Africans, while about 700 foreign athletes, mostly from Western countries, were attracted by the promise of lavish expenses-paid hospitality.

Stan Wright, chairman of the men's track and field committee of the US Amateur Athletics Union, observed: 'None of the athletes chosen to represent South Africa were selected through an open championship based on merit; segregated seating prevailed through the Games, and the existence of four separate teams based on colour violated international rules.' And after the event brave voices in South Africa pointed out the reality of such multi-national games. The

leading white South African liberals and a friend of Steve
Biko, saw the elimination of sports apartheid as important
to establish points of inter-racial contact, and the first step
in the gradual elimination of apartheid itself. Koornhof, says
Woods, 'felt that while South Africa remained excluded from
international sport this constituted a political pressure-point
against the whole Afrikaner Nationalist regime and the main
body of political apartheid. While he agreed that non-racial
sport would help build useful bridges between South Africa's
alienated communities, and that this was a good thing in
itself for the sake of racial peace, he saw it mainly as a means
of buying time for his Government's general policies.' In
short, Woods wanted to end sports apartheid in order to
hasten the breakdown of general apartheid, while Koornhof
wanted to end sports apartheid in order to prolong general
apartheid.

But Woods warmed to Koornhof, who seemed to have a
greater sensitivity on the race question than most of his
cabinet colleagues. Soon Woods began to act as a go-between
for him. The white South African Cricket Association had
persuaded an unofficial Australian cricket team to tour South
Africa. But they would come only if every South African
team they played had at least two non-white players. Both
Koornhof and SACA were very keen on the tour; for the
Government it would mean breaking the cricket isolation
that had prevailed ever since the 1970 England tour had
been cancelled – although since then white entrepreneurs
such as Derek Robins had brought teams over to South
Africa – and for the white cricket association there was the
revenue and the chance of satisfying its white supporters that
it was keeping cricket going. But SACBOC saw it as mere
tokenism: two non-white players in every team during the
tour, then back to the daily reality of apartheid sport.

Koornhof called the white and the non-racial cricket
bodies together for a confidential meeting in his office to
which Woods was invited. Also at the meeting, from
SACBOC, was Kemal Casoojee, a South African of Indian

descent, who had a reputation in East London of being something of a playboy, but was now the leader of non-racial cricket in that part of Cape Province. Woods recalls: 'Koornhof thought he was being gracious and non-racial and he started by saying to us all, "I want to tell all you chaps about this nice weekend I've had with Rashid Varachia [a leader of SACBOC] and his wife. Let me tell you I've met Mrs Varachia and let me tell you she is a very nice civilized lady." He thought he was being gracious, but I could see the assembled SACBOC delegates stiffening. Then Kem [Kemal Casoojee] came up with the classic line: "Which of his wives are you referring to?" Of course Rashid only had one wife, but it threw Koornhof and he suddenly realized that he was in deeper waters than he had anticipated.'

The meeting did, however, persuade SACBOC that a deal was possible with Koornhof. If the Australian side, organized by Richie Benaud, was allowed in, maybe concessions could be rung from Koornhof. Woods recalls how Koornhof startled everyone by saying: 'Gentlemen, you've got no reason to trust me. As far as you are concerned I'm one of those Afrikaner Nationalist bastards who have been buggering you around for years. But now we've all got a chance to achieve something. I ask you to trust me now. If we don't trust each other and come to this agreement we are going to fuck the whole thing up!' This, says Woods, broke the ice and everybody started laughing, and a deal was done. Richie Benaud's side came and SACBOC hoped Koornhof would lift the ban on inter-racial club cricket.

This, as Woods accepts, did not happen, although Woods and Casoojee managed to make a dent in the ban by promoting the Rainbow Cricket Club. This club selected players from across the colour range clearly on merit and its existence had already thrown the local white cricket organization into something like panic. Woods and Casoojee had three blacks, two Indians, three Coloureds and three whites, and initially the white cricket authorities refused the application to hold matches on the ground that multi-racial cricket was any of the other apartheid legislation. What I was saying was that sport should be exempted from them. In other words sports facilities should be exempt from the liquor and licensing laws, would therefore enable everybody to have a drink after the game in the club bar, which then was illegal. I insisted that, when playing away from home, sportsmen must be exempt from the pass laws, which required that people of one colour required a permit to go to an area of another colour. The Group Areas Act and the Reservation of Separate Amenities Act – the two key acts of apartheid – which enforced racially segregated facilities, had to be amended for sports. In short, Vorster would have to take through Parliament a bill which exempted sports from all the apartheid legislation.'

It was this proposition that Hain put to Woods. Hain also told Woods that if the meeting with Koornhof was going to work, the South African government would have to lift the banning orders on black sports administrators, who were prevented from leaving South Africa and presenting their case abroad.

Koornhof did not think Hain's conditions were impossible: they would be difficult but they could be met. A few months later Woods was travelling again to Europe to present the case for the South African Chess Federation. The Soviet Union had convened a congress to urge the expulsion of South Africa from international competitions. Woods was planning to go to Lucerne to argue that the South African Chess Federation abhorred apartheid and had abolished it from its chess clubs at tournaments. A week of two before his departure, Koornhof rang suggesting further contact with Hain and Brutus and asked Woods to fly from Lucerne to London. The result of the call was that Woods's trip was now being financed by the South African government, although he told the Chess Federation that it was 'an anonymous chess fan'. Just as he was due to leave, however, Koornhof asked him to come to Johannesburg to meet General Van den Bergh, Head of the Bureau of State Security (BOSS).

No sooner had Woods checked into the hotel at Johannesburg airport than the general arrived, and he made it very clear that he thought Koornhof was going too fast with the sports initiative. He claimed to be a friend of Koornhof, wanted to 'protect' him, and had decided that the meeting between Koornhof and Hain, Brutus and other members of the sporting anti-apartheid movement in London would have to be called off. It seemed there had been a leak. The general announced that he would now like to meet Hain.

Van den Bergh also wanted to gauge the strength of the Soviet lobby at the chess congress. A fascinating conversation developed between the man who was seen as the symbol of the armed might of apartheid and Woods, one of his outstanding white liberal opponents. When Woods explained to the general that he was going to the congress to attack all apartheid laws and policies, that he would put as much distance as he could between the South African Chess Federation and apartheid, Van den Bergh said, 'Ya, naturally – that's what you must do to get the Western votes.' 'But that's not the only reason,' Woods replied. 'We in the federation are against apartheid.' 'You don't have to tell me that,' the general replied. 'But,' Woods continued, 'you should know what I told Dr Koornhof from the beginning: I'm doing this not only to end sports apartheid but to weaken *all* apartheid.' 'I know that, man,' replied the general rather testily, 'but if Western delegates at any international forum support a South African organization, it helps South Africa's name, of course.'

The exchange could not be more revealing. All those who supported sports contact with South Africa had always argued that by isolating South African sport, the protestors were not achieving anything against apartheid. Sports in South Africa had nothing to do with the Government, they insisted: if anything, the boycott mainly hurt the whites who opposed apartheid and the blacks. But as the above conversation shows, the Government clearly regarded the sports boycott as a dangerous strike against its apartheid policies. By the same token, in the South African government's eyes, all those who opposed the boycott, particularly the politicians and sports administrators of the Western nations, were providing a great moral boost for apartheid.

Woods left for Europe with the good wishes of the general and the suggestion that a meeting with Hain should be fixed for Paris, where the general's friend, a French nobleman, would provide a house. London was to be avoided at all costs: the general feared the British Secret Service and thought they would know the minute he got there.

At the chess congress in Lucerne Woods got the support of the Western delegates, including the Scandinavians, with Victor Korchnoi, the exiled Soviet grandmaster, openly supporting the South Africans. However, with the entire Soviet bloc and the Third World delegations against him, Woods knew he would lose out when it came to the vote. But as he sat listening to some of the speeches being made against the South Africans, particularly the speech by a Nigerian delegate, Woods began to change his mind about maintaining sports contacts with South Africa. The Nigerian's speech made the greatest impression on Woods when he said that, even if the South African Chess Federation barred apartheid, chess could not be viewed in isolation. How could a black player be on an equal footing with a white when they came from environments which were so unequal? Woods connected this up with what Steve Biko had been telling him and began to think that integrated chess clubs and cricket clubs were 'little more than fiddling while Rome burned'.

It was then that he decided not to initiate a meeting between Peter Hain and General Van den Bergh. When he returned to South Africa, where he was hailed as a hero for winning over the Western block at Lucerne, he explained to Van den Bergh and Koornhof that he could no longer act as go-between for such a meeting. They didn't seem to mind. They were so pleased at the Western support he had got that, he recalls, 'the other issue hardly seemed to matter to them any more. And that disturbed me too.'

In London Peter Hain waited for a call from Woods. It was about the middle of summer and he was planning to take his family to the Lake District for a holiday. He had told Woods that he would be quite prepared to fly from the Lake District to Switzerland in order to meet Koornhof. Today he cannot recall ever being told about a possible meeting with the general, and soon he received a call from Woods saying the whole thing was off – that Koornhof had been warned off by the security services and the meeting would not now take place. However, Woods had started a chain of events which was to rumble on for some time yet.

After his meeting with Hain during the golfing trip, Woods had gone back to South Africa and spoken to Dannie Craven. Suddenly one day Hain picked up the telephone in London and heard a voice saying 'Craven, South Africa, here.' Before Hain recovered from the shock, he realized he was speaking to Dannie Craven, South Africa's Mr Rugby, the man who had been his mortal enemy in 1969–70 when he was leading the Stop the Seventy Tour and disrupting Craven's rugby team's tour of Britain. At the time they had even had some verbal clashes; but now Craven was coming to London and he wanted to meet Hain. 'Where?' asked Hain. 'Could you come to the South African embassy or alternatively to my hotel in London?' asked Craven. 'No,' said Hain, 'I'll be happy to see you if it is on a private basis, but I'm not going to the South African embassy nor to your hotel. If you want to see me, by all means come to my house.' 'Fine,' said Craven. He turned up in a taxi at Hain's home in Putney 'looking very nervous, and a minder saw him out. Then we had a long chat. I offered him a drink, a beer I suppose. My son was then a year old and Craven took a lot of interest in him. We got on very well, actually.'

Hain told Craven what he had told Woods: 'I was not demanding the abolition of political apartheid. This was a very important message. I had always talked in sporting terms, never the wider politics. And I told Craven, "Look, we are not calling for the abolition of the entire apartheid system." He seemed to be quite startled by this, and thought there was a lot of common ground. I said, "Look, you go back and get your Government to take this bill through. You integrate your rugby, starting with school rugby, and I'll be happy to lead the call to welcome you back." '

Hain also mentioned that the banning orders on non-white sports administrators would have to be removed, but Craven shrugged his shoulders and said this was a strictly political matter. However, the talks ended so cordially that Craven presented Hain with a Springbok tie.

Craven was soon followed by Rudolph Opperman, president of the white South African Olympic Committee. In 1968 he had been even more arrogant than Braun: he was a member of the Broderbond and in 1971 had sat on a committee which advised the Government on the legislation that would ban non-whites from using the Springbok emblem. Now he was more conciliatory. He, in turn, was followed by Ali Bacher, who was just making his way into the Transvaal cricket administration and was acting as some sort of emissary of the white South African cricket body, or so Hain understood.

All this coming and going demonstrated how the boycott was forcing white sports administrators to compromise. But on the political front the Government was as hardline as ever. In 1975 Put Jansen, deputy Minister of Bantu Education, was asked if he had consulted Africans about having to speak Afrikaans. He replied, 'No, I have not consulted them and I am not going to consult them.' A year later Andries Treurnicht, an equally unreconstructed racist, who took over from Jansen, said, 'In the white areas of South Africa, where the Government pays, it is certainly our right to decide on the language division.' Sports administrators, having faced nearly a decade of isolation, had lost some of the arrogance of their political counterparts.

'Ali Bacher was quite different from Craven,' Hain recalls.

'I've always thought you can do a deal with an Afrikaner. English-speaking South Africans I've always been suspicious of – even though I was one myself. Bacher was much more aggressive. Basically he said, "Look, you know, we are doing what we can. You are asking for the impossible." I replied, "I'm actually taking a step which, in anti-apartheid circles, might be regarded as compromising in asking for sport legislation to go through." No, I was not very impressed with Bacher, then, and the feeling increased during the rebel sports tours later. In the end, I grant you, he saw the light sooner than anybody else.'

Just as Woods's proposed meeting between Koornhof and Hain had run into the sands of time and circumstances, so did these various meetings with Hain and the white sports administrators. Within a few weeks of Woods's return to South Africa his great friend Steve Biko was murdered by the security police. They initially denied all responsibility and claimed that he had died while on hunger strike in detention. They failed to explain how a lack of food had caused his terrible head wound.

Woods, campaigning to reveal the truth behind Biko's death, was himself silenced by a banning order which was so restrictive that he was allowed to be in the company of only one person at a time, even in his own home. This would eventually force Woods to flee South Africa and take up the life of an exile.

Biko's death had come just over a year after the student uprising in Soweto when, in the words of Alan Paton, 'black South Africans said to whites, "you can't do this to us any more" '. On that day 10,000 black Soweto school children gathered at Phefeni school in Orlando West to protest at compulsory instruction in certain subjects in Afrikaans. Faced by these unarmed pupils the police opened fire, killing scores of children and sparking off a general uprising.

Biko's murder seemed to confirm the fear of many blacks that none of their leaders would be allowed to survive by white South Africa. The events of 1975–7 were greeted with revulsion throughout the world and marked a turning point in the history of apartheid. If they did not lead to quite as big a flight of capital as the massacre of Sharpeville had done, they caused unease and a growing sense of self-doubt among the white population. It was after the Soweto riots that Ali Bacher began to think seriously of emigrating from South Africa and going to live with relatives in Canada.

Even if the crisis of apartheid created by Steve Biko's death had been avoided it is extremely doubtful if Woods's initiatives would have led to anything. By the mid-1970s the campaign against apartheid sports had developed into what might be called third-party activity. South Africa was by now such a sporting pariah that it had almost become infectious: any country or individual who had even the briefest sporting association with her risked being ostracized by sports authorities throughout the world. This had been amply demonstrated in 1976 when the African countries had boycotted the Montreal Olympics because the All Blacks had toured South Africa. The New Zealanders hardly did their cause any favours by arriving in South Africa even as the blood was drying in the streets of Soweto. The African boycott was to prove a seminal moment in the campaign to isolate South African sports. The tactics employed by SANROC during the Montreal Games was to split the movement, with its leading figures, Dennis Brutus and Sam Ramsamy, travelling along very different routes. Ramsamy, a South African of Indian origin, had, like Brutus, been forced to leave South Africa one step ahead of the Special Branch, and he was now taking charge of the organization in London. Brutus, living in the United States, was becoming more and more alienated from the movement he had helped create. The rift between the two created at Montreal was to widen over the years and has never really healed.

The boycott led to fears that other sporting events could be hit by such third-party action. The Canadians were very worried about the Commonwealth Games, to be held at Edmonton in 1978. They were regarded very much as the 'good guys' of the Commonwealth by their black fellow members, and many prominent Canadians felt something must be done to prevent the Games from being disrupted. Leading up to the Commonwealth Prime Ministers' meeting in London in June 1977 there were hectic consultations with Shridath ('Sonny') Ramphal, Secretary-General of the Commonwealth. 'At that stage,' recalled Ramphal, 'we had a limping kind of action but nobody was doing very much about trying to develop an international boycott. I thought the Commonwealth had a duty to give leadership to the international sports boycott movement. People like Malcolm Fraser and Michael Manley [Prime Ministers of Australia and Jamaica respectively] wanted to see the London meeting do something on sport.'

Jeremy Pope, a New Zealander, had just then joined the legal department of the Commonwealth secretariat at Marlborough House, London. 'One day I got a telephone call from John Syson, who was in Ramphal's private office. He said, "The Secretary-General wants you to draft something on sports." The gist of his message was that "Jeremy's bastards" (meaning the New Zealanders) have got us into this mess, he can get us out of it. I was very worried. I just did not know what to do. I discussed it with Kutlu Fuad, the Turkish Cypriot head of my department. He said there were precedents for Commonwealth leaders issuing "stand-alone" declarations on particular issues. He and I sat down at a table in Marlborough House and hammered out a draft.'

The big question was who would sell it to Robert Muldoon, the New Zealand Prime Minister? He had come to power in 1975 on a right-wing platform skilfully using the country's love of rugby and desire to play South Africa as a winning election slogan: 'I want to see the All Blacks team go to South Africa,' he had said during the elections, 'and lick the pants off the Springboks. If I can personally be there to cheer them on, so much the better.' He had done nothing to stop the 1976 All Blacks tour, so why should he now agree to a statement proposing such boycotts? Ramphal,

Pope and a few others from the secretariat discussed long and hard as to who could try to break the news to Muldoon. Eventually they decided it would have to be Michael Manley, whose charm is legendary. The location was the Gleneagles Hotel in Scotland, where the leaders were to have a weekend retreat. Muldoon would later describe how he and Manley hammered out the declaration in a bar of the Gleneagles hotel. The bar certainly played a part but there were also long hours spent in a hotel suite where Ramphal had got together a small group which, apart from Manley and Muldoon, included General Yaradua, representing the Nigerian President. 'I wanted to have Malcolm Fraser in the little working group, but Muldoon was unwilling. He knew he had to yield, but he did not want to be seen to be yielding to Fraser. This was Pacific politics. So Fraser was kept very close to the group but was not actually in it.'

Muldoon made the predictable and already totally discredited points about how politics had no part to play in sport; then, as the time came to sum up, Ramphal produced the draft, saying, 'Might we find consensus on something like this?' The compromise with Muldoon meant some changes but they were largely cosmetic. Muldoon was more interested, recalls Pope, in 'shafting the anti-apartheid movement in New Zealand'. Ramphal is sure that, while the declaration was couched in 'very careful language derived from Muldoon's rather negative position, I got 80 per cent of the draft I had started off with from London – a very substantial agreement'.

So, in one of the many ironies of this story, Gleneagles – which is associated above all with a sport, golf, that had always been notoriously lukewarm towards any boycott of sporting white South Africa – lent its name to what was the first and most stringent political commitment given by Governments against apartheid sport. The essence of Gleneagles was clear enough: Governments should use their best endeavours to make sure their sports people did not engage in sporting contact with South Africa. The crucial part of

The architect and the builder of apartheid. Verwoerd (*above*) made it clear that there could be no non-racial sport, while Vorster (*below*) helped spark the boycott. (Johannesburg *Sunday Times*)

The stark contrasts of black and white sport in South Africa. These photographs of white thirteen-year-old Roger Wentzel and black fourteen-year-old Paul Masilo were taken just before Gatting's rebel tour arrived in the winter of 1989. (*John Rogers*)

Paul and Roger came together for a fleeting moment of apparent equality on the cricket field as a result of the township programme initiated by Ali Bacher. (*John Rogers*)

The last all-white South African cricket team to tour England, 1965. Ali Bacher is seen on the back row, seventh from the left. *(John Rogers)*

'The Dirty Dozen'. The first rebel tour of South Africa, organized by Peter Cooke *(seated, centre)*, flanked by a bearded Graham Gooch and one of the architects of the tour, Geoff Boycott. *(Peter Cooke)*

Ngconde Balfour *(left)*, who tried to persuade Gatting not to come to South Africa, with Morne du Plessis *(second left)*, once a rising star of white rugby who saw the error of his ways and began to advocate change. *(Morne du Plessis)*

Steve Tswete *(left)* the godfather of the new South African sport, with Dannie Craven, the godfather of white rugby. (Cape Town *Argus*)

Ali Bacher raising funds for his township programme, just after he had announced Gatting's rebel tour. *(John Rogers)*

Bacher surrounded by his adoring family, including wife Shira and daughters Lyn and Ann. *(John Rogers)*

Bacher with Hoosen Ayob *(left)*, his lieutenant in the township programme and part of the lost generation of black and brown cricketers. *(John Rogers)*

One of the growing band of black female teachers coaching cricket in the township. *(John Rogers)*

Bacher *(right)* with Sunil Gavaskar *(left)* and Sir Garfield Sobers in Soweto to look at township cricket, a symbolic moment that marked South Africa's acceptance by the international cricket community in June 1991. *(United Cricket Board of South Africa)*

Bacher introducing his protégé, Walter Masemola, hailed as the South African Wes Hall, to Sir Garfield Sobers. *(United Cricket Board of South Africa)*

Bacher with Hoosen Ayob *(left)*, his lieutenant in the township programme and part of the lost generation of black and brown cricketers. *(John Rogers)*

One of the growing band of black female teachers coaching cricket in the township. *(John Rogers)*

Bacher *(right)* with Sunil Gavaskar *(left)* and Sir Garfield Sobers in Soweto to look at township cricket, a symbolic moment that marked South Africa's acceptance by the international cricket community in June 1991. *(United Cricket Board of South Africa)*

Bacher introducing his protégé, Walter Masemola, hailed as the South African Wes Hall, to Sir Garfield Sobers. *(United Cricket Board of South Africa)*

the statement stated that Commonwealth leaders 'accepted it as the urgent duty of each of their Governments vigorously to combat the evil of apartheid by withholding any form of support for it, and by taking every practical step to discourage contact or competition by their nationals with sporting organizations, teams or sportsmen from South Africa'.

Strictly speaking Gleneagles was neither an agreement nor a declaration, and nobody signed anything. It was a press statement endorsed by the Commonwealth leaders. However, within six months the United Nations General Assembly issued a declaration against apartheid sports and Ramphal is right in saying that Gleneagles set 'an international benchmark; it was the starting point because it represented inter-governmental commitment, inter-governmental undertakings. Even Mrs Thatcher could not get round it. She always took the position that Britain had signed the Gleneagles agreement and maintained that the British Government was fulfilling its obligations under Gleneagles.'

The Commonwealth leaders may have felt Gleneagles was the final word but, as Ramphal himself admits, 'Gleneagles depended on whether you had the political will.' Some countries went much further than Gleneagles required – as for instance Guyana in February 1981, when Robin Jackman was flown there as a replacement by the touring England cricket team. Jackman had married a South African and spent many winters coaching and playing cricket there. He was English and his presence in the England team did not violate Gleneagles. But Guyana thought otherwise and banned him. The England party left at once, the Georgetown Test match was cancelled, and for a time it seemed the entire West Indies tour might be in jeopardy. But the other Caribbean Governments did not follow Guyana's line and the tour continued. As Ramphal observes, 'Guyana was further out than most. Gleneagles didn't oblige them to ban Jackman, but you cannot stop a Prime Minister or any Government from taking action that they regard as valid and necessary.'

A few months later in New Zealand Muldoon put a very

reverse, it was the comfort factor of the sport to the apartheid movement. Removal of that comfort could hardly be described as interference. Muldoon and other apologists kept saying that Gleneagles was premised on discrimination in sport in South Africa and that therefore even if you did nothing about apartheid and somehow you cleaned up sport, Gleneagles lost its rationale. That was nonsense. Gleneagles was about apartheid, it was about sports in an apartheid country. Gleneagles sustained its relevance so long as the struggle against apartheid was on.'

For white South Africans this was 'moving the goalposts'. They had been made a pariah in international sport because they would not allow multi-racial sport. Now that they did allow it, they asked, why were they still being ostracized? The fact is that such multi-racial sport as was possible in South Africa was just as distorted, unreal and absurd a version of the real thing as any played under Vorster's bogus 'multi-national' policy. In the months after the New Zealand tour, through the South African spring and summer (September to March 1981–2), the white Parliament debated amendments to the three pillars of apartheid: the Liqour Act, the Group Areas Act and the Blacks (Urban Areas) Consolidation Act. The changes had been prompted by a 1980 report of the Human Science and Research Council which had been asked by the Government to study sports and recommended that sports bodies, being autonomous, could now 'differentiate' as opposed to discriminate on the basis of race, culture, language and religion.

The whites' faith in apartheid remained undiminished. Just before the tour, in the whites only elections held in April 1981, four fifths of the electorate had voted for parties that supported racial segregation. Nor was anybody under any illusions what these sporting changes meant. In October 1981, as the white Parliament discussed the amendments, an opposition spokesman described them as providing blacks a 'license to be white for the short time they are engaged in sporting activities, but reduces them to a lower status as soon as they leave the club premises. They cannot go with their team-mates to the movies and they cannot ride with their team-mates in the same public transport in most cities in this country. Unless a hotel in South Africa has been given special permission they cannot stay in such a hotel . . . unless somebody telephones the Hon. Minister and gets special permission for them to do so.'

Nationalist MPs hastened to reassure their constituents about the changes. As one of them said, 'Individuals or clubs who do not wish to compete against other individuals or clubs if people of colour are participating, do not have to.' Government ministers made no bones about the fact that these cosmetic changes were unwanted but were necessary in order to help the white sports bodies keep a toe-hold in international sports. D. J. de Villiers, Minister of Industry, Commerce and Tourism, speaking during the debate on the amendments to the Liquor Act, said, 'He [a member of Opposition] must keep in mind the position in which South African spokesmen and sporting bodies find themselves in the world today and the almost desperate effort of our sports administrators to retain a foothold in international sport.'

Not surprisingly, the changes could not hide the absurdity of trying to dress up apartheid as something different, and soon after they became law white South Africa once again showed how little things had changed. A black trampolinist was chosen to represent the country in a contest in the United States. But he could not use the recreation centre in Johannesburg for training, and after public protests the general manager of the Parks and Recreation department said, 'The centre's facilities are reserved for whites only but we would be able to make the necessary arrangements to have him practise on his own.' He was allowed to use the centre once a week, at a time when no whites were there.

The next few years would produce many such examples and South African whites seemed unable to comprehend the point that would soon be made most vividly by the sports writer Frank Keating. After explaining why South Africa overwhelmed by such feelings one day at the Wanderers when he saw Eddie Barlow badly injured in the hand by a ball from Clive Rice. As he saw his favourite cricketer leave the field, Cooke thought, 'Well, that's the end of an incredible career, and a wonderful era in South African cricket. Almost simultaneously I started to ask myself; why, why should we not play international cricket?'

Any rational examination of the moral issues would have provided the answer. But white cricket and its followers, secure in the privileged world of apartheid, could see no reason why they should be ostracized.

While in principle, like the majority of English-speaking whites, he was against apartheid (though as an English passport-holder he did not even have the vote) Cooke could see nothing wrong in accepting all the economic, social and legal advantages of apartheid, and cocooned in this distorting world felt that it was almost his moral right to try to organize a tour of English players who would provide the South Africans with some international competition. Since the boycott a number of international teams had made tours, but none of them had approached Test standard, and Cooke was determined to change all that.

In December 1980, when Boycott came to South Africa for his regular winter sojourn, Cooke, while bowling to him at the nets at Wanderers, unburdened himself. Boycott sympathized and said, 'Meet me in Trinidad.' So it was that, while the cricket world was recovering from Guyana's expulsion of Jackman and the consequences this might have for international cricket, a much bigger threat was being hatched by Cooke and Boycott around the Trinidad pool.

Cooke's plans met with a ready welcome in South African business circles, with the South African Holiday Inn chain keen to sponsor it.

Once this had been confirmed and Cooke had signed up many of the players, the South African Cricket Union came into the picture. Apart from one sceptic, Cooke met with universal approval. Joe Pamensky, head of the cricket body, was very enthusiastic. The big worry for the rebels was whether the English Test and County Cricket Board would try to stop them. In August Boycott and all the contracted county players received a letter from the TCCB. The letter warned that by taking part in tours to South Africa the players 'could make themselves ineligible for future selection for England'. The TCCB was in fact reacting to an 'English Counties XI' tour being organized by John Edrich, the former Surrey and England opener. Seventeen players had signed up for it. Cooke's tour was still a secret, and Boycott and company felt that if enough of the current England side went there would be safety in numbers. By September, the Edrich plan having been aborted, Cooke was ready to roll.

That month Stuart Banner of Holiday Inn flew in to London, and it seemed to him that nearly the entire English Test team was keen. The money was certainly tempting: half a million rand was available for 14 players plus Bernard Thomas as physiotherapist-manager. Boycott was acting as leader and Banner told him of the secretive meetings that had taken place between him and the other players: Gooch, Dilley, Knott and Gatting at a London hotel; Gower, Botham and Willis on the phone. Phone lines also buzzed between London and Australia as Gooch spoke to his close friend John Emburey, who was holidaying in Australia; he was just as keen. Holiday Inn had made it clear that both Boycott and Botham, who had just enjoyed his magical summer against the Australians, were absolutely essential for the tour. Botham, then holidaying with Vivian Richards in Antigua – a point of some significance, as we shall see – once again indicated his willingness to tour. The only drop-out was Gatting, who was advised by his solicitor that he might be in breach of his contractual arrangements with Middlesex. But he promised not to leak details.

Initially the tour was to have taken place in October 1981. However, the heat generated by the Jackman affair had made Boycott and company wary. England were due to tour India that winter and it would not be politic for England players to go to South Africa just before that. So it was decided to tour South Africa at the end of the Indian visit. But would the Indian tour take place at all? Although the negotiations for the Cooke rebel tour remained a secret, Boycott's past seemed to be threatening the Indian tour. The Indians did not much like the fact that he and Geoff Cook had been on coaching assignments to South Africa, and until the last minute the tour to India was in doubt. Boycott was asked to give public assurances that he would not go to South Africa and to condemn apartheid. He refused to do so. Now everything depended on 'Madam', as the Indians called Indira Gandhi, the then Prime Minister. Just before the tour she attended a conference in Mexico. Returning home via London, where the English cricketers waited fearfully, she gave the tour the go ahead. Boycott, in a cricket book, had said that he abhorred apartheid as much as communism. Mrs Gandhi concentrated on the first part of the sentence and, content with that ritual denunciation of apartheid, sanctioned the tour. When Boycott arrived in Delhi he presented Mrs Gandhi with a copy of his book. Mrs Gandhi accepted it, remarking, 'You caused us some trouble.'

As the England players toured India, moving from hotel to hotel, Boycott and the other players would meet to discuss details of the rebel tour. For most English players India is a hard place to tour: the people strange, the food literally hard to stomach, the water undrinkable, the heat unbearable. The richness and variety of Indian culture seems to be beyond them and, rather like British holiday-makers abroad, they detest the absence of home comforts and amusements. Boycott had turned down tours to the subcontinent three times. Now, on his first tour, he was unable to come to terms with it. He whiled away the hours with endless discussions on the forthcoming tour of South Africa. Gooch, too, bored with the cricket and the tedious evenings, slipped into a 'depression' which, he claims, drove him to tour South Africa. As such rationalizations go, it was about par for the course.

Boycott and the other players would meet in each other's

hotel rooms to discuss the changing plot: the money on offer, the guarantees and so on. Gower wanted £150,000 spread over three years, Gooch £40,000 a year with a prospect of another two or three years. Dilley £60,000 upfront plus an extra two years. Botham was worried about how a tour of South Africa might affect not only his international career but also his commercial endorsements. His 1981 exploits against Australia had made him the biggest catch in cricket. His greatest fear was that both might be in jeopardy if he took the krugerrands.

The plotting came complete with code words borrowed from the world of chess. Cooke's nickname was Karpov, and whenever the players wanted to discuss South Africa they would say to each other, 'How are Karpov and Spassky getting on?' Or 'It's a cool (k)night but do you fancy a trip to the Maharajah's castle?' On 21 November, in the Express Hotel in Baroda, at a meeting in Willis's room, he, Gower, Boycott, Dilley and Emburey gathered to thrash out how much money would tempt them to tour South Africa. It was agreed to ask for £150,000 over three years. Holiday Inn was still keen and within a week their representative Peter Venison had flown out to Bombay. As England prepared for the first Test against India, the details were finalized: £45,000 would be paid up front for the first year, there would be a 5 per cent increase for the second and third years, and wives and girlfriends could accompany the tour with all their expenses paid. The money would be paid into the players' accounts before the tour started, and they would pay no South African tax. But, recalls Cooke, Venison upset Boycott 'very, very much because Geoffrey was not prepared to be pressurized'. Suddenly cracks began to appear, not on moral grounds, but purely commercial ones. Botham had signed lucrative commercial contracts and was advised these would be at risk. 'Venison upset Botham very badly,' says Cooke. 'Botham flew his manager out to India [Reg Hayter, who was advising him, and his solicitor Alan Herd suddenly arrived in Bangalore]. Principally, Botham did not want to lose his

Volvo contract; but Volvo had pulled out of South Africa. That is when the shit hit the fan.' But still no public details emerged.

England were playing India with the Fleet Street media in attendance, but despite Hayter's sudden arrival in Bangalore – it says much for the investigative instincts of the cricketing press, and I include myself in that company – none of us twigged that anything was afoot. Nor did Raman Subba Row, the England manager, although on one occasion as he entered a room where the players had gathered, the discussion suddenly ceased. For a moment Subba Row wondered what it was all about, but soon dismissed it from his mind.

Later Botham would try to take the high moral stand, saying he couldn't have looked Vivian Richards in the eye if he had toured. As we have seen, he had initially agreed to tour while gazing at Richards as they holidayed together in Antigua. Boycott says bluntly in his autobiography that he found such self-exculpatory comments 'unnecessary and puke-making'. Morality had been no concern of the players. Boycott saw this as a 'business proposition of the type that might be considered by any professional in any walk of life. . . . There was no talk of bridging ideologies or nurturing international understanding.' Gower, too, had no moral qualms about going to South Africa. He pulled out (during the third Test in Delhi) only because he had now developed business interests in the West Indies which might be in danger if he went. Botham's withdrawal had put a giant spoke in the plans, and now with Gower pulling out it seemed the tour could not go ahead. Then during the fourth Test in Calcutta, Boycott, sick and unhappy, went AWOL and as soon as it was over he was sent home, weak and listless, to recover from a viral infection.

Cooke was determined the tour should go on. 'After Botham pulled out, Holiday Inn started getting nervous. I said to Pamensky, "Look, we are this far down the road. I'll find another sponsor." Geoffrey was not helping me any-

more. He had been sent home – he wasn't feeling well, his
mother had died and he had pulled out of my negotiations.
I was now dealing with Graham Gooch and John Emburey.
Gooch was more reserved and John was my chief liaison
man. I would send messages to John Emburey saying, "The
chess tournament will take place on such a such a date. You
play so many matches, etc, etc." My messages would be
signed "Karpov". After India the boys went on to Sri Lanka.
We had tremendous difficulty communicating. From South
Africa I couldn't get through to Sri Lanka.'

With Boycott unable to help and Gooch and Emburey in
Sri Lanka, Cooke flew out to England to sign more players.
Cooke's philosophy was that safety lay in numbers: England,
he felt, could not just sack its entire Test team. The amazing
thing was that the tour was still being kept a secret. Brenda
Gooch had nearly given the game away in Colombo when
in front of journalists she looked at a map and traced the
route from Colombo to Johannesburg, but still the journalists
did not cotton on. However, a new sponsor was yet to be
found, and this only came in the last week of February as
Cooke returned from yet another trip to England. The
moment he got off the plane he went to the Wanderers
ground for the final of the South African one-day tournament.

'It was a Saturday. As I walked into the Long Room, I
saw Joe Pamensky. He said, "I have got you a sponsor." Peter
Savary [of South African Breweries] came up to me and I
told him the story about Holiday Inn pulling out. He asked,
"How much do you need?" I told him how much I needed.
He said, "It will be in your bank on Monday. You bring
them back on Tuesday and by then we will be ready." I went
straight back to London with my lawyer.'

Cooke arrived back in London just as the England team
was returning from India and Sri Lanka. They were due to
arrive at Gatwick. Cooke's plane was due in at Heathrow
where he had a helicopter standing by to take him to Gatwick. However, owing to fog his plane could not land and

many of the South Africans very well. Then at the last minute Pamensky told them the tour sponsors had decided they didn't want Kallicharran in the squad. Boycott was disgusted and at one point threatened to go home. He was eventually persuaded to stay, but resigned as team captain, Gooch being chosen as the new skipper. It was clear that the South African Cricket Union, rather than Cooke, was now in charge of the team.

The English players had to play the first game before their contracts became operational. 'Once they had played a game,' recalls Cooke, 'there was no backing out. As long as they didn't play they could always get out. On the day of the first match, just before it started, I got a message from the British consulate relaying an official request from the TCCB to call off the tour. I had to take a chance. I decided to speak to my committee. They said it was my decision. I told them I would probably get into less trouble than them and I decided we would go ahead.'

George Mann, then chairman of the TCCB, rang Pamensky to say if he called off the tour England would propose South Africa's membership of the ICC. But Pamensky, fearing election would again be blocked by India, Pakistan and the West Indies, refused.

Before the first international match, spuriously billed as the first Test match, Cooke persuaded Geoff Humpage, the Warwickshire wicket-keeper/batsman, to join the team. Humpage was playing in the Orange Free State for a club called The Greys, and he had soon become aware of the South African way of life:

'It was strange going to the off-licence and seeing one entrance marked for whites, and another for non-whites. But it did not bother me. At the club all the menial jobs were done by blacks. I grew up in Birmingham, so I know what a multi-racial society is like; in any case I played in a multi-racial Warwickshire team. I just accepted this segregation in South Africa. When you get involved with the whites there I suppose you wear the same blinkers as they do.'

Humpage's reflections illustrate that, contrary to the
bridge-builders' glib theories about contact opening minds,
those who went to white South Africa often had their own
multi-racial minds closed. Humpage's sojourn in South
Africa closed his mind so tightly that when he returned to
Birmingham he could not understand why his participation
in the rebel tour should have caused such problems. His
photograph had been removed from his school's hall of fame.
When the headmistress of his old school asked if he would
have played cricket with Nazi Germany during the Second
World War, Humpage replied, 'Germany doesn't play
cricket.' He seemed to believe the only reason why the
teacher might want to ask such a question was that 'she is
married to a coloured chap, so she is affected by it'.

On the tour the English players, cocooned in the welcoming bosom of white South Africa, knew little of the fuss the
tour had caused in the wider world or the outrage many in
England felt. The British press published cartoons depicting
them as pirates carrying away swags of money. The players'
chief concern was to get eleven fit men on the field so that
the tour could go on, a matter of some urgency after Emburey
broke a finger and did not play again. In Cape Town Cooke
himself had to field when Lever injured his back.

As we have seen, the players were handsomely rewarded.
The most fiercely argued debate was whether such tours
aided apartheid. The South African Cricket Union strenu-
ously claimed that they were for the good of the game, that
they were multi-racial, and that they had nothing to do with
the Government. SACU also insisted that they did not accept
any Government money. (During subsequent tours Pamensky
would, amid much publicity, reject Government offers of
help.) It is true there was no direct Government money. But
the tours, as Cooke admits, were in effect Government
funded. 'In actual fact,' says Cooke, 'the Government was
actually financing it, if truth be known, through colossal tax
breaks. They were a form of incentive during the years of
isolation to encourage companies to export their goods.

Bacher had now started jetting around the world in pursuit of the best West Indian talent:

'In 1982–3 I saw Larry Gomes in New York, Viv Richards in Taunton, Gordon Greenidge in Hampshire, Malcolm Marshall in Portsmouth and Desmond Haynes in my sister's house at Gateshead. I knew from Kallicharran that the West Indian cricketers had no financial security. Vivian Richards was charming, but he said he couldn't come to South Africa. Greenidge was dour; I spoke to him in a cafe for an hour. My talks with Marshall and Haynes went well. Haynes was offered $200,000 for two years to come and play, including club cricket in Durban; Marshall would get $250,000 for three years and would also play for Transvaal. Just before Christmas 1982 Marshall rang from Melbourne, reversing the charges. He said he and Desmond were in, and asked me to arrange the tickets. But then Peter McFarlane broke the story and they vanished. The West Indians just took them away.'

Gregory Armstrong, however, had managed to secure Lawrence Rowe, the Jamaican who had looked like he might become as great a batsman as George Headley but had failed to live up to his early billing. With Rowe as captain, Armstrong was able to get quite a strong side after playing on the fears and insecurity of the West Indian cricketers. The first tour, in early 1983, was a short one; but the second, in 1983–4, proved quite dramatic. That was when Peter Cooke got involved again:

'The first tour was over very quickly – a very short trip. On the second tour they were much more aware of the situation, having been back home where they had been threatened. They wanted help and an ally in South African terms. By the time they came for the second trip, they were very well organized, had worked out what they wanted and what they could get out of it. I was called in to help them with local knowledge. All the rebel-tour players came with no recourse to their own unions. They were completely on their own.'

In Cape Town harsh apartheid reality struck. The fast bowler Colin Croft, travelling by train from Newlands to the city centre, got into the compartment meant for whites and was thrown out. This was not the first time West Indians had come up against so-called petty apartheid. Sometime earlier when Kallicharran was playing for Transvaal he had gone with a white friend to a hamburger place in Johannesburg and been refused service because of the colour of his skin. But Kallicharran meekly accepted it as part of the 'customs and traditions' of the country. Croft's experience combined with the publicity focused on this rebel tour made the headlines. Cooke is convinced Croft was testing the system: 'He tested the system on purpose, he was a highly intelligent man and things were being exposed, the window dressing was going, the shop was now starting to crumble.'

But it was not only South African social life that was starting to crumble under pressure from the West Indian presence. The local cricket administrators, too, had problems. 'What was being exposed,' says Cooke, 'was the inexperience of the South African administration. They were dealing with international players, which was unusual. If in England there is a tour and there are problems, the English administration deals with the tourists' board. The rebel overseas players had signed an agreement with the South African Cricket Union. This was not what I had planned. I had intended it should be an independent organization which would act on behalf of the international players as though it was their home board. But the South African Cricket Union overruled that and entered into contracts directly with the overseas players. They treated them as schoolboys.'

As so often happens in such situations the basic problem was money. The West Indians, says Cooke, felt that SACU was going back on its word. When the West Indians arrived SACU had no sponsors for the one-day matches. Eventually, with just a day to spare, Holiday Inn agreed to sponsor the first match (Yellow Pages agreed to sponsor the others). If the West Indians themselves had secured the sponsorships man who had qualified for Australia, but would later resume South African nationality and captain his country. This dinner, however, attracted enormous publicity – much of it hostile – and Bacher withdrew to his brother-in-law's flat in London to conduct his negotiations in great secrecy.

He decided the best person to help him would be Bruce Francis, a former Australian cricketer who had formed a strong attachment to white South Africa. Francis had been discussing a rebel tour for many years with Pamensky, and a year earlier, in May 1982, Bacher had rung him to ask his help in organizing one. Now, receiving Bacher's summons, Francis flew to London, where amid great secrecy they began meeting the Australians. But one of the Australian players leaked the meetings to the journalists covering the World Cup for the *Adelaide News* and Bacher was forced to put the tour on hold. It remained there until Easter 1984, when Graham Yallop met Francis, Pamensky and Bacher in Johannesburg. Yallop was the ideal recruit for a rebel tour: a former captain of Australia, he had not only lost that job but found it difficult to hold on to a place in the side.

It was two years since talks on an Australian rebel tour had started, and both Yallop and Francis were very keen to bring it to a conclusion. Francis had become something of a consultant to both white cricket and white rugby and for good measure fallen in love with a white South African woman. He was another in that long line who, arguing for sporting contact, effectively make an apology for apartheid. He would make ritual denunciations of apartheid – but then contest every idea to combat it.

Yallop's Johannesburg visit got things going and by October 1984 many Australian rebels were ready to move. Bacher flew to Singapore and set up shop at the Marco Polo Hotel. Most of the Australians who joined Bacher there were on their way home from a tour of India; others came from Australia. The group at this stage included Yallop, Graeme Wood, Carl Rackemann, David Hookes and Dirk Welham. No agreement had yet been made with the then Australian captain Kim Hughes, and when he checked into a hotel next door to the Marco Polo, Bacher took fright and he and Francis moved to the Paramount Hotel.

Bacher had learned from the West Indian rebel tours. He told the players everybody would be paid equal sums from a budget of three million Australian dollars, with each player receiving A\$200,000 after tax was paid in South Africa. The meeting at the Marco Polo went on until four in the morning, with much of the discussion centred on the players' concern about the money. Nothing was decided and Bacher and Francis returned to Johannesburg. But, within a month, nine of the Australian players who were facing the West Indies in the first official Test of the series at Perth had secretly signed to play in South Africa: Dyson, Wood, Rackemann, Hogg, Maguire, Wayne Phillips, Yallop and Alderman. There was a provisional contract with Kepler Wessels, while Rod McCurdy and Dirk Welham had contracts signed on their behalf.

The negotiations remained secret for almost two months. Then in January 1985 Chris Harte, of the *Adelaide Advertiser*, received a phone call from a Cape Town contact. Harte recalls: 'My article appeared on 30 January 1985. Once it was in print a lot of pressure developed. Players denied it. The Australian Cricket Board in their usual fashion denied it. They knew exactly what was going on. The *Adelaide Advertiser* had given my unlisted home number to Bruce Francis and he would ring me two or three times a day. The next real explosion came when selectors announced the team to tour England. By this time Kim Hughes had been replaced as captain by Allan Border. After the Brisbane Test against the West Indies, with Australia being constantly hammered, Hughes could not stand the back-stabbing. He resigned, shedding both literal and metaphorical tears. Hughes was told he would be in the team to England; he had taken a house in England and even arranged a nanny for his children. Just before the team was announced he got a phone call to say he was not in the team. As a sop he was chosen for a short tour to Sharjah. While he was in Sharjah he was approached by Graeme Wood, his Western Australia colleague, about the South African venture. Later, Bruce Francis met him in his home at Perth. Hughes got on the next plane to Johannesburg. News of this soon broke. Hughes had booked himself under a false name in the Johannesburg hotel – but it turned out to be the real name of a visiting American professor, who started getting calls in the middle of the night from Australian journalists demanding to know what he was doing there.'

Despite such problems the South Africans got Hughes to sign in May 1985, and this was clearly a big catch. Once again the South Africans had preyed on those unhappy and disillusioned. The Australian board reacted by deciding to take legal action. They had got the players to sign contracts. But, says Harte, 'you could drive a horse and cart through those contracts. After the Australian board started to take legal action, Bacher, Pamensky and Dakin asked if they might come and discuss matters with them. The immigration minister refused to give them visas, but Bob Hawke (the then Prime Minister) overruled him. Eventually the matter was resolved. The South Africans had to agree that the Australian board's contracts were correct and valid, and they had to pay the board's A$120,000 legal costs. In reality the Australian board did not put any blocks on the rebel tour: it was the usual dubious freemasonary between cricket administrators.'

After the rebel tours were over Harte, who wrote a book on it, was shown a file by Bacher which had faxes from the Australian board which suggested they were willing accomplices in the recruitment of their own players. 'I saw faxes in which the Australian board even suggested players the South Africans could recruit.' (During the rebel tours four of the 14 directors who made up the Australian board flew to South Africa to see some of the matches in the rebel series.)

Unlike the Cooke-engineered English tour, when the South Africans had been able to control all the pre-tour publicity, the Australian one was being undertaken amid a barrage of media attention and the players, anxious to avoid anti-apartheid protesters, met in dribs and drabs. They travelled to Singapore for training, booking themselves under the name of the Willow Group, before flying on to Johannesburg via Frankfurt.

They were followed by Harte and other Australian journalists. The expectation was that there would be violence; but there was little apart from one bomb attack on the team hotel when they were in Welkom. But, recalls Harte, there was political resentment among the Cape Coloured and the Indians: 'Krish Mackerdhuj – then head of the non-racial SACB (South Africa Cricket Board) – told me, "I don't talk to fascist journalists." I may be many things but I am no fascist. I heard he told his supporters that if they went to watch the rebel tour matches they would be banned from SACB matches. The blacks, to my surprise, did not resent the presence of the Australians. On Christmas Day we got lost in Soweto. Our bus had "Australian Cricket Team" emblazoned on the outside. When we got to a bus station in Soweto about 100 blacks surrounded us. But they smiled and said, "Hey, man, you beat the Springboks. You are our team." '

Yet again, as with all the rebel tours, the question was who paid for them. On both tours the so-called 'Test' matches were sponsored by National Panasonic and the one-dayers by Yellow Pages. But, says Harte, 'the cost to them was no more than 10 per cent of the total because of massive Government tax rebates. When I was South Africa I was told the rebate was 90 per cent. I was later to learn it was 160 per cent. So the Government was letting them trade without paying tax and the taxpayer footed the bill.'

The rebel tours were, in fact, Government-funded operations which brought aid and comfort to the apartheid regime and to the whites. The organizers of the rebel tours and their supporters denied it then and would do so even now; but Governments do not give such tax concessions unless they believe they are going to benefit from it. This point is of some importance because supporters of the rebel tours, particularly in England, pictured them as breaking down apartheid. But the South African organizers such as Cooke and Bacher never justified it on these grounds. Cooke's reason for organizing the first rebel tour was that cricket in South Africa was dying. At the Wanderers, where they once fielded 16 sides at the week-end, they could field now only eight, and he was saddened by the thought that his children were not able to see international cricket.'

Joe Pamensky, while claiming to oppose apartheid, also opposed the sports boycott and cannot even now accept that there might ever have been any need for it. For him the sports boycott was merely a cheap way for the politicians to hurt South Africa through its love for sports.

The white South African cricket authorities almost to a man insisted they were opposed to apartheid, but they were quick enough to accept in effect the financing of the rebel tours by the apartheid Government. However, even while travelling on this route, one man took a diversion that led him to another, more exciting, place. That man was Ali Bacher.

6

The Doc Awakens

Many years after Ali Bacher's township cricket programme
had become famous and he was on his way to being hailed
as 'Comrade Ali' in Soweto, he would tell Lawrence
Mvumvu, one of the men who helped him get the programme
started, 'You know, Lawrence; I have been sleeping for decades.' Lawrence replied, 'Doc, thank God you have woken
up from your long sleep.'

So far we have seen several faces of Bacher: triumphantly
captaining an all-white team, contentedly playing in front of
crowds that were segregated; one Sunday playing against a
non-white team in his native Johannesburg on their own
wretched ground – but then on the Monday returning to
his all-white comfort and forgetting all about his week-end
experience; and, finally, organizing rebel tours to keep white
cricket going at the highest level. Now, in the middle of the
rebel tours he began to discover something that was to have
a dramatic impact both on him and on sporting South Africa.
It would play a crucial part not only in bringing white South
Africa back into international acceptance but in making
cricket a symbol of the 'new', reforming, non-racial South
Africa.

The idea of township cricket had come to Bacher on one
of his early morning jogs with Alvin Kallicharran some time
in 1982. Bacher had brought Kallicharran to South Africa
because he was keen, as he says, 'to get a black player and
set the ball rolling.' He had come via the Warwickshire
connection, an exercise in bridge-building – although not in

145

quite the way its supporters envisaged it. It had been a bridge between English and white South African cricket, with English cricketers regularly going out to South Africa. Since his playing days Bacher had kept in touch with David Brown and it was he who had suggested Kallicharran as the ideal black player for Transvaal. Bacher, who had just been put in charge of Transvaal cricket, signed him to play in South Africa's domestic competition. Getting Kallicharran to play was a big step that in the South Africa of the early 1980s brought Bacher into conflict with the laws. Under the Group Areas Act Kallicharran, a Guyanese of Indian descent, could not live in the white suburbs that Bacher and the cricketers of Transvaal considered their home. But Bacher got around this by finding him a flat at Don Pasquali, just up the road from the Wanderers. 'The owner,' recalls Bacher, 'was quite helpful and let Kalli live there, although strictly speaking this was against the law.'

Like Bacher, Kallicharran was an enthusiastic jogger and in the early mornings as they pounded the streets of the northern white suburbs of Johannesburg together, Bacher was told about beach cricket in the West Indies. This, said Kalli, was how black kids in the West Indies learnt their game. They first played with a soft ball, so they did not have any fear of getting hurt. A small child has only to suffer one hit from a hard ball for his confidence to be destroyed. This was a whole new world for Bacher who, before meeting Kallicharran, had known little or nothing about West Indian cricket. Ever an eager learner, he lapped up tales of beach cricket. Then the talk turned to the idea of introducing such a soft-ball mini-cricket in South Africa, and soon Bacher began to feel quite passionate about it.

As managing director of Transvaal's cricket organization, Bacher was boss of the most important white provincial cricket body in the country. One of his first acts in this job was to dismantle the cages at the Wanderers ground. To many, this and the introduction of Kallicharran may have seemed like tokenism. But given the lack of moral courage shown by his predecessors, who were known as the lions of the gin-and-tonic circuit and the meekest of lambs when it came to backing their denunciations of apartheid with any worthwhile action, this was heady stuff.

How much Bacher's crusading passion derived from his Jewish upbringing is hard to say. Certainly a decisive influence, as so often in Jewish homes, was exercised by his mother. (There is a famous, and true, story of how his mother persuaded him to declare the innings closed during a match at the Wanderers. It was his first as captain of Transvaal; he was only 21 and it was the third day of a match against Eastern Province. A declaration was due and Bacher's mother could feel the restlessness of the people around her in the stand. Suddenly, she decided to act. 'I ran from the main stand to the players' pavillion: "Ali," I said, "you must declare." ' Bacher walked into the dressing room and said, 'Chaps, my mom says I must declare.' Actually, mom had been too patient. She should have told him to declare earlier, for Easter Province held out for a draw.)

His mother, born Rose Nochomouwitz in Slonim, Poland, had come to South Africa with her father just before the Second World War and married Ali's father, who had come from Lithuania.

Bacher showed quite early on a taste for leadership and captained his Johannesburg school at soccer, tennis (which at one stage was considered his best game) and, of course, cricket. And it was cricket that made possible the extraordinary story of this Jew becoming a great sporting hero of white South Africa who, by his success, inspired Afrikaners to excel at this very English game. Even odder was that, in a society where the merest hint of dark blood could mean a person being classified as non-white, Bacher has distinctively dark, swarthy, looks which make his nickname Ali (his real name is Aron) very plausible. Indeed, he has often been taken to be an Indian. When he played in that match against D'Oliveira and the other non-whites, Hoosen Ayob, who was in the crowd, wondered, 'What is that Indian boy doing playing for the whites?' Apart from the odd occasion, however, Bacher has never encountered any problems with pigment-obsessed officialdom in South Africa.

By 1986 Bacher had moved from Transvaal to become managing director of the white South African Cricket Union and was ready to implement his most radical plan: taking cricket to the townships. P. W. Botha, who had succeeded as the Nationalists' leader after a scandal had forced Vorster to resign, was trying to attract the Coloured and Indian peoples to his side in order to break the anti-apartheid front. They were even given the vote, although not for the only elections that mattered – the ones that choose the all-white Parliament. Botha's hopes that the Indians and Coloureds would be fooled by his political con trick were soon dashed, the elections for the Assemblies showing derisory turn-outs.

The blacks did not have this essentially symbolic vote: they were supposed to be content with their Bantustans. But Botha tried to woo well-off blacks by creating an urban middle-class that had a stake in the economy and could be weaned away from the revolutionary politics seething in the townships. The job-reservation schemes which had reserved all the best jobs for whites were done away with, and in 1979 black trades unions had been legalized in the hope of drawing their militancy. By 1985 blacks were permitted to own freehold land in the townships, and some black businessmen were allowed to trade in 'white' business districts. But the pillars of apartheid were essentially unaltered and political power remained firmly in white hands. When a so-called 'Eminent Persons' group came from the Commonwealth to suggest avenues that might lead to a negotiated end to apartheid, Pik Botha, South Africa's Foreign Minister, ended the talks by saying the Government was not interested in 'negotiations about a transfer of power'.

As invariably happens when regimes are on their last legs Botha soon discovered that his 'reforms' were too little, too late. The response of the dispossessed was to form the United Democratic Front, which became the front organization of the banned ANC, while in the townships the mood, a quarter of a century after the banning of the traditional political parties, was truly revolutionary. Indeed, in July 1985 Botha imposed a state of emergency over many parts of the country, arresting over 8,000 people; and this repression intensified still further the following year, when the state of emergency was reimposed and extended until 1990. By June 1988 it was estimated that over 30,000 had been arrested; thousands more were to join them in the following two years, and some kept in detention without trial for well over two years.

It was against this background, and after Botha had imposed the state of emergency for the second time in June 1986, that Bacher made his move. Bacher likes to describe himself as a 'very impulsive man', and there can be little doubt that the idea of taking cricket to the townships required courage. It meant challenging the conventional white South African wisdom that the blacks do not play cricket, and confronting white fears about going into the townships. Bacher was well aware of the disgusting inequalities of the apartheid system which, apart from the administration of justice, were most evident in school education and sports. In 1986–7 R2,299 was allocated by the state to educate each white child; the figure for each black child was R368. In white schools each teacher taught on an average 16 pupils, in a black school each teacher had to cope with 41 pupils.

Bacher had been to the townships before, but his first organized cricket visit is engraved on his mind. '20 October 1986 was when we first went into Soweto'. Although the nearest township to his luxurious white home was that of Alexandra, hardly a five-minute drive away, he was determined to go to the biggest and politically the most resonant of the black townships. Going in there was like going into Beirut: the army was still there, the kids had not been out of the township for three years, and around the world it had became the symbol of the black struggle against apartheid. 'We went in two cars, Volkswagens,' recalls Bacher. 'We were all white and we got lost. We ended up in the middle of Soweto, and I was frightened.'

In the end the whites managed to find their way to the Elkal Stadium in the middle of Soweto, a far cry from Bacher's beloved Wanderers and very like a soccer field. Here they hoped to conduct a cricket clinic for black kids. As they arrived they could see nobody – just the bare, intimidating veldt. Waiting with Bacher was Hoosen Ayob, who on that Saturday morning was just as scared. 'The townships were exploding. People were not interested in a game like cricket and as we waited I thought, "What are we doing here?" '

Hoosen, a tall, handsome man with an eye for the ladies, considers himself a true South African: his grandfather was an Afrikaner, known as The Dutchman, who married a Sotho woman; his mother, classified as Coloured, married an Indian. A fast-medium bowler, Hoosen had played all his cricket under the constrictions of apartheid, which meant that as a non-white he never played against whites. 'We never had a blade of grass. The ground would be littered with stones and glass where we had to prepare and mark the wicket. We would roll the pitch ourselves, lay the mat, and our cars provided the only changing room.' Despite this he felt he might have played for South Africa had white cricket provided the opportunity. But not only did it deny him on the field, off it it made him suffer even when he came to watch cricket at the Wanderers. He would have to sit behind the cages, which were beyond backward point or deep mid-wicket. Until the cages came down, when Hoosen was well past his prime as a cricketer, he had never seen cricket at the Wanderers from behind the bowler's arm – a great deprivation for a bowler whose trade was to make the ball swing and swerve:

'I used to walk from school, 10 or 15 kilometres away, and I watched Peter May's side from that cage. It was terrible. Once you got here and it was full, you couldn't move. When Alan Davidson came I wanted to see how he swung the ball but I could not sit behind the bowler's arm, that space being reserved for whites. So I could never appreciate his technique.'

Hoosen had been in contact with Bacher ever since the cancellation of the 1970 English tour, developing a genuine fondness for a man who was so different to the normal run of white cricket administrator. 'It was Dr Bacher who got rid of the cages,' he says, 'and I shall never forget that.' Their formal alliance began when Hoosen come over during the short-lived unity of the mid-1970s and stayed with Bacher even when other Indians and Coloureds went back. It was Hoosen who had introduced Bacher to Lawrence Mvumvu who, like many black Africans, had learnt cricket while working for a mining company in the 1940s.

Mvumvu was a teacher in Soweto and on that Saturday Bacher had asked him to bring along a few black coaches. Radio and television appeals had also been used to try to get the kids to come. But as the sun grew hot and Bacher and Hoosen waited they began to get the feeling that the whole thing would flop. Finally, at about 8.30, the first kids started arriving – and in the end there were about 1,000 of them.

For three and a half hours Hoosen and Bacher taught black kids the rudiments of the game. 'We just showed them what the game was all about,' recalls Hoosen. 'Various aspects. Ali and I both played, and although these kids did not know anything about cricket, they enjoyed hitting the ball and running.'

'We went,' says Bacher 'for eight consecutive Saturdays. By the third Saturday I realized the kids, given the opportunity, could play; they had co-ordination and rhythm. I should have realized this decades ago. That Saturday I turned to Mervyn King, an ex-judge, and I told him we needed dough. Through the South African Executive Cricket Club, the business community pledged to raise a million rand in a year.'

But even as Bacher recognized that there might be cricket potential in Soweto, he was conscious that his very venture into the township could be interpreted as just another expression of the old-style white man's behaviour. 'In essence, what we had done was move in and take over. We felt the consequences on the sixth or seventh Saturday: the. kids' numbers started to dwindle. I realized there was a problem. The kids loved the game, but it emerged that the teachers had started telling them not to go. People had begun to criticize me for going into the township without permission. What they meant was not political permission but educational permission. That was my first lesson of the township. The days of the whites making decisions for blacks, which was part of South African history for over half a century, had gone.'

Slowly, however, the township cricket programme took off. In the process Bacher discovered that the great majority of the teachers in the black schools were female. So, in a remarkable break with cricket tradition, he encouraged these teachers to learn cricket. Soon it was a common sight to see in Soweto and Alexandra middle-aged black ladies teaching young black kids the game. By this time coaches of all colours were going to Soweto and the other townships quite regularly, and Bacher had launched not only a new cricket form – mini-cricket, played with a soft ball – but a new kind of cricket coach: the female teacher.

Was Bacher's township programme part of the Government's campaign to win the hearts and the minds in the townships? Even those who accept that the township programme was innovative and welcome, wonder about this. André Odendaal is an admirer of Bacher, but is worried by the fact that Bacher started his programme just as Botha's Government was trying desperately to win black support. This was also a time when even sports administrators, including colleagues of Bacher (though not Bacher himself), promoted the 'total strategy' that Botha had enunciated. This strategy was underpinned by the typically paranoid conviction that any opposition to apartheid, including the sports boycott, was part of an all-embracing world-wide communist plot against South Africa.

Odendaal's fears seem misplaced. Bacher's flair for public relations and marketing may be acute but he is no machiavellian plotter. He had gone to the townships because he felt strongly about cricket and in the power of the game to achieve things beyond the reach of politics. From an early age he had been obsessed with cricket. Of course, this obsession did have a certain political fall-out, but not in quite the way Odendaal may suspect. Its impact lay in the fact that by taking cricket to the townships Bacher was, perhaps unwittingly, opening up another front. Until Bacher went into Soweto, the racial argument in cricket had been between the whites on one hand and the Coloureds and Asians on the other. Although black Africans had produced some striking cricketers – notably the legendary Frank Roro, who had hit 100 hundreds for Crown Mines and scored 304 against Main Reef in 1942 – there was no great tradition of black African cricket. For young blacks in the townships, the favourite game was football: in 1984 Soweto had four cricket pitches and 140 soccer fields. At that time 'non-white cricket' meant Asian and Coloured cricket – the game that had produced D'Oliveira, Tiny Abed, Cecil Abrahams and Hoosen.

As township cricket got into its stride Bacher was forced to accept what the anti-apartheid protesters and organizers of the boycott had always insisted – that the response to the boycott had produced only cosmetic changes. You cannot suddenly have equality at the age of 21 if for all your childhood and adolescence inequality has been brutally forced upon you. In sport, only an imbecile could believe that you could have equality among players at club level if such equality does not exist at school level.

The success of Bacher's township programme had the effect of outflanking the non-racial bodies opposed to SACU, which had been far too busy trying to keep their organizations going in face of the onslaught by the forces of apartheid to do anything about taking cricket to the black kids. They still had a membership that was largely Indian and Coloured.

Although Bacher almost certainly did not intend it that way, his foray into the townships meant a largely white organization had exposed the non-racial body's limitations. For the first time since the boycotts began there had now been a counter strike. By reaching out to young black kids the white sports world had, for the very first time, made a positive move in the direction of the non-whites. It would have important consequences.

7

Abnormal Becomes a Cul-de-Sac

Ever since the late 1970s, opposition to sporting contact with apartheid South Africa had been summed up in the phrase: 'No normal sport in an abnormal society'. The slogan had been coined by Hasan Howa, who had rallied the anti-apartheid sports movement in the country after Brutus's departure and, although his remit was cricket, he was soon seen as the spokesman for all the dispossessed of sporting South Africa. Like Brutus, Howa was what white South Africa classified as a Coloured and he was proud of the fact that he was a true South African:

'Early Portuguese adventurers in Goa injected red hair into my Indian ancestry and, on my mother's side, I can boast a minister of the Dutch Reformed Church as an ancestor. Chapman of Chapman's Peak [Cape Town] married into the family. Our bond is really very close. How can one be anti-white or fight against whites under these circumstances? It may be your uncle you are fighting, your own blood and people. There are people sitting in Parliament who would blush if they were aware of their ancestry. I am a true South African. Not a black, white, yellow, pink, or green South African.'

There had been a brief moment in 1976, as the white and non-racial cricket bodies merged, when it looked as if Howa might relent. He led his non-racial body in but then, having discovered that the changes were purely cosmetic, he led them out again. Howa would later see the riots of 1976 as the turning point, confessing that he was wrong to go into the merger talks just thinking of cricket, that he should have heard the cry of children for a normal society. It was after this that his famous slogan was articulated. It had the merit of simplicity, one that the world at large could understand. But accepting Howa also meant accepting his iron discipline and his rule that nobody who played cricket for his non-racial organization could even watch any of the white, establishment cricket. To do so meant a cricketing death. So after Sedick Conrad returned home on 23 November 1973, having watched a game between a South African invitation side and Derek Robins's XI at the Newlands, he was rung up by Howa and asked, 'Were you at Newlands today?' 'Yes, I was, Mr Howa,' replied Conrad, an answer that led to his expulsion from Howa's cricket. Conrad, as captain of Western Province, had never much liked Howa's style of autocratic leadership and in the end took the matter to the Supreme Court before walking across the racial divide to join the mainly white cricket body.

Later, Omar Henry was also to be pushed into the white body's arms by Howa. Henry, a Cape Coloured, had grown up in Stellenbosch in the Cape, the area that was also Howa's home, and experienced the rigours of apartheid.

'At that stage the "multi-racial" cricket was being played under permit. That year I went to Durban to play a match for Western Province versus Natal. We were due to play at Tillscrescent, a Coloured area, but the game was cancelled due to rain. On the way back (we were staying in a hotel in a white area) we passed Kingsmead [Durban's Test ground and headquarters of Natal's white cricket]. It was after tea-time, there was no gate charge and we went in to watch the match for about 10–15 minutes. When I came back to the Cape I was summoned to a meeting by Howa. It was held in Stellenbosch in a coloured hotel and was like a kangaroo court. We were accused of being traitors and sell-outs. I was told I must ask forgiveness, and when I refused I was banned and told I must never ever attend white sports. After the banning I had to make a decision. I loved the game and

wanted to carry on with it.' So Omar Henry defected
and eventually ended up playing for Orange Free State in the
wake of Kallicharran. In November 1992, when India played
South Africa at Durban in its first home Test for 22 years
and its first ever against India, the man who had been banned
by Howa for watching a game at Kingsmead made history by
walking on to the same field and becoming the first non-
white to play Test cricket for South Africa. By then Hasan
Howa was dead and his slogan 'no normal sport in an abnormal society' had been repudiated even by those who had
long campaigned on it. In doing so they both exposed its
limitation and its contradiction.

The contradiction was that most people interpreted
Howa's slogan as meaning that South Africa could be
allowed back into the international sporting community only
when it had one man, one vote. But Howa had no such aim;
in fact, he was opposed to it. In *Cricket in Isolation*, edited
by Odendaal and published in the glow created by the short-
lived cricket unity, Howa, having argued persuasively that
sports and life at all levels should provide equal opportunity,
firmly declared this opinion: 'One man, one vote is wrong
for South Africa. With approximately 20 million Africans
and only 4 million other people [Howa was writing in 1977]
it cannot work, it cannot be a viable proposition.' Howa
feared that one man, one vote would 'swamp' Indians like
him, who would always be outnumbered by the blacks. No
white man could have expressed his fears more clearly.

Until the mid-1980s such contradictions mattered little.
The South African Council for Sports (SACOS), the umbrella
body for the internal anti-apartheid sports movement set up
in 1973 and allied to SANROC, had made Howa's slogan
its anthem and barred membership to any organization
taking part in 'multi-national' sports. At one stage it had even
placed sports facilities in black universities out of bounds for
its affiliate organizations. SACOS members would earnestly
debate whether its coaches ought to be trained overseas.
Would this not break the sporting isolation of apartheid

South Africa? In the end it allowed such coaching, but not without some misgivings.

But by the mid-1980s, with black trade unionists setting a different agenda, the question was: where next? When isolation had started there was hardly any non-racial sport in the country. By 1984 there was a fair amount of it and that year some members of the SACOS began to say that total opposition to any sporting contact was actually harming non-racial sports in the country.

'We started the debate within SACOS in 1984. It was a hot debate. No normal sport in an abnormal society was all right but it was not a solution. It was a cul-de-sac. Just to repeat the slogan was a weakness. We could blame apartheid for everything – but that wouldn't get rid of apartheid. We had to do something to normalize sports. SACOS policy meant that it did not come out with any position. You went to a meeting, condemned apartheid and waited for the next meeting. There was no real drive to do something.'

The words are those of Muleleki George, only in his late 30s but already one of the most powerful sports administrators in the country. His rise to sporting prominence shows how the power equations inside South Africa, particularly within the anti-apartheid sports movement, were changing. George hails from the Xhosa-speaking blacks of the Eastern Cape. The first Africans to be subjected to British rule in 1820, they took to western sports in quite a significant manner. As early as the 1850s Xhosas were interested spectators at cricket matches and horse races in King William's Town, George's birthplace.

The sport George was brought up on was rugby, a very popular game among the blacks of the Eastern Cape – indeed, their only game until cricket arrived in the 1950s. George loved rugby but of course he could play only black rugby. 'We would play in the black townships: open fields, no changing rooms. You changed in the corner of the field. The young boys would surround you while you were taking off your shorts.'

George played almost all his rugby in East London and recalls with pride playing as scrum half against Welsh High, a famous black school in the area. He is convinced that had South Africa been a free society he would have represented his country. But his youth coincided with the heyday of apartheid and he can vividly recall the time when the liquor laws were so strictly applied that blacks could not even buy a drink. 'You had to have a Standard 6 certificate to buy liquor. Or you would hang round the liquor shops and ask a passing Coloured or Indian person to go in and buy a bottle for you. Invariably, they charged more.'

When he was 18 or 19 he broke his neck playing rugby. 'I went into a trap gap and broke it, although I didn't feel it immediately.' The result is that it has now given him a distinctive appearance – but such is the power of myth that I was told, not by George but by some of his white friends, that his broken neck derived from torture at the hands of the South African police for his political activities. He was tortured, but they were careful not to leave such obvious physical marks on him: 'I was arrested in East London in 1978 and taken to the Cambridge Police Station. There I was stripped naked and beaten with fists and rubber batons. Then I was bundled into a car and taken to Uitenhage. Here it was more sophisticated, electric shocks were given. My balls and penis were attached to pliers which were then fixed to a table. Then when an electric current was passed and my body went zzzzzzzzz the pliers would pull my penis and balls towards the table. It was extremely painful.'

George's list of the cells where he was tortured reads like a tour of the modern circles of hell: in East London, in Uitenhage, in the Sanlam buildings in Port Elizabeth and in Protea police station in Soweto. At every place he was stripped naked and asked questions while policemen devised various ways to beat him up. At Port Elizabeth six policemen took turns to, as he says, 'torture me to the best of their ability'. On one occasion he was hung upside down, quite naked, from the ceiling. In 1979 he was sent to the final,

innermost circle of modern South African hell: Robben Island
penal colony. After his release from there in 1982 he was
sent to Ciskei, the black 'homeland' near East London, but
even here he was a suspect and spent much of the time
between 1985 and 1989 in and out of Ciskei jails. The
torture regime did not change, except this time it was black
policemen who inflicted the pain.

'Robben Island,' recalls George, 'was the home of politics.
That is where we learnt our politics and by the time we came
out we were politically hot.' It was after his release, and
despite being in and out of Ciskei jails, that George began
to organize a dissident faction within SACOS. While George
was a member of the ANC, many people in SACOS derived
their inspiration from Steve Biko's Black Consciousness
movement, with its philosophy that there should be no truck
with whites, while others followed the Unity Movement,
which had always been strong in the Cape and had developed
an ultra-left Trotskyite line on most issues. The South African
Government may have painted the ANC as the most radical
of the non-white organizations, but its stance on sports was
to prove much more conciliatory than that of many in
SACOS.

As with almost everything in South Africa, there was a
racial angle to this. SACOS, personified by people like Howa,
was largely Indian or Coloured, and was very strong in the
Indian and Coloured areas. It had a sprinkling of educated
Africans but it had never really penetrated the townships.
'Soweto,' says George, 'was not part of SACOS, nor was
Umlazi or Lamontville [black townships in Natal]; these
places were not involved in SACOS, which represented only
one section of the non-white people.' Race combined with
politics to make a split inevitable.

George and his friends decided to reinterpret the Howa
slogan, insising there was not one South African sport but
two. There was apartheid sport, which needed to be isolated
and boycotted, and there was non-racial sport, which had
developed and grown over the years, and needed to be

encouraged. 'It was,' says George 'not easy to promote this idea. We were accused of being sell-outs. But we said we can't wait for society to be normalized. The normalizing of society and the playing of normal sport needn't be locked into the same timetable.'

George's arguments gained greater force when he pointed to the fact that the world outside was not waiting for SACOS. In 1985 the anti-apartheid movement had won a major victory in New Zealand in which SACOS had played no part. There the rugby authorities were planning yet another All Blacks rugby tour of South Africa, but two New Zealand rugby players took their home union to court alleging that by sending the All Blacks to South Africa the authorities were violating their own constitution, which required them to promote and advance the welfare of the game.

The case brought Rev. Arnold Stofile, a member of the non-racial South African Rugby Union and an activist of the UDF (United Democratic Front), to New Zealand to give evidence. It turned out to be a brilliant move, with Stofile proving very impressive in court. The players had sought a temporary injunction. The New Zealand Rugby Union estimated that if they, the union, eventually won the case after a temporary injunction had halted the tour, they would be in a good position to sue the two players for anything up to a million New Zealand dollars in damages. The players clearly faced the possibility of bankruptcy, and at this stage their lawyer Ted Thomas, in some desperation, telephoned a friend of his, Jeremy Pope, in London. Pope recalls:

'We had only 24 hours in which to find a solution. I turned to Sam [Ramsamy of SANROC] and within an hour we were meeting with [Bishop] Trevor Huddleston. Within minutes he was on the phone to lawyers and to major donors who provided money for the Defence and Aid Fund [which aided victims of apartheid]. It was able to give Sam a guarantee of up to a million dollars should damages be awarded against the rugby players. But for political reasons they did not want to be named. Sam gave the rugby players his own personal

guarantee and I was able to telex a written assurance to Ted
Thomas to the effect that Sam would be able to pay if need
be.'

Armed with these guarantees, Ted Thomas was able to go
ahead with the application for an interim injunction. The
rugby union's attempts to take the case further fizzled out
and for the first time legal, as opposed to Government, pressure had forced a tour to be cancelled. The judgement was
hailed as an historic victory, it caused a legal sensation and
was written up all over the world and much studied by
lawyers. Stofile returned to South Africa a hero of the anti-
apartheid movement but a villain in the eyes of the white
Government, who soon had him arrested. But his testimony
had done wonders for the prestige and authority of the UDF.
However, burdened as it was with its political work it could
hardly take on sports as well. And so it was that many in
the UDF now began to think that the front needed a sports
arm of its own in South Africa – but that arm could *not* be
SACOS.

It took three years for talk to be translated into action.
This finally happened in 1988 when George and his dissident
group set up the National Sports Congress (NSC). Had they
not done so they probably would in any case have been
expelled from SACOS. The divisions, as George admits, were
too great to be combined within one organization. While
public pronouncements made it out that the anti-apartheid
front was still intact there was, for anybody who cared to
see, a clear divergence of ways. The split widened when,
later that year, George and his friends went to Harare
(Zimbabwe) to meet the ANC.

Waiting for George at Harare was an old ANC friend.
They had first met on Robben Island, and he, too, had been
doing a lot of thinking on how to cope with the changes in
sports. And while his name would not become familiar to
the outside world for some time yet, he was to become the
most influential person in the re-emergence of South Africa
into international acceptance. Four years after this meeting

in Harare he would be hailed in the South African press, both by whites and blacks, as the godfather of South African sports, his every utterance scrutinized, his photographs plastered all over the papers, and his words determining whether South Africa could once again compete overseas or remain doomed in sporting isolation.

8

The Man Who Started Rugby on Robben Island

That man was Steve Tshwete. His status in the new sporting South Africa that has emerged was strikingly evident on the evening of 29 December 1992. South Africa had just beaten India at Port Elizabeth – its first victory in Test cricket since its return from 22 years of sporting isolation. As is usual on such occasions, the captain, manager and the man of the match held a press conference. Presiding over the conference were Ali Bacher and Krish Mackerdhuj, president of the United Cricket Board. But sitting between them, smoking his pipe, was Steve Tshwete. He did not say anything because he was not asked any questions; he just sat there, surveying the scene like an indulgent father.

Nothing could have pointed out more starkly the contrast between the old and the new South Africa. Tshwete had no formal position on the United Cricket Board. His own political party, the ANC, was locked in argument with the white Government about talks on a political settlement – which at that stage seemed as far as away as ever. But as far as South African cricket was concerned, its greatest moment for 22 years would not have been complete without the presence of a man who did not even have a vote in his own country. What was even more astonishing was that the white South Africans accepted his presence as if it was a rightful one. Even the white ladies present – most of whom considered Nelson Mandela to be a murderous revolutionary and the

164

ANC an evil communist organization – referred to him as 'adorable Steve'. It is the gift of great men to encompass such contradictions, but few could have predicted such a destiny for Steve Tshwete. By the time George met him at Harare in 1988, Tshwete had established himself as one of the coming men in the ANC, a man who had suffered for his beliefs but had not allowed the unspeakable cruelty the apartheid regime had visited on him to destroy his humanity or his faith in the capacity of human beings to redeem themselves.

Tshwete's story reads like a modern African fable. Like George and Mandela he was born a Xhosa at Springs (near Johannesburg) and grew up in a village called Peddelton near what is now Ciskei. The year was 1939, Jan Smuts ruled South Africa, apartheid was still a gleam in the eyes of Malan and his nationalists but for blacks living in this white heaven, life was no picnic. His father worked near Johannesburg, 500 miles to the north, earning £2 a week. Steve, the oldest child of five children – four boys and a girl – was brought up by his mother. Peddelton was and is unremarkable: a few shacks in the veldt, the only work for blacks was as farm labourers or house servants for whites, some distance away. In 1948 the Nationalists came to power. That year, too, came a drought which destroyed most of Steve's family's livestock. Already poor, the family now faced a crucial choice: they could afford to educate only one of their children. Which of them should it be?

Steve was the fortunate one: 'I was the one who would go through primary and secondary education, so that when I got my general certificate I would go on to a teacher's course. The idea was that I would augment the family earnings and so assist in the raising of the other kids.'

Right from the beginning Tshwete had a passion for sports, particularly ball games, which he played at week-ends: 'When you are looking after cattle the whole day, you play cricket with a tennis ball, using sticks for bats and our tucked-up jackets for wickets. Then, when you are tired, you go swimming. Once you have finished you get hungry, steal

would feel angry that this was happening to our people, but not to the whites. They could go wherever they wanted to. But if I wanted to travel from East London to see my aunt in Cape Town I had to get a permit from a resident magistrate. Without it I was liable to be thrown into prison.'

The wider political world also made an impression. He followed the treason trials of 1956 which featured Nelson Mandela, Oliver Tambo, Joe Slovo and others, and had already begun to get a grasp of the struggle being waged. At Forbes Grant the principal, Henry Mjamba, introduced him to the ANC, of which he was a member. Soon Steve was explaining to his parents why he had to identify with 'the aspirations of our people'. They were not only God-fearing but believed that the suffering of their people was ordained by God. It would be righted only if the Lord so decided. Steve disagreed and, much to the disappointment of his father, left school in 1961 after gaining his matric.

Steve was offered a job in the Native Affairs department, which regulated everything to do with blacks, including the issuing of passes, but he turned it down, convinced that he must not work for his oppressors. His parents were furious: 'I was chased away from home by both of them – they threw me out. They said I was useless, I was of no assistance to the family. My mother had had to go back to work to help me get my matric and now they were disenchanted with me.'

By this time, in 1962, Tshwete was already an ANC organizer and in trouble with the Government. He was a black without a job in East London, which meant he could be sent back to his village of Peddelton. He had opposed De Ventel, the Minister of Bantu Affairs and Development, when he announced that the rugby stadium where Tshwete's club played could be used only by Bantus. This did not affect Tshwete personally because he was classified as a Bantu, but it meant he could not play with Indians or Coloureds who were also members of the rugby clubs he played for and against. Moreover, the restriction also meant that Tshwete, as a Bantu, could not play on Indian or Coloured grounds.

Ventel's order meant dissolving the East London Sports Board, which was making use of the ground. Some of the blacks accepted this but Tshwete wanted to fight it. 'I said we should not be dictated to by that department. What they were doing was in line with the idea of separate development, and if playing rugby meant rugby under those conditions, then to hell with it. I led the split and we formed our own union, taking seven big clubs with us. We had no ground to play on since ours had been taken over by the puppets, so we played in open fields without any posts.'

Soon Tshwete had bigger worries. On 24 June 1963 he was arrested after being 'shopped' by a colleague who turned out to be an informer. As part of the regional command of Umkhonto weSizwe (Spear of the Nation), the ANC's military wing, Tshwete had been involved in a sabotage campaign against pass offices, telephone poles, railway lines, and other structures. The ANC observed 26 June as freedom day – on that day in 1955 its historic Freedom Charter had been adopted – and Tshwete was determined to observe it. He put out a bloodcurdling leaflet calling on his fellow blacks to 'prepare for the bloodbath' to liberate South Africa. Against the advice of an older colleague, he used a typewriter, confident that with all the Olivettis around, his machine would not be traced.

Tshwete was arrested in East London and interrogated at the Cambridge police station. At first it seemed as if he would get away with it. The first policeman who questioned him, an old man called Smith, believed his story that he was not politically involved and that he was preparing for church. Every time he locked him up they knelt together and prayed. But then the typewriter was discovered, Tshwete's lies were exposed and now an Afrikaner took over the interrogation. He promised to 'sweep the room with me' and threatened to hang him from the walls. 'You want to be white, I'll beat you till you are white.' He was stripped naked, made to stand like that for hours in the interrogation room, and then given what he calls a 'good hiding'.

Curiously, Tshwete preferred the beatings to the questions: 'I wanted them to beat me so I could get over the shock of being a victim. I felt, I believed, that if they were going to persist with pure interrogation they might break me in some way, but I wanted them to physically maul me. One thing I was not going to do was to give them the chance to say that they beat the hell out of me and that I had eventually confessed.'

Tried at Queenstown Supreme Court, away from East London so crowds might not gather, Tshwete was acquitted on the charge of sabotage but convicted of belonging to the ANC. In April 1964, with his mother watching – she had come up every day not only to cook for him but bring clothes – Tshwete received 15 years.

Tshwete was transported to Robben Island on 6 April 1964 in leg irons and handcuffs and on the notorious 'Ferry of Tears' he and his fellow prisoners were sjamboked throughout the eight-mile crossing from Cape Town. On Robben Island the cells measured 8 ft by 6 ft and were ranged on each side of a long corridor. Each cell had two barred windows, one opening onto the small yard, the other onto the corridor. The prisoners slept on the bare floor on which had been spread a tiny mat, with a thin blanket for cover. The food was mealies and porridge. The beatings were constant.

The island regime was designed to make the prisoners succumb to a sense of utter despair. From five in the afternoon until seven the following morning they were locked in their cells; then from eight in the morning until four in the afternoon they broke rocks. When the pile of big rocks had all been broken into smaller ones, these were taken away and dumped and more big rocks were brought in. All the time they could hear the sea, but they could never see it because of the high walls surrounding the compound. And all the time there were the tortures, beatings and the sight and sound of people dying in agony. The winter of 1964 was the coldest in South African records. The prisoners were scantily dressed, barefoot, underfed and overworked. 'You came to think of your survival in terms of hours. Your thought was, if I can survive from 6 pm to 8 pm, thank your stars.'

Tshwete describes the years 1964–72 as 'hell on earth'. For the first 11 months of his sentence he was locked away in solitary confinement; the only people he saw were his torturers. Apartheid South Africa seemed to have succeeded in convincing most Robben Island prisoners that there was no hope and that nobody outside cared for them. It was only in the 1970s that things began to improve. Tshwete's Christian faith in the rightness of his cause had sustained him so far. Now there was international pressure, with the International Committee of the Red Cross agitating for improved conditions. One of the major concessions involved his beloved rugby.

'Eventually they allowed us to play games, starting with football; they were reluctant to introduce rugby because they felt it was going to be a drain on state expenses. But we insisted and eventually they conceded. Initially we said that we were not going to tackle, it would just be a touch and then we would drop the ball. Their fear was that if we played tackle rugby, we would get injured and would have to be taken to Cape Town at state expense. We played touch rugby for just a few weeks – but soon it was the real thing.'

The original field of play was just an open, bare piece of ground in the middle of the prison yard. 'Then one day the common-law prisoners were removed from a prison next door to a place further away – the authorities feared we would influence them politically. So we had to pull down their jail. We immediately saw that this area would make a better rugby pitch. We planted grass there and at night we would open one of the outside water taps and let it run all night. Our plan was not discovered, and soon we had a very beautiful green pitch.'

The football that had been played had been along political lines, with the ANC and the Pan-African Congress each fielding seven teams. Tshwete was keen to get away from such divisions, and set about writing a constitution for Robben Island rugby. Finally adopted on 30 January 1972 as the constitution of the Island Rugby Board, and signed by Tshwete as president, it must be one of the most remarkable documents to emerge from a prison.

Just nineteen hand-written pages, it was as if Tshwete and his fellow rugby players were writing the constitution of a new South Africa.

Initially there were three teams. Tshwete's club was called 'Ikwezi (Morning Star); then there was Ixhalamga (Vultures) and Igguala (Experienced Old Men). Tshwete also started a sporting newspaper, *Island News*, to record details of the matches.

Tshwete's rugby career on the island had a distressing symmetry: he was injured in both the inaugural match and in his final match just before his release. The first match of the Island Rugby Board had nearly proved Tshwete's last. The captain of the Vultures had been a rival of his back in East London, playing for Winter Rose when Tshwete played for Spring Rose. In those days of freedom, Winter Rose often beat Spring Rose. Now, in the winter of captivity, Tshwete was determined to extract revenge.

The Vultures had a gifted youngster playing at centre for them. Tshwete decided he would get that player. 'He was the boy I was going to get out of the field before the second half. I had taken the decision that if we got the boy out before the second half, we would win. When we got on to the field, somewhere towards the end of the first half, that boy was in possession. He was a terrific runner and I went for him. He was running very fast, jinking and swerving, and mine was really a foul tackle. But I missed the monkey. I bruised my forehead and there was not even a blade of grass on the ground as I fell. Instead of taking him out, I had to retire injured. I felt very dejected, and we lost the match.'

Almost seven years later, in 1979, just as he was about to be released after serving 15 years, they decided to give him a send-off match and although aged 39 he played. 'I was moving with the ball and somebody had his leg tangled round mine and I cut the tendon in my knee. I had to go out on a stretcher!'

Although much had changed in South Africa in those 15 years, the situation for non-whites had scarcely improved. He was supposed to have been driven from Cape Town to East London, but because of his knee injury he had to be taken there by train. As a black he should have travelled third-class, but since he was being accompanied by prison warders who were white, and therefore could not travel third-class, Tshwete travelled first-class. He also had beer for the first time in 15 years.

His pleasure in his release was dulled by his sadness that his mother had died while he was on Robben Island. In any case, his freedom turned out to be partial, to say the least. He had thought he would be released in East London, but he was driven to King William's Town – and even as he was being taken out of the police station he was served with one of the notorious banning orders. This stipulated that for the next five years he was forbidden to go to East London – he was confined to Peddelton – and that for the first two years he could not be in the company of more than two people. Jimmy Kruger, the police chief who had joked in public about Biko's death, signed the order, claiming he was satisfied that Tshwete was engaging in activities furthering the aims of Communism. So, although he had served his long and brutal sentence, he was now under fresh restrictions without any further trial. 'I mean, here I had been imprisoned for 15 years, and then I'm confined for two years on the grounds that I'm a threat to the peace of the country even before I have left my cell. This certainly embittered me. It strengthened my resolve to do everything in my power to remove this Government.'

When his banning order expired in 1981, Tshwete became involved in the new trade union movement and in 1983 became one of the founders of the United Democratic Front. He was elected a member of its national executive and president of the Border region, which included East London and King William's Town. But although the UDF's declared aim was peaceful and non-violent and it was not a liberation movement in the way the ANC was, Tshwete's involvement with it was enough for him to lose his job as a teacher in Ciskei. He also served a four-month jail sentence there in 1983. UDF members inevitably became involved in violence but, as Tshwete sees it, this was 'never a question of organized groups going to attack people or anything of that nature. It was not done with the participation or encouragement of the UDF. It was an expression of the anger of the people.'

This may seem a hair-splitting argument, but the fact is that the apartheid regime harassed the UDF in much the same way that it had harassed the ANC even before it took to the gun. By 1984 Tshwete was getting some very definite warning signals. Many of his friends in the UDF had disappeared mysteriously. Some were later discovered, hacked to death – the first clear signs that Government-sponsored death squads were in operation. In 1985 Tshwete decided he must go into exile. 'My friends were being assassinated and I was on the hit list myself. I decided to go on the run when I was declared *persona non grata* in South Africa by F. W. de Klerk, who was then in the Home Ministry.' De Klerk's order meant that Tshwete would have to seek shelter in one of the Bantu 'homelands' or go into exile abroad. If he wished to come to South Africa he had to be in possession of a visa and a temporary resident's permit. He went first of all to Lusaka (Zambia) and over the next few years led the life of an exile so familiar to many other South African leaders, travelling to various parts of the world and attending meetings to whip up support for the anti-apartheid movement. However, as a member of Umkhonto weSizwe he also received some military training in East Germany, eventually becoming number two to Chris Hani, then leader of the ANC military wing and a member of the South African Communist party.

In 1987 the ANC appointed Tshwete organizing secretary of the celebrations to mark the movement's 75th anniversary. By now it was clear that the Botha Government's mixture of repression and vague promises of future amelioration was going nowhere; nor was there any future in its policy of trying to preserve apartheid by recruiting a cadre of non-white collaborators. More significant, however, was a new-found realism among Afrikaner intellectuals. For years English-speaking whites in South Africa had ritually protested their opposition to apartheid, but had hardly managed to dent it. Alan Paton's Liberal party had long since been dissolved, and while there were some brave voices – Helen Suzman's in Parliament, for instance, and Nadine Gordimer's in her writings – actively campaigning against apartheid, the liberal opposition in general appeared to have exhausted its ideas about how to end apartheid. Now, however, the Afrikaner resistance to apartheid emerged.

Rian de Villiers, now managing editor of *Leadership*, says: 'Before then, real militant resistance to apartheid in the Afrikaner community was very, very limited. You could count the people on the fingers of your hand who really stood up and allied themselves to the progressive movement. In the mid-80s it began to change. There was real dissent at Stellenbosch University, where students protesting about apartheid were baton charged.'

De Villiers helped set up *Die Suid-Afrikaan*, an Afrikaans magazine which also published articles in English; its editors included André du Toit, de Villiers's old mentor from Stellenbosch. This began to provide an intellectual home to those Afrikaners who opposed apartheid. The new movement received a tremendous boost in the summer of 1987 when Van Zyl Slabbert, an Afrikaner who had formerly been leader of the Progressive Party, decided to cross the ultimate barrier and engage in dialogue with the ANC. In one of the great historic steps in recent South African history he took a group of Afrikaner intellectuals to Dakar to meet the ANC leaders, one of whom was Tshwete. De Villiers accompanied Van Zyl

Slabbert to Dakar and recalls: 'That trip accomplished an enormous amount. Slabbert legitimized extra-parliamentary politics. It was a very, very significant contribution to South African politics. It had to be planned in complete secrecy. The whole idea was to legitimize the ANC: the ogre would become human. Slabbert identified the people he wanted to take, but not everyone he approached agreed to come. Our fear was that if our plans became known P. W. Botha would stop us from going. The story did actually break on the day before we left, but nobody was prevented from leaving. Once we reached Dakar it became a huge controversy at home: Botha thundered away and with the press making the most of the story it had a huge impact on South African politics.'

The Dakar conference made Tshwete into a nationally known political figure. Well before the conference De Villiers and others knew quite a lot about some of the ANC people they were going to meet. Thabo Mbeki, the ANC's foreign affairs spokesman, for instance, had often appeared on foreign television, and Mac Maharaj was a hardened member of the movement. Tshwete, however, was a complete unknown and he intrigued de Villiers, who spent a considerable time with him and published a long interview in *Die Suid-Afrikaan*. De Villiers explains: 'The major thing that was traumatic for us was the fact that the ANC planted bombs in our country. How could they justify this? There was a lot of dialogue about that in Dakar. They explained to us why they thought this was legitimate. We thought that if we hoped to make the ANC more understandable to the whites, one of the things we had to bring out were the reasons why they thought the armed struggle was legitimate. They put the arguments to us very strongly in our discussions, emphasizing that they had tried peaceful avenues of negotiations within the political process but the doors had been shut on them. They had no other recourse. With the greatest of reluctance, they had turned to violence. That is the way they spoke about it.'

Much of de Villiers's four-page interview with Tshwete, in

question-and-answer form in English, was about the justification for violence. The introduction to the interview showed the careful path de Villiers and the magazine had to tread: 'Mr Tshwete is not a listed person in terms of South African security legislation and may therefore be quoted.' (At that time, South Africa had more than 125 laws and regulations restricting the areas of political reporting in which the press could operate. Raymond Louw, a former editor of the Rand *Daily Mail*, observed in 1984 that the press laws were so framed 'that it is virtually impossible for an editor to escape prosecution'.)

Tshwete also profoundly impressed the white South Africans at the human, personal level. One of the first things he did when he met de Villiers and André du Toit was simply to touch them, to hold their hands and give them a gentle squeeze. As de Villiers notes, 'We Afrikaners are not given to touching each other, hugging or that sort of human contact – certainly not the males. That is our Calvinist tradition. When Steve did that with me and others it made a big impression – it was so African. It seemed to establish human contact and later, when I spoke to him, I realized what a very nice, very charming, warm person he was. I don't want to over-romanticize the thing, but it was a significant gesture.'

Until the later 1980s, sports had not featured significantly in ANC policy-making. Although the international sports boycott had proved a critically important strike against the apartheid regime – unlike the protests in South Africa (before they were banned) or the military activities since then – it had not begun as an ANC initiative. As we have seen, it was individuals such as Brutus, Hain and others who had started the movement rather than the ANC.

Sometime in 1987 the full executive of the ANC (apart from those in jail) met in Lusaka and adopted a position paper on sport and culture. 'Basically,' says Tshwete, 'the paper said that when we left the country in 1960 to go into exile the rallying slogan for the international community and ourselves was "Boycott apartheid sport and culture". At that time, when we talked of South African sport we referred to white South Africa. As far as the Government was concerned, black people were never considered to have any interest in sport. All resources were channelled towards buttressing apartheid sport. But, over the years, the struggle for non-racialism in sport gathered momentum. By the time we came up with this position paper South African sport was divided into two distinct elements: on one hand apartheid, racist, establishment sport, and on the other alternative, non-racial, democratic sport. We had now to decide if it made sense for us to ask the international community to continue its overall boycott of South African sport. We decided, on the contrary, that we should ask the international community to support the non-racial, democratic sports structure that was beginning to emerge, and to provide it with the expertise it required and with moral and material support, so that it could grow and itself become a prominent force against apartheid. Furthermore, we resolved that if non-racial democratic sport was going to take its place in the international community, we felt we must eat into the body of racist sport to weaken it.'

Such a programme, of course, ran completely counter to Hasan Howa's slogan, 'No normal sport in an abnormal society'. Surely South Africa was even more of an abnormal society in 1987. 'Ah,' says Tshwete, 'in any political struggle, particularly the South African struggle, we cannot rely only on the politics of the heart: we have to use our brains and become flexible enough to respond to objective situations from time to time when taking up political positions.' Tshwete's voice here is that of the trained Marxist, with his references to 'objective situations', a favourite Marxist phrase. But, shorn of jargon, what the ANC was saying was this: 'We know the Government has painted us as an evil organization – the modern personification of the black who impales small white children on his spear. But we have something to give to the whites, something which shows that we have tremendous international clout and that we can help to change things.'

That something was sport, and the possibility that the ANC could play a decisive role in bringing about the ending of the international boycott.

A year after the position paper was adopted Tshwete got an opportunity to put its ideas into practice. In 1988 he was co-opted on to the executive, just as Muleleki George and his friends arrived to discuss the formation of the National Sports Congress (NSC). It marked the start of Tshwete playing the role of the sporting godfather. His first 'client' was his own beloved rugby. White rugby, under great external pressure, needed to change and Tshwete could help it change.

9

Tommy's Try

The rugby initiative had come from rugby people themselves and, most surprisingly, from white rugby. Until after the England tour of 1984, rugby's establishment saw little reason to change. For some years such tours had provoked protests in the visitors' home country; and for journalists accompanying the players to South Africa they provided ample evidence that the country had changed little. Visiting journalists often ran the risk of falling foul of South African 'practice and custom'. On the British Lions visit in 1980 there had been the famous incident when Chris Lander was thrown out of a disco for having escorted, along with colleague Ian Todd, a black girl. As he left, Lander paused on the stairs and told the manager, 'When the revolution comes, I hope they get you first.'

In 1980 Frank Keating ran into somewhat similar problems. In one of his dispatches he narrated how at a disco in Cape Town one of the Welsh friends he was with brought along a pretty girl from the car-hire firm. But a tall woman being escorted by an English friend objected, 'Why did he have to bring a girl like that?' 'Only then,' wrote Keating, 'did we realize the car-hire girl had a tiny touch of the tar brush. Nobody spoke to the tall woman again, and she soon departed, chin jutting in a righteous huff, amazed at our lefty leanings. The car-hire girl looked sad and frightened.' Soon after this was reported in the *Guardian*, Keating was on his way out of the country. Peter Preston, editor of the *Guardian*, was told he was not welcome, and at one stage there was the possibility that if Keating was thrown out the paper would withdraw David Frost and the great Welsh coach, Carwin James, who were also reporting the tour. But it turned out that Keating had arrived without a visa. British passport-holders, provided they are just visitors and have not come to work, do not require visas. He was summoned to a Cape Town police station and asked to return to Britain to get a visa. They agreed to let him stay until after the first Test; then he came back to London – and he has never returned.

It was the cancellation of the 1985 All Blacks tour that first began to put the real squeeze on the white rugby authorities. Initially, white rugby reacted much as cricket had done, by organizing rebel tours of various kinds, including one from Fiji and Samoa and then a side from New Zealand which consisted of virtually the entire All Blacks team that was originally coming on the official tour. They called themselves the Cavaliers but in South Africa everybody treated them as if they were the real All Blacks. It was following these tours that external pressure began to change things, and reformers noticed how receptive the white rugby authorities were to dialogue even with the enemy.

One of the reformers was Tommy Bedford, who had been vice-captain on the disastrous 1969 rugby tour hounded by Peter Hain and the equally traumatic 1971 tour to Australia. Bedford's path to meeting ANC and Tshwete is very interesting and tells us a great deal about the changes taking place in white rugby. Bedford grew up in an Afrikaans-speaking town in Orange Free State. After attending an English-speaking school and, later, after gaining a Springbok cap, he went to Oxford: 'It was in the mid-1960s when the Vietnam issue provoked all those protests. I saw the power of demonstrations including the one in Grosvenor Square [1968]. I met Tariq Ali, who was such an exceptional figure at Oxford then, one could not help being influenced. It was just a whole broadening process. Then when I got back to South Africa in the middle of 1968, having been away from the country for so long, I suddenly realized how things had changed, particularly in rugby, where there seemed to be much more of an Afrikaner influence.'

Already Bedford was more aware of the world than most of his contemporaries and this became evident the night before the white South African team left Johannesburg for London on their 1969 tour of England, what Bedford calls the 'demo tour'. A grand reception was held for them at the Casa Mia Hotel in Johannesburg's Hillbrow, now one of its thriving multi-racial suburbs but then a strictly whites-only area.

'A great many speeches were made on the evening before we left. We had Vorster speaking, wishing us well. I think Jim Fouche, the then President, spoke. I made the second to last speech. Everybody had said how well things were going to go, and we shall overcome, etc. I said that I had seen the power of demonstrations in England and was extremely worried about the tour. It was difficult enough to play inter-national rugby at the best of times, and if there were going to be demonstrations like the ones I had seen we would not do well at all. This went down like a lead balloon.'

The next day, as Bedford boarded the Boeing 707, 'a fellow asked me if he could have a chat. I sat with him up near the top. He said, "The players seem very confident. But how do you feel? You were at Oxford." I told him what I had said the night before. He said, "My name is Richard Kershaw. I have done a television interview with Vorster for the BBC. When it is shown the tour will be in great difficulty." Later, I watched it in black and white, which seemed to emphasize Vorster's big jowls and big glasses. It was no help at all. What was worse, the tour management, led by Corrie Bowman, did absolutely nothing to defend the team. They did not have to apologize for apartheid, but it was important to separate the players from the policies of the Government. All those officials sitting back in sunny South Africa should have sent somebody to try to defuse the situation. Nobody came, nobody dared appear on television, not even Dannie Craven.

'I played in the first Oxford side which fielded a black Blue. I felt our rugby players could take back a very positive image if only they would mingle with people here in Britain. But if you are rarely allowed out of your rooms and once outside you only see the back of policemen, you form your own laager. All one saw was the face of anti-apartheid on television. I hated Peter Hain for what he was doing. But when the dust settled I thought maybe he had a point. That point was finally made for me on the tour to Australia. I realized then that Hain had a very good point. Maybe his *was* the route that would change things. It was simply impossible for us to carry on the way we had.'

The trouble was 'there were no dynamics in South African rugby. It was totally dominated by those who had been there for ever. They could not take aboard any new thoughts; you had to conform to the system. If you said anything else, people just thought you were stupid.' And Bedford, a lone voice among top Springbok players, was ostracized.

Bedford remained within white rugby, but he became an increasingly outspoken critic. He found he could do nothing about the inequalities of sports facilities at school level, but after much soul-searching he felt he had found a way of getting involved with black and brown players to bring them up to a standard. 'The system in the country meant they could not aspire to Springbok standards. However, they could qualify at club level. I felt that was important and that is where I concentrated my efforts. Eventually I was instrumental in arranging successful tours to England and the United States by black and black and white sides.'

However, such tours made no impact on the white rugby authorities, 'who were still trying to organize tours to New Zealand and from England. As long as the international contacts were maintained, nobody was really listening to what one was saying.' Bedford's testimony is, of course, another demonstration of the absurdity of the 'bridge-building' argument.

It was only when the tours – including the ludicrous clandestine Springbok tour to Chile – stopped that Bedford began to sense that people might listen. It was this that led to meetings with ANC and Tshwete.

Bedford had been the only sportsman among the white South Africans on Van Zyl Slabbert's mission to Dakar. 'Dakar was crucial to everything that has happened in South Africa. It was the process that got everything going. It made things happen more quickly. It enabled certain things to be pointed in a new direction.'

Soon Bedford began to plan a meeting between the rugby authorities and the ANC. 'There were meetings in London and Frankfurt because some ANC people were not allowed into South Africa at that time – people were banned, people were under surveillance, phones were tapped. It was a long process and a difficult process, and not only the rugby world was involved.'

Even today Bedford refuses to reveal the contacts that helped him set up the ANC meeting, claiming that it is too dangerous to reveal all the details. Tshwete is more forthcoming: 'There were meetings with Louis Luyt [an Afrikaner businessman who was president of the white Transvaal rugby body] in the UK and Germany. Luyt rang me himself and I met him in London and Frankfurt. It was provoked by the desire to get back to international competition. They realized that the key to that lay with the African National Congress. As far as we were concerned the issue was for a single rugby-controlling body in South Africa. Once that was achieved the prospects of South Africa competing internationally would be brighter.'

Eventually a meeting was arranged in Harare (Zimbabwe) for October 1988. Bedford took with him Dannie Craven, still the supremo of the white South African rugby board, and Louis Luyt. It was an odd team to take to Harare to meet the ANC. While Craven was credited with resisting the Broderbond, he had once famously declared that no black would ever be a Springbok. After the 1986 rebel New Zealand tour Craven gave vent to the following imbecility: 'This

tour has done wonders for the country. Rugby has changed
the front pages of newspapers. We no longer see Mandela's
name, he has been removed to page six so as to accommodate
rugby. And to me this is wonderful. In time to come we
should erect a monument to honour these New Zealand
players, for they have changed the face of South Africa.'
Bedford had only recently started talking to Craven again,
the two men having fallen out in a big way back in 1984
when Bedford had opposed the England tour to South Africa.
Luyt was probably the most surprising member of the trio,
having been involved in the 'Muldergate' scandal in which
The Citizen newspaper was secretly launched by the Government in 1978 with taxpayers' money, but without taxpayers'
knowledge or consent, as a pro-Government mouthpiece
while posing as an independent national daily. But, whatever
their past, these men now sought the help of the ANC to
get their sport back.

Craven and Luyt had realized that an alternative would
have to be found to the rebel rugby tours which, however
popular with the diehard, pro-apartheid Afrikaner element
in the rugby establishment, represented a blind alley and were
causing increasing aggravation among players and public at
home and abroad. With no imminent end to apartheid in
sight, Craven and Luyt sought some kind of accommodation
with and limited acceptance by other rugby organizations
in Africa. Groups of academics and politicians had already
travelled to meet the ANC in exile; so, with few other options
available, Craven and Luyt agreed to the Harare summit
where, they were told, they would meet rugby officials from
other African countries.

In the event, the officials they met were from their own
country – from the non-racial South African Rugby Union,
led by Ebrahim Patel. Waiting for both parties at the Shera-
ton Hotel in Harare was a nine-member ANC delegation,
including Tshwete. 'We had been sending signals,' says
Tshwete, 'that we would like the rugby bodies to merge and

we saw ourselves as facilitators in an attempt to bridge the enormous racial divide in rugby.'

The problems to be tackled at the meeting were immense. Rugby, even more than cricket, was infected with white South Africa's racist way of looking at things. Since the 1960s there had been attempts to develop a strong non-racial rugby body, but although by the early 1980s Patel's body had 26,000 members with 26 provincial affiliates, they had to contend with three other bodies which collectively had more members and were organized along strictly racial lines. Bedford puts it thus: 'In cricket there were two: a white body and a black and brown body. In rugby there were four bodies: a white body, a black body, a brown body and a black and brown body. The white body, black body and brown body formed an alliance. The South African Rugby Association (SARA) was for blacks, the South African Rugby Federation (SARF) for coloureds, and the South African Rugby Board (SARB) for whites. The black and brown body opposing them was Patel's South African Rugby Union (SARU).'

Bedford is reluctant to concede that SARU was non-racial: 'It was really for black and brown, hardly any whites. Let us say it aspired to be non-racial but wasn't. The South African Rugby Federation and South African Rugby Union were integrally related to one another from way back. So from the 1970s white rugby always had a black and a white body associated with it. The relationships continued until the amalgamation of 1992. Cricket never had anything like this: when the amalgamation took place in cricket it was between a white body and a brown body. But in rugby it was between four bodies, each representing players of different colour.'

In reality the black and coloured bodies allied to the white rugby body did not amount to much and the negotiations were between the two principal bodies – the Craven-led SARB and the Patel-led SARU. Despite the problems and the distrust Bedford returned from Harare enthused by 'the tremendous meeting. They went remarkably well because the objectives were good. It came out absolutely productively with an agreement that they would proceed with basic unity. It was a major breakthrough which ultimately led to the March 1992 unity.'

Edward Griffiths, then sports editor of the Johannesburg *Sunday Times*, is not so sure, 'The meeting achieved little in those terms, with rumblings that Craven and Luyt had been lured into a political public relations coup by the ANC. Accused of going cap in hand to terrorists, they were derided.'

Harare created as much angst in the South African sporting world as Dakar had done in the political. True, Bedford did not have the same fears after Harare that he had had after Dakar, but 'immediately after Harare de Klerk crapped on us for daring to meet the ANC. He castigated Craven, Luyt and myself and called us traitors. And the ostracism process carried on from Dakar.' De Klerk, then Minister of Education and responsible for sport, called Luyt to Pretoria and demanded an explanation for the meeting. Luyt attended, was publicly slapped on the wrist, but emerged declaring, 'No man is my master. I answer to no one.' Griffiths says, 'Craven was also undermined, not least by his vice-president, Fritz Éloff, an acknowledged member of the Afrikaner establishment, who cynically distanced himself from the meeting. High-ranking policemen in Pretoria denounced the initiative as plotting with the enemy.' As the writer J. M. Coetzee has pointed out, with white South African rugby heavily militarized criticism from this quarter was of grave importance.

At that stage, with P. W. Botha still in power and with de Klerk more famous for his remark that he would not want his child to sit next to a coloured child than for any reformist zeal, the rugby officials certainly showed a lot of courage in going to meet what was a banned organization whose leader had been sentenced to life imprisonment on Robben Island. Griffiths is right when he says, 'Luyt and Craven had demonstrated outstanding vision in realizing that South African sport would not advance from its pariah status without the blessing of the ANC.'

But despite the head start that Harare was to give rugby, it failed to build on it. It was cricket that was to claim the limelight when the new South Africa was created. By the middle of 1992 cricket had already had two major international tours involving South Africa, while rugby was just managing to unify itself after four years of tortuous negotiations. And when it did stage its first unified international, it succeeded in having a row with the ANC.

Such a scenario must have appeared even more unlikely at the beginning of 1989 for a year after white rugby had made what seemed like a great breakthrough with the ANC, cricket still appeared obsessed with its bad old ways. Bacher had not been inactive while rugby made the waves. But when he finally emerged with a plan it seemed like more of the same: in the summer of 1989 a shocked cricket world learnt that Bacher was organizing yet another rebel tour. It would prove the most explosive one of all, and it nearly ruined Bacher and cricket. Yet from its ashes would emerge the new sporting South Africa, with Bacher showing the way to all other sports, including rugby.

10

Bacher's Last Fling

Bacher had started 1989 in the cold of a London January, waiting for news from the ICC. The Conference was meeting at Lord's on 23 and 24 January, for its long-awaited special session on South Africa. After a tortuous three-year process the ICC had at last finalized a range of penalties for players who maintained 'sporting contact' with South Africa. The previous autumn had provided a painful illustration of the ICC's failure to deal with this issue. The 1988–89 England tour of India had been cancelled because the Indians objected to England's choice of Graham Gooch as captain and John Emburey as vice-captain – the positions they had held on the first English rebel tour of South Africa in 1982; their names were on the United Nations blacklist of sportsmen who had played with white South Africa. When England refused to bow to Indian Government pressure, the tour was called off, almost 20 years to the day since the D'Oliveira affair had forced another cancellation.

The parallels with D'Oliveira did not end there. After the latter fiasco the MCC had lost control of English cricket, the responsibility later passing to the Test and County Cricket Board. In the winter of 1988 Raman Subba Row, chairman of the TCCB and well aware of the political sensitivity of such selection, was appalled by the selectors' choice of Gooch and Emburey. But when he raised the matter with Peter May, chairman of the selectors, he found him quite oblivious of the fact that in choosing Gooch and Emburey he had, in effect, shown two fingers to the Indians. However,

189

Subba Row found that the TCCB, unlike the MCC, had no power to veto the choice of the selectors. For a time Subba Row considered calling a TCCB meeting and sacking the selectors, but in the end he gave in, and it came as no surprise to him when the Indian Government objected. He then moved swiftly to confer the power of veto on the TCCB.

Supporters of white sporting South Africa such as the MCC secretary Jack Bailey castigated the Indians, arguing that since Gooch and Emburey had been allowed into India in 1987 for the World Cup the decision only a year later by the Indians was, in Bailey's words, 'a supreme example of political cynicism'. The charge was made in an article in *Wisden* which revealed a marvellous mixture of emotion and illogic. For him, the white South Africans were, as he wrote in his book *Conflicts In Cricket*, 'time honoured and trusted friends' who had 'fought side by side with England during the war'. (Presumably he did not mean Vorster and his friends, who were jailed for a time for their Nazi sympathies.) Yet, as the narration of facts in Bailey's article itself made clear, the Indian decision, far from being an exercise in politics, was that of a country exasperated beyond endurance. The Indians had allowed entry to Gooch and Co in 1987 because they believed that the ICC would at last do something about their association with South Africa at their meeting in 1988. The issue had been hanging fire since 1986. In 1987 a select committee had been formed and its report was to be considered at the 1988 annual meeting. It was the failure of the 1988 meeting to agree on a recommendation that made Mr Salve, the then president of the Indian board, warn that the England tour might be in trouble.

The cancellation by India forced the English authorities to recognize that they were running out of friends. They tried to replace the Indian tour by one to New Zealand. But New Zealand had come a long way since 1981, let alone 1976, and did not want to jeopardize the Commonwealth Games which were due to be held at Auckland. Australia, too, made it clear that it was not prepared to endanger international cricket for the sake of the 60 or so English professionals who spent their winters coaching and playing in South Africa. So, by the time the cricket administrators gathered at Lord's on January 23 there was unanimity about what should happen. The meeting decided that as from April 1989 cricketers would face bans of between three and five years, depending on the nature of their sporting contact with South Africa, 'contact' being defined as active participation by any administrator, coach or player above the age of 16. It was almost 60 years since white South Africa had dictated to England and had Duleepsinhji dropped from the England Test side. Now the world cricket authority dictated what would happen to any cricketer who plied his trade in South Africa.

Not surprisingly, Bacher was thoroughly depressed by the ICC decision. The one ray of hope was that he and Joe Pamensky were given leave to address the full TCCB at a meeting in the Oval. But even this was a close run thing: on the morning of the meeting the TCCB executive met and tied 4–4 in a vote on whether to hear the South Africans. Raman Subba Row, who had always felt that contact should be kept open and considered Jackie McGlew as one of his friends, cast his vote in favour of the South Africans. He then took Bacher out to lunch, and left him with few illusions. Back in 1986 Subba Row had walked him around Edgbaston and told him: 'There is no way England can play with South Africa unless the political situation changes. Otherwise England would have nobody left to play with.'

Bacher also talked with Lord Bramall, President of the MCC and Chairman of the ICC. Bramall had presided over the Lord's meeting, and he told Bacher to look on the bright side: the ICC decision meant cricketers now had a clear-cut choice; they either did not go to South Africa or they went and risked a penalty. This, reasoned Bacher, left South Africans free to organize another rebel tour.

His recruiting campaign started soon after the ICC decision. As always, he worked on more than one level. The year 1989 was the centenary of white South African international cricket, and Bacher set about celebrating this in style. He invited cricket notables from England, including journalists, to join the celebrations, with all expenses paid. One of the invitees was Graeme Wright, then editor of *Wisden*, who had never been to South Africa, didn't want to go and disapproved of what was happening there. 'I felt, without having been there, that I knew enough to know that I didn't want to go.'

As luck would have it Bacher's phone call to Wright came just as Wright had posted a letter to Bacher inviting him to speak at the annual *Wisden* dinner. Wright, a man of interests far beyond cricket, had felt that South Africa might be on the brink of dramatic change. There was much talk of peace: after years of illegal occupation of Namibia, the white rulers of South Africa seemed ready to accept UN resolutions and grant that country its freedom; in Angola, where the South Africans had fought proxy wars on behalf of the Unita rebels against Cuban-supported government forces, there was talk of an end to that war; there were even rumours that Nelson Mandela might be released from jail.

What really intrigued Wright, however, was Bacher's township programme. Surely, he reasoned, this must have had at least the tacit approval of the ANC, and Wright was convinced Bacher was au fait with their thinking. 'The letter that I wrote to Ali Bacher,' he recalls, 'was still in transit when he phoned me and asked if I would like to go to South Africa as part of the celebrations they were having. This put me in a slight quandary as I'd just asked him to come here. I hummed and hawed and had what I thought was the perfect excuse: I said that I had already made plans to go to New Zealand at that time and that I didn't think I could make it. He said that was not a problem – I could come to South Africa en route to New Zealand. So in the end I compromised my moral stand and went to South Africa.'

Bacher, in his usual way, set up a very special welcome for Wright and his other guests, which included journalists John Thicknesse, Jack Bannister and many others. 'At Johannesburg we were taken in through the back door. We went through customs but our passports were never stamped. We were guests of the South African Cricket Union and they met all our expenses. Some people even got envelopes with money. I heard about this afterwards. I don't know what the money was for. I think it was for out of pocket expenses like drinks in the bar or something like that. It didn't happen to me. I think it made a lot of people uncomfortable but I suppose people entertained in their rooms and there were laundry bills. I knew I was going back to England in two weeks, so my dirty laundry just stayed in my case.'

Bacher charmed Wright, who was much taken by the fact that he seemed more European than a typical white South African. There was little of that defensive aggressiveness that so many whites display and which had so often grated on Wright. In the end Wright was glad he had gone because, after being taken to the townships, he was able to appreciate the complexity of the racial situation: 'It wasn't just a question of black and white. I realized that there was a definite political strategy to keep all the different groups in opposition. I spoke to African teachers who were at the bottom of the scale, with more money for Asians and a bit more money for Coloureds. I started to see how the apartheid system works. Also how, within African groups, some people had money and some didn't. Then through a publishing contact I met with liberals who were opposed to the Nationalist Government but who were afraid of what the Africans would do because they had no understanding of them. Their education hadn't prepared the whites for living with another culture. I realized how difficult it would be to get some form of government that would work.'

How much the centenary celebrations helped Bacher present the acceptable face of his cricket is difficult to say. Some leading English cricket dignitaries didn't come. The previous year Ted Dexter had come to see the township programme, and Bacher had even instituted the Dexter Cup for a township competition in his honour. But then he was a mere commentator and PR man. By the time the centenary came around he had become chairman of the new England committee and as the chief man responsible for selecting English Test players he declined. However, Bacher was successful in using the celebrations to make a partial convert. Peter Roebuck, the former Somerset batsman and now a cricket correspondent for a national paper, had been a strong supporter of the boycott but had accepted the invitation. While he was there Bacher was not sure what Roebuck was up to. 'He arrived, then took off to do his own thing. One day he came back to tell me, "It's all right, your township programme has the approval of the ANC." I must say I found him strange. He wouldn't look me in the eye and all his conversations with me came via Woodcock.'

In contrast, Wright found Roebuck a most open-eyed travel companion and relished his arguments with John Woodcock who, as ever, seemed incapable of seeing anything wrong with white South Africa, let alone the need for a sports boycott. 'Some of my friends,' recalls Roebuck, 'like Dudley Doust and Matthew Engel, were upset that I accepted Bacher's invitation. I had a furious fight with Dudley. But I had told Bacher I would come but do my own thing. I flew with Woodcock and as we arrived at Johannesburg we saw a black man. I said, "Wooders, what you have to remember is the black man does not have the vote and the white person does." Woodcock said, "I hope you will not be writing that all the time"; but he was smiling. Ever since I was young I have always felt very strongly about apartheid, but I saw nothing wrong in going to see it in action, even allowing Bacher to pay for my tickets, as long as I could do what I wanted and go where I wanted.'

Roebuck went to Black Sash meetings, and met a French priest who told him people were still just disappearing. Before his visit to South Africa Roebuck was seen as part of the Rev. David Sheppard and Mike Brearley school of sports boycott supporters. He returned to argue that the boycott should be selectively lifted; that, having wielded the stick for so long, a bit of carrot should now be offered. Just the line Bacher was preaching, in fact.

The celebrations provided the right launching pad for what Bacher called his 'Out of Africa Will Come Something New' speech at the *Wisden* dinner. He was well aware of how important the speech might be. So it proved – although it would later generate a wonderful, very English anecdote. The menu at the East India club where the dinner was held included boiled ham, and some sharp-eyed reporters noticed that Bacher did not touch it but ate salad instead. How crass, they thought, of English cricket to serve ham to a Jew. But Wright had checked the menu with Bacher, who did not mind the ham: he was so nervous he could hardly eat a thing.

Bacher's nerves were understandable for he was seeking to project a new face of white South African cricket. In his speech he spoke of his Jewish heritage, with a reference to the Holocaust, and his Lithuanian Jewish background. As we know, his story had not been a matter of sporting prowess leading to riches: his father's business in Roodeport had prospered sufficiently for Bacher to have a comfortable upbringing. But the imagery was deliberate. It was meant to convey to his audience that this was not just another well-off white but one who had used cricket to reap vast benefits and could see how the black children of the townships might do the same. Cricket had been good to him. He felt he could help make it good for the benighted black kids of Soweto and Alexandra.

The speech was certainly an extraordinary tour-de-force and perhaps the most remarkable ever delivered by a white sports administrator. No *Wisden* dinner had ever heard so many references to wider political events and changes in society. Bacher spoke of how South Africa was a censored society, acknowledged that white South Africa had for years shunned black communities, accepted that the boycott had been necessary in the 1960s. And then he described how, through the township programme, his cricket union was trying to attack the foundations of apartheid, such as the

Group Areas Act, the Separate Amenities Act, and the ignor-
ance and fear that apartheid both fed on and generated.
Township cricket, he claimed, had made white cricket sensitive to black feeling, now it was necessary to build for the
post-apartheid society he was sure would emerge. Wright,
listening intently, thought this was just the sort of speech a
white ally of the ANC would give.

'Because of the fact that he would be speaking after the
papers went to bed we arranged with David Lloyd of
the Press Association that I would get a copy of Bacher's
speech and send it to the PA; and we decided that we might
as well give it to certain journalists at the dinner who
might want to phone something through their night desks.
So on the afternoon of the dinner I went to Ali's hotel, where
he was still going through his speech and waiting for bits to
be phoned through from South Africa. Certain parts of the
speech had to be adjusted, and I am convinced Bacher's
speech was approved by the ANC.'

This was a bit wide of the mark. Bacher was in touch with
township opinion and knew what influential people who
sympathized with the ANC thought. His old school friend
Chris Day, for instance, had put him contact with a couple
of key soccer officials who were close to the ANC. One of
them was Legau Mathesathe, who was principal of the
Soweto school where the riots of 1976 had started. But at
this stage there had been no formal link between Bacher and
the ANC.

In any case, Bacher also told his audience that he would
still have to organize tours to South Africa. Just as English
cricket could not survive without Tests, so, he argued, South
African cricket, particularly the initiative in the townships,
could not prosper without the money that international tours
generated. The argument had a certain plausibility and drew
warm applause at the dinner – not surprising given that
many in the audience had, like Jack Bailey, never cared for
the boycott and wanted to restore links with white South
Africa as soon as possible. But Bacher added a rider. These

should not be called 'rebel' tours; and drawing on what Bramall had told him (without, of course, mentioning Bramall by name) Bacher argued that, by penalizing those who went to South Africa to play, the ICC had clarified the alternatives for players.

This was a clear hint he was planning a rebel tour. What his audience did not know was that Bacher had already started casting his net for players. By the time he returned to England in July there was hardly a player of consequence that Bacher had not contacted. As he admitted afterwards, there was more than a touch of James Bond about some of the contacts: 'I met Phil DeFreitas in the Manchester station buffet. I also met Graeme Fowler, Gehan Mendis, Neil Fairbrother, Martyn Moxon, Ashley Metcalfe, Paul Allott, Jonathan Agnew, Mark Nicholas, Neil Radford' – and many, many others. Emburey was again on Bacher's list, but the one player he didn't approach was Gooch. According to Jack Bannister, Emburey, who is close to Gooch, told Bacher, 'You are just wasting your time. Forget it.'

The two crucial meetings for Bacher were when he rang Mike Gatting. 'I phoned him myself. His mother-in-law had just died and we met at Enfield cricket club.' Gatting had been sacked as England captain after his problems in 1988 and was a disaffected cricketer. He would have returned as captain against Australia in 1989 had Ted Dexter and Micky Stewart, the England manager, got their way; but the TCCB vetoed the choice, and Gatting, having played only one Test against Australia that summer, was unsure whether he might play for England again. Like Kim Hughes in Australia, he was ripe for picking. He was also the obvious captain of the rebel side. Bacher also spoke to Ian Botham. 'Alan Herd, his solicitor, was there and we spoke about Botham's remark about not being able to look Viv Richards in the eye if he came to South Africa. He said, "Don't worry, I have cleared it with Viv." But we couldn't afford him. He wanted £600,000. Even if we had had that sort of money, we couldn't have paid it – it would have got out.'

Boycott offered to be manager, but Bacher went for a player-manager in David Graveney. In recruiting players Bacher extensively tapped his considerable English contacts and throughout that summer almost everybody on English cricket who knew Bacher got a call. Kevin Mitchell, then working for the *Sunday Times*, was in its office in Wapping, when he picked up the phone one day to find a female voice saying: 'It is Dr Bacher for Robin Marlar' [the paper's cricket correspondent].

Another useful contact was Jack Bannister, then secretary of the Players' Association. As we have seen, he was an old friend of Bacher's; the two would often discuss ideas about ways to change the game, like using substitutes. Bannister had been going to South Africa since 1958 but, as he quaintly puts it, 'the rough side of the country was hardly made apparent to me and I didn't go looking. Call it naive, call it what you like.' Was it possible for a white player to go to South Africa and not be aware of the 'rough side'? 'Yes,' insists Bannister, 'it was.' On his second trip in 1960 he did play in an all-white side got together by Peter Walker against a Coloured XI at Natalspruit, which might have been a hint to him that not all South African cricket was played at the Wanderers: 'The day before the game the police warned Peter and said, "We probably won't arrest you all, but we don't want the game to take place." Peter rang all of us, and I asked him, "Do you want the game to go ahead?" He said yes, and so we played. Their ground was very rough and ready, with no changing facilities. We changed in our cars and I played on a mat for the first time. It was also the first time I came across a young man called Basil D'Oliveira. He shouldered arms to my first ball which pitched on a length on the off-stump and I thought, "Thank you, bowled first ball!" But it went about 18 inches over the top of the stumps. The second ball I pitched up a touch more – and they fetched it out of the stand. That was my first lesson, which Basil rammed home and rammed home. After that I was a bit aware of what was going on. But you could have spent months in the country and not be aware.'

By 1989 Bannister had became widely known in South Africa as a television commentator. He was now more aware of apartheid; but he was convinced the rebel tours were justified as without some international matches South African cricket would decline. But he vehemently denies that he had acted as recruiting sergeant for Bacher. 'The principle that he was going to do the tour he had discussed with me, and that was that. In actual fact, when the names were announced, I hadn't talked to any of the 16 players who were eventually named. The whole thing was done by Ali and David and somebody else whose name I can't remember. I had nothing to do with it.'

What particularly pleased Bacher was that he had succeeded in securing two black Test players in Philip DeFreitas and Roland Butcher. But once the news was announced, they came under such great pressure from the black communities in England, and also from some black sportsman such as the runner John Regis, that they withdrew. Bacher was left with an all-white team, something he had not wanted, and a venture that was seen by many people as ill-timed.

The players led by Gatting justified it on the grounds that they were only doing what professionals should do; that their cricket careers were short and they had to take what money they could get – an estimated £50,000 a year for a three-year contract. But as Graeme Wright, in his editor's notes for *Wisden*, said, '. . . the argument devalues the professional in this instance'. And while he had doubts about the ICC's imposing the penalties, he also felt that 'the South African Cricket Union has made a mistake – politically and tactically – in staging this tour. In recent years it has been improving its credentials, both as an opponent of apartheid and as a non-racial administration, through its cricket development programme in the black townships. Now it is gambling that goodwill on a venture that can be seen only as "sanctions busting" by the country's black leaders. If, as a result of the tour, the community leaders turn against the township programmes, it will be a tragedy: not for South African cricket, but for those underprivileged children to whom cricket had offered a means of expressing themselves beyond their segregated environments. Had SACU waited a year, such is the promise of change in South Africa politically, that the ICC decision of January 1989 might have been seen as coming too late to be meaningful. As it is, who knows what harm will be done?'

Wright was to prove remarkably prescient. Bacher himself was not unaware of the dangers he was courting. All the time that he was recruiting players he was also busy weighing up how the tour would affect the township programme. Wright may not have been quite right in thinking that Bacher was in direct touch with ANC, but he was in indirect touch through Van Zyl Slabbert. And during his visit to London in July Slabbert had arranged a meeting with the ANC: 'I had lunch with two executive members of the ANC – Mendi Msinang and Aziz Pahad. They came to the Westbury Hotel. Aziz came first at 12.45. At 1 o'clock Mendi came with three security men, who watched the entrance the whole time Aziz and Mendi were there. Aziz and Mendi were there for an hour and a half and were very courteous.'

Bacher and Pamensky also had a crucial meeting with Dennis Brutus in a London hotel. Although Brutus was president of SANROC, this was very much a nominal post, with the organization being run by its executive chairman, Sam Ramsamy. Brutus seemed to suggest to Bacher and Pamensky that it would be possible for South African cricket to get into international competition. When this got out, it further widened the breach between Bacher and Ramsamy.

Bacher returned to South Africa, conferring with Van Zyl Slabbert, Ebrahim Patel of SARU, Hasan Howa and others in an attempt to gauge the effect the rebel tour would have on the township programme and, in particular, how the ANC would react to it. The withdrawal of DeFreitas and Butcher meant that Bacher had no black players who could act as role models for his young township cricketers. As protests began to mount, and it became clear that his own coaches in the townships were opposed to the tour, Bacher began to wonder whether the rebel cricketers would be prepared to coach in the townships. In England much had been made of the fact that they would play a big part in this evangelical process. In October of that year Bacher told me: 'When the tourists arrive, and if the climate is good, and if the townships agree – then they will coach. The days are gone when you can tell the blacks what to do.'

To add to his pressures, 1989 had seen the creation of the Mass Democratic Movement, bringing together the UDF and the Congress of South African Trade Unions. Unlike its constituent bodies, the Movement was not a formal organization, and so was not subject to the legal restraints imposed on the others. And while it was linked to the ANC, it acted as an umbrella organization for many other bodies. No sooner had Bacher announced the tour than it became clear that the MDM opposed it. What's more – as I was to discover in October 1989 when I met Bacher in Johannesburg – at least one member of Bacher's own family was in the MDM. This was his daughter Lyn, who came out firmly against the tour. What concerned Bacher most was that if the Gatting tour threatened the township programme it would also damage the social engineering process that was part of it, whose effects, Bacher was hoping, would extend far beyond the cricket field.

11

The Gatting Fiasco

Through the summer of 1989 Bacher agonized over the Gatting tour, but by the end he was confident he would have the tour and preserve the township programme. In August 1989 P. W. Botha had gone; de Klerk had taken over and in September won a whites-only election which had seen the far-right Conservative party increase its support and become the official opposition. De Klerk had fought the election on a vaguely worded Five-Year Plan of Action and campaigned in language all too familiar after 40 years of Nationalist rule: no 'one man, one vote' and 'group rights' to be protected – the latter being code words for white rule to be protected, with any new constitution to be based on 'consensus' rather than majority rule. The non-white reaction to the election had been to organize more protests, including a successful two-day stay-away and schools boycott which involved 3 million workers and students; while only a fifth of the Indian and Coloured electorate voted for the essentially toothless Indian and Coloured assemblies.

But then de Klerk, hitherto identified as a conservative, suddenly started showing signs that he might be a reformer. Walter Sisulu and other long-term ANC prisoners – but not Mandela – were released from Robben Island. I was with Bacher on that day and he was buoyant with hope. 'You know, by January this [meaning Gatting] could be the official English tour, with Colin Cowdrey [chairman of the ICC] flying out to watch the matches.' By the end of the week he had met Gerrit Viljoen, the Constitutional Minister, then second only to F. W. de Klerk in the Government. 'They mean business, they want to change,' bubbled an optimistic Bacher.

De Klerk did mean business and Bacher's optimism was understandable. For at that stage his opponents in the anti-apartheid sports movement seemed to be in disarray. There was the growing and very visible split in SANROC, with Brutus appearing to be the moderate and Ramsamy the hard-liner. Within South Africa the challenge to SACOS that had started in the mid–1980s was now formalized. In June 1989 the National Sports Congress (NSC) was formally launched at the University of Witwatersrand. SACOS had done some good but had now outlived its usefulness: it was no longer able to penetrate the African townships or, equally crucially, mobilize white support.

In September Krish Naidoo of the NSC offered Bacher what seemed like a historic compromise: if Bacher called off the tour, Naidoo would arrange to get all the various sports bodies together, so that, even before apartheid was abandoned, South Africa could be back in international sports.

For Bacher this was too vague, too imprecise. He could call off the tour, but how could Naidoo guarantee that South Africa would be back in international cricket in, say, a year or 18 months' time? Naidoo, a lawyer, refused to put anything in writing, and Bacher refused even to consider calling off the tour. In any case he believed that his township programme had forced the anti-apartheid sports movement onto the back foot, and indeed that the National Sports Congress had been created because of the success of his township programme. What he failed to appreciate was that the NSC also had the muscle to stop the programme. Long before Gatting and Co arrived, Naidoo had warned that, although Bacher's township development programme was good, 'if the tour goes ahead the township programme will be killed'.

Bacher could be excused for not taking their threat seriously. In the past SACOS had often made such threats. Even as Naidoo was warning about the township pro-gramme, the white South African Rugby Board held its centenary celebrations, hosting two Tests between the Springboks and a World XV. Ramsamy had warned of the dire consequences for world sport, but nothing happened – although there was just a hint of what was to come when, despite the state of emergency, demonstrations were held both before and during the matches. In the past, as we have seen, rebel tours had generated considerable controversy in the country from which the players were recruited. But once in South Africa they seemed to be behind a cricketing iron curtain where no demonstrators could touch them. All this was to change with the Gatting tour.

The decisive change with Gatting was that there were people in the NSC who were hardened political activists, men who had been to prison and suffered violence and torture for their beliefs but who had also developed an interest and involvement in sport. In September one such man flew to London to try to persuade Gatting not to tour. He was Ngconde Balfour. Two days before he flew to London he had been released from prison, having spent nine months in Pollsmoor charged with 18 offences under Section 29 of the Internal Security Act. Although his prison experience was nothing like that of Tshwete, he had by this time spent some six or seven years in prison on various charges, but had never been convicted. And he experienced the full force of the South African police: 'I was once interrogated in a building near the harbour in Cape Town called Culuemborg. I had to take off my clothes and stand there naked and answer questions. A young white policeman got so fed up with the way I was answering questions that he pulled out his service revolver. I was handcuffed with my hands behind my back. He pushed the service revolver into my mouth. He was screaming at me and punching and kicking me all the time. My God, I was thinking, he's going to blow my head off – right on the wall. But he decided not to do it. That was about 10 or 11 in the evening. I was made to stand until six in the morning. No food. No water. The next morning, as I was about to be taken to Pollsmoor, in handcuffs and in leg irons, we passed a room and I saw the back of a person. It was my wife. I got in the car and saw her standing there. I didn't know what she was doing there, what was happening to her, to my children. I had a real sinking feeling. I felt like a lost soul. My wife had gone there with clothes for me. She didn't know I was in the building. That was a painful moment. There were many such painful moments. After I was released I went to work for Archbishop Desmond Tutu. I was asked, didn't you cry? I said I did. You didn't cry in front of your captors, but I believe crying is a sign that you are human, after all.'

It was fresh from these experiences that Balfour flew to London to try to persuade Gatting and Co not to tour. With him was Krish Mackerdhuj, who had replaced Hasan Howa as President of the South African Cricket Board. On the face of it the visit achieved little. Initially, the gatemen at Lord's refused even to allow Mackerdhuj in. Then, after he had made a fuss, Lt Col John Stephenson, Secretary of the MCC, came down and the NSC delegation was allowed to see Gatting and Emburey in a Committee Room. Although in the media Gatting was getting most of the flak, Balfour found him more receptive than Emburey:

'We spent an hour and a half with Gatting and Emburey. Gatting, I thought, had a soft underbelly, a big soft underbelly. He also had a chip on his shoulder about [Pakistan umpire] Shakoor Rana and the barmaid incidents. He was not a thinker but a doer. Emburey was a little bit cunning. He'd had a taste of the krugerrands before. He was saying things in India were pretty bad. He was on the UN black list and he did not care. There was nothing he could do to change the situation – he could only play cricket. I felt we were getting through to Gatting but not to Emburey.'

Failure or not, this meeting showed the new face of black South African sport. Mackerdhuj had a long record as a black sports administrator, had been a member of the ANC since 1958 and, like Brutus, was a product of Fort Hare; but he was not a political activist like Balfour. While Balfour was a member of the ANC military wing, Mackerdhuj was a sports administrator in the style of Hasan Howa and, like Howa, had been refused passports to travel outside the country. In the past, if SACOS had attempted such a London visit, the people concerned would all have been of the sports-administrator type. NSC's involvement meant people like Balfour were coming into the picture.

The advent of such political activists in sports became all the more evident when in November 1989, in a conference room at the Johannesburg Sun, the NSC met with Bacher's cricket union to try to persuade them to call off the tour. As far back as 1988 Lig Nosarka, a board member of the Transvaal Cricket Union, had suggested that it might be worth talking to the NSC. Krish Naidoo brokered the meeting and he and Geoff Dakin acted as co-chairmen. The NSC delegates included Balfour and Muleleki George. But, as Mthobi Tyamzashe, another NSC delegate, remarked, it was very much a case of a rich, powerful cricket body, which had been going for 100 years, sizing up a young, seemingly upstart organization that had been launched barely six months before.

The meeting broke up without a decision being taken. Few of Bacher's colleagues were impressed with the NSC. They were used to hearing threats from SACOS that in the past had amounted to little more than hot air. Ewie Cronje, one of the delegates, observed: 'I knew very little about the NSC. I didn't think they had much standing. They made it out we should not carry on with the tour and that it would be a wrong thing. I thought these chaps were just threatening and that they had no power.'

The next day Tyamzashe and Muleleki George flew back to East London. As luck would have it one of Bacher's delegates, Robbie Muzzell, President of the white Border Cricket Union, sat between them on the plane. George asked, 'What have you decided? If you have decided negatively you will feel the wrath.' Muzzell, uncomfortable sitting between two opponents, murmured: 'Later on you will know what we have decided.'

The decision to carry on with the tour hardly came as a surprise. But the surprises came thick and fast once Gatting and his men had landed on 19 January 1990. The plane carrying them from London was delayed by a bomb scare. Unaware of this, demonstrators gathered around Jan Smuts, and although police roadblocks prevented thousands from getting into the airport, a group of 150 did succeed and they were met with all the force the police could muster. The British media were already in Johannesburg in considerable numbers and, hearing the flight was late, delayed their arrival at the airport. So they missed the police action, but wrote up the story based on what facts they could subsequently gather. According to Colin Bryden, one British journalist, Paul Weaver of *Today* went further: 'He wrote a lurid eye-witness account which described how blood was still damp on the steps when Gatting's men arrived after "violence that left me weak and nauseous". He then described in graphic terms the viciousness of the dogs, the brutality of the police and their physical resemblance to young Nazis.' Bryden, who had been the PR consultant to Bacher's union throughout the rebel tours, feels that for the Gatting visit the British press contingent 'was dominated by a tabloid hit-squad whose appreciation of the evolving political situation in South Africa appeared to be non-existent, but who displayed a remarkable inventiveness in portraying events to their readers'. Weaver, in his view, was the worst.

Today subsequently agreed to publish a full-page article by Bacher but before this could be done two white policemen suddenly arrived at Weaver's hotel and told him he had to leave South Africa by night-fall. He was being deported in the style so common to South Africa.

Weaver accepts that he did not see the airport battle, but argues: 'I had spoken to the witnesses and the blood *was* damp. It was quite a savage beating of the demonstrators. No one seriously denied that what I wrote was true. I never claimed I saw it. I arrived there within minutes of the incident. I spoke to black and white eyewitnesses who were emotionally affected by the gratuitous violence. There was even one policeman bitterly complaining that they wouldn't let his dog off the leash to have a go at the demonstrators. . . . Ali Bacher, against whom I have no complaints, tried to quash the deportation order, but it had been taken out of his hands. Before I was thrown out I had threats on my life. I had calls in the night. The whole atmosphere was very poisonous. In Bloemfontein we met police officers who were so paranoid they accused us of starting riots, placing stones in rioters' hands. The fact was that the British journalists there would not accept the propaganda line.'

That initial airport confrontation set the stage for what was to prove the most violent sporting tour of South Africa. White South Africans got a taste of the sort of violence their own overseas tours had provoked in England in 1969, in Australia in 1971 and in New Zealand in 1981. George had warned Muzzell of the wrath and this was evident as soon as the tour started, showing the tremendous power the NSC could wield. At two large luxury hotels there were protest strikes by staff belonging to the South African Commercial, Catering & Allied Workers Union.

The first match was due to be played at East London, the heart of the area where George and Tyamzashe hailed from. Bacher, sensing this was not going to be like other tours, switched it to Kimberley in the Orange Free State. Surely here, in the heart of Afrikanderdom, it would be back to the sun-filled days of *braie* (barbecue), cricket and fun. But this was 1990; there was a new mood amongst the blacks which astonished the whites. Ewie Cronje drove to Kimberley from Bloemfontein: 'As I drove I could see the demonstrations. I had never seen such demonstrations, there were police everywhere with helicopters flying about, and I thought back to what the NSC had told us in November.'

Soon after the game started at the De Beers Country Club in Kimberley Bacher was approached by Krish Naidoo at the head of a small delegation. 'The police are stopping our people from demonstrating,' he said. Bacher drove two or three kilometres to find a line of policemen blocking several thousand marchers in a quiet residential area. The police told him the demonstration was unlawful. The NSC, as a matter of policy, had refused to ask permission for the demonstration. Their question to Bacher was: 'You said we will be allowed to demonstrate. Why are we not?'

Bacher had never had to face demonstrations, but with that quick thinking that has always characterized him, he explored the possibility of making the demonstration legal. This required the permission of the local chief magistrate. Bacher rang Gerrit Viljoen, then Minister of Sport, who told him he should speak to the Police Minister, Adriaan Volk. While Bacher phoned, the sun grew hotter and the police moved in men with teargas. It seemed an explosion could not be far away. When Bacher asked the men to be moved, the police moved the journalists away before they were checked by Bacher. 'Not the journalists, the police.' Eventually Bacher defused the situation by telling Naidoo that he would have no objection to a demonstration outside the ground provided it was peaceful. Bacher himself went to the chief magistrate and then to the town clerk to get permission. It was now legal to stage demonstrations outside the ground, although the NSC was furious that Bacher had 'obtained permission on behalf of the NSC under false pretences'. As Tyamzashe says, 'He took the wind out of our sails, because now we couldn't get angry about being refused the right to demonstrate.'

But not all Bacher's off-the-cuff adroitness could disguise the fact that there was now a new sporting and political phenomenon in South Africa: the legal demonstration. Next day at the De Beers club white spectators watched in astonishment as thousands massed outside the ground with only a wire fence separating them from paid-up spectators. Apart from one white spectator who threw a bottle, the demonstrators were allowed to sing and *toyi-toyi* their protests. At the first demonstration Gatting had revealed his naiveté; when asked about it he said, 'As far as I'm concerned there were a few people singing and dancing and that was it.' As the tour progressed through Bloemfontein and Pietermaritzburg, where 10,000 demonstrators gathered, it was clear it was much more than that.

The first so-called Test was played at the Wanderers ground, but in the most unnatural of circumstances. The police refused to allow a march from central Johannesburg to the suburb of Illovo; police helicopters hovered overhead and dozens of police vehicles were dotted around the ground and its environs. Moreover, the tour had now been overtaken by wider events. On 2 February de Klerk, opening the white Parliament, announced the unbanning of the ANC, the Pan-African Congress, the South African Communist Party and 33 other organizations. He also announced that Nelson Mandela would soon be released. The changes reverberated round South Africa like a thunderclap. Politically, South Africa could never be the same again and the rebel tour era had to end.

Bacher feared what would happen when the tour moved to the Cape. There, waiting for him, was Balfour and his organization: 'In Western Cape we had gathered our support. Even cricketers supported us. We were working on Peter Kirsten; we were quite close to him, and he was caught in the middle. We were preparing a warm reception for Gatting and his men. We were going to close down the airport. Any access to and from the airport would be closed. It would be a really good reception. We were prepared to spill on to the runway. We were going to close off Newlands cricket ground. We would use graders, those big things that chip the roads, and old cars to blockade the streets around Newlands. We would drive our cars on to the Newlands outfield. We had obtained 1,000 tickets to get our supporters into the ground. They would invade the square, take out the wickets, and sit on the pitch.'

A week before Gatting and his men were due to arrive, a

bomb went off outside Newlands. Was that Balfour's bomb? 'I didn't say that,' he says; but clearly it was an ANC operation. A warrant was issued for Balfour's arrest, and he spent a night in the cells. But he was then released on his own cognizance and the case never reached court. The next day the tour was cancelled.

Moves towards this began in London, where Thabo Mbeki, the ANC Foreign Affairs spokesman, was meeting some South African businessmen, who said they were anxious to settle the cricket tour. On Saturday 10 February Krish Naidoo received a telephone call from Mbeki in London, followed by a second call from Sam Ramsamy. Both Mbeki and Ramsamy were anxious to keep the ANC out of the picture. On the Sunday Krish Naidoo, with a couple of colleagues, met Bacher at the home of Michael Kez in the plush Johannesburg suburb of Athol. According to Naidoo, 'Dr Bacher offered the cancellation of the second leg of the tour as a compromise. This offer was rejected and we stated our position that the tour be called off in its entirety. Dr Bacher then made a second offer – that the second leg of the tour be cancelled as well as the second Test of the first leg, which was due to take place in Cape Town the following week.' Naidoo wanted to consult on this, and they agreed to meet again on Monday.

Bacher called a meeting of his board for the Monday and for five hours they discussed what could be done to rescue the tour. In the end it was agreed that at least four one-day internationals should be played on the present tour and that a decision on the second tour would be made later. Later that day Bacher and Naidoo met again, and they talked through much of the night. There were arguments about the venues for the four so-called one-day internationals; eventually, after much haggling, it was agreed that they would be played at Bloemfontein, Johannesburg and Verwoerdburg. Naidoo's colleagues were very reluctant to allow a match in Durban, but eventually this was accepted as the fourth venue. On his part, Bacher agreed (although at the time he had no mandate to do so) that Gatting and his rebels would not return the following year.

On 13 February Geoff Dakin announced the curtailment of the tour, justifying it on the grounds of the dramatic political events of 2 February and Mandela's release from prison on 11 February. According to Bacher, Krish Naidoo then leaked the cancellation of the second tour. Naidoo claims that he did so only because Bacher, at his press conference, had indicated the second leg was still on the cards. 'For this reason the NSC decided to expose cancellation of the second leg.' Bacher now faced a storm from his own board. Dakin insisted that Bacher had no mandate to decide on the second tour. Bacher, at that moment busy with his daughter's wedding, had to cope with something quite unexpected: revolt in his own ranks. Stormy board meetings followed, and for a time it seemed that Bacher himself might go. But Bacher had a trump card up his sleeve:

'I had got hold of BBC news clips which showed how the police had clobbered the demonstrators. This had not been shown on South African television. I showed this to the board. Then I left, as I had to go to an award evening. But it resulted in a very lively meeting. No, I didn't threaten to resign. In the end the board agreed the second tour was not possible. We would have been mad to contemplate another tour. We were cutting our losses. In any case, I had the support of the business community.'

But although Bacher had squashed the rebellion in his ranks, there was no disguising the defeat he had suffered:

'The development programme was closed. Hoosen could not go into the townships. He was bottled up in the office and we were paying all this money. At that period in March and April I felt battered. For the first time in my life I lost confidence in myself. I used to go home early from the office. I would not take calls.' For Bacher to shun the telephone was almost revolutionary and indicated his despair. It seemed everything Bacher had worked for all the years since he had gone into Soweto that day in October 1986 was now dead and buried. A few short weeks had ruined almost everything – all his time, work and dedication, was wasted. The man who had tried to balance rebel tours with township cricket now found he had lost both.

12

Out of the Wilderness

Slowly Bacher came out of his despair, but it was April 1990, two months after Mandela's release, before he could begin to think of a way to get back into the townships. The Anglo-American company had provided R.1 million to build a multi-purpose sports complex in the Alexandra township. The problem was that, even with this sort of money, the Gatting fiasco meant that Bacher could no longer just walk into the townships. Eventually contact was re-established, however, and on the night that Bacher was to receive the Newsmaker of the Year award at a Wanderers dinner sponsored by the breweries, a meeting was arranged for him in the township. Bacher received the award, then slipped away to Alexandra to meet the local ANC branch and delegates from Congress of South African Students and the Women's League.

It was not an easy meeting for Bacher. 'The issue here was that during the Gatting tour, when the so-called Test at Wanderers took place, the police closed off Alexandra. Students from Alex who were going to march to Wanderers were not allowed to get out and were clobbered. Some of them were badly beaten up. There was obvious bitterness. And I was not well received.' Bacher listened, acknowledged mistakes and expressed regrets. 'We came to terms and decided to call a media conference. I went on the 8 o'clock news and said I accepted the tour was ill-timed. It had been brought to my attention that people were hurt, and we were profoundly sorry.'

Even then the township people would not accept Anglo's money until they had a few questions answered: why was Anglo spending such a large amount, what was in it for them? This was the new reality of South Africa to which Bacher and everyone had to adjust. Bacher persuaded one of the senior people at Anglo to go to the township with him and address a meeting. Probably, says Bacher, for the first time ever a senior man from the heart of white South Africa's capital had been to the township. After the meeting he confessed to Bacher, 'I have never had an experience like this.'

However, while all this was a gain, there was still the larger question: how could Bacher's cricket union come back from the Gatting fiasco? It was now that Bacher turned once more to Van Zyl Slabbert. 'I'll never forget what he said to me. He said, "Ali, if you made the wrong decision, don't worry. If you misread the political scene or the scenario that was going to evolve, you are in good company. F. W. [de Klerk] caught the whole ANC with their pants down. Don't you worry, you are in very good company." And we spoke and spoke and spoke. I explained to him the seriousness of the situation.'

Then in April or early May there was the first ever business conference with the people from the ANC who had come home from exile in Lusaka. 'A whole lot of them came down. They had a big conference at the Carlton Hotel. Gavin Relly from Anglo-American was there, so was Mandela. It was the first ever get-together of high profile business leaders and ANC, and Slabbert phoned me at 10.30 that night. It was a Wednesday and he said, "Ali, on Friday night I want you to go to Mdanstsane [a big township in East London] and I want you to meet Steve Tshwete." I had never heard of him – I didn't know who the hell he was.'

To get to Mdanstane Bacher needed a black guide. This was provided by his great friend in East London, Robbie Muzzell, who was running the Border province of Bacher's cricket union. His guide was Muzzell's black driver. 'This driver fetched me from the airport and we drove into the township. It was a cold, wet, wintry May night. The house was a bit better than most township houses. Steve was not there, but three others were (I later learnt that between them they had spent a total of 50 years on Robben Island).' Shortly before Bacher arrived they had been rung up and told to expect Bacher. They did not much like that, and Bacher waited in frosty silence hoping Tshwete would arrive soon.

Tshwete had not been too keen to meet Bacher. 'I had never met him before but I had heard about him and the rebel tours. I had just come back into the country from Lusaka and felt I had to know the lie of the land before I could get involved in intricate discussions of that nature. I knew how very sensitive unity in sport was. Also, having just returned from Zambia, I was squatting in somebody's house in East London. I got delayed that evening and when I arrived I found Ali watching television. It was all very quiet and nobody was speaking to him.'

Bacher's first impression of Tshwete was his size. 'He walked in and there was this big chap, and he had at that time very thick-rimmed glasses. We sat facing each other. The chair he was sitting on was higher than my chair, so he really perched over me. I remember speaking for half an hour about the development programme, the need for it, how the kids wanted the township to be open and that the process should be allowed to continue. There had been errors, and we acknowledged them. For half an hour he just looked at me. At the end of it he thought and he thought. He didn't say much, only "OK, that's good, and we'll meet some other time." '

In concrete terms this first meeting between the head of the white cricket body and one of ANC's most important executive members had not achieved anything significant. Tshwete had not squeezed Bacher's hands the way he had done with de Villiers in Dakar, but human contact had at least been established, the ice broken. As Tshwete saw Bacher out of the house to the car, he became very concerned, 'I took him out into the darkness of the township,' recalls

Tshwete, 'and there was a possibility that he might get into trouble – a white guy driving through the township at that hour, anything could happen. He assured me he was safe and that he was going to be picked up somewhere by a guy who turned out to be the prospective President [of the United Board, Muzzell]. He had a black driver with him who was going to take him there.' Bacher, always sensitive to any human touch, is sure that is when Tshwete began to 'thaw and the warmth started to come out of him'.

June 1990 saw the formal relaunch of the National Sports Congress. It was now to be called the National and Olympic Sports Congress (although most people continued to refer to it as the NSC). The ceremony saw the ANC emerge in all its pomp, with Tshwete giving the keynote address. He was referred to as Comrade Steve Tshwete and photographs showing his smiling gap-toothed face and the thick-rimmed glasses were everywhere.

Bacher was not slow to appreciate the significance of the event. In the autumn of 1989 he had perceived the NSC as having been set up in response to his own township programme. Now he was very aware that they were the new sports power in the land and that he had to get to know them. If South African cricket was to get back into the international fold it would do so only through the sponsorship of the ANC and its partner in sport, the NSC. And this meant cultivating personal friendships. The rugby establishment had met Tshwete two years previously, but they had failed to establish any personal links. Bacher was not to make the same mistake.

In August he flew to East London and, through Robbie Muzzell, met Muleleki George and Mthobi Tyamzashe. Nothing could better have illustrated the divide in South African life than this meeting. Muzzell and Tyamzashe lived in the same city, but Muzzell lived in the white area and Tyamzashe in the Coloured area called Buffalo Flats. Neither had ever visited the other's area, although they were only a few miles apart. When Bacher decided to visit Buffalo Flats

Tyamzashe had to give Muzzell directions to find it. Some months later when Tyamzashe visited Muzzell's house it was the first time he had been to a white area.

Such meetings of sports officials after decades of mutual enmity and distrust was still fraught with danger. Soon after this introductory meeting with Bacher, Tyamzashe had to be in Johannesburg to report to an NSC executive meeting and Bacher offered to put him up in his house for the night. He picked him from the airport but within five minutes of entering Bacher's home there was a strange happening. The phone rang and a voice asked, 'Is Mr Tyamzashe there?' By the time he was called to the phone the line was dead. A few minutes later it rang again. This time Tyamzashe made it to the call in time. The voice said, 'Tyamzashe, read the *Sowetan* tomorrow.' Tyamzashe, recalls Bacher, was scared. He could barely sleep that night haunted by the thought that the leading black paper in the country would splash the news that he had spent the night in the home of the man still seen as the evil mastermind of rebel tours.

Next morning at 5 am when Bacher returned from his jog he found Tyamzashe packed and ready to go. He was desperate to get a copy of the *Sowetan*. Bacher went with him to get the paper, not normally available in white suburbs. Tyamzashe breathed a sigh of relief when he saw that there was no mention of him in the paper. But still his nerves were on edge. He reluctantly agreed to Bacher driving him to Jan Smuts, but insisted he drop him some distance from the airport lest they be recognized.

So it was in this climate of suspicion and distrust that the first talks between Bacher's cricket union and the non-white cricket board took place at the Elangeni Hotel in Durban on 9 September. Mackerdhuj offered Tshwete's services and Bacher accepted with alacrity: without him the talks would surely have broken down. Tshwete was in the chair acting as facilitator and he was well aware of how difficult the task would be. 'The first meetings were very difficult because those attitudes from the past were still lingering and there was an element of hostility.'

Tshwete's presence meant that, despite the deep divide, the two sides agreed to meet again for a further meeting at Port Elizabeth on 16 December. 'That was a very difficult meeting,' recalls Tshwete. 'There was a very, very hostile atmosphere. The talks nearly foundered just on the point of whether or not to adopt the Statement of Intent. The cricket board in their own Statement of Intent came out with a number of purely political demands, but we didn't think that a sporting body should be involved in the provision of houses and the many other amenities denied to the blacks by reason of the prevailing political situation. Eventually Geoff Dakin proposed that we should dump the adoption of a Statement of Intent because it was controversial and would lead to the foundering of the talks. I said there was no way we were going to allow that. I said without the Statement of Intent I didn't think we could consider any of the items on the agenda.'

Tshwete then called for an adjournment and took the members of the South African Cricket Board to another room. He said to them: 'Guys, I understand why you are feeling the way you do. But we must not lose sight of the fact that we are founding not a new political organization but a sporting body. So it would be in our interests to put aside all the demands which are political in content and character because if these talks founder – and Bacher's Cricket Union will not accede to this kind of political statement – you will be isolated in the country, you will be seen as irresponsible. The mainstay of the Statement of Intent should be the principle of non-racialism but we should confine it to sports.'

Tshwete had called for a 10-minute adjournment; 10 became 15 as the argument raged before he finally got the Cricket Board to agree. It was only after this that the Statement of Intent, including a moratorium on international contacts, was agreed. It would form the basis on which South

African cricket, more than 100 years after it had first played international cricket, finally acquired a single, united cricket body. Unity and development were now to become the two watchwords of what was increasingly being referred to in the media as the 'new South Africa'. And, as ever in South Africa, these words were loaded: 'unity' meant black and white bodies coming together; 'development' meant white bodies providing funds so that the sport could be taken to the townships.

Cricket, in comparison to other sports, had an advantage in that it already had a development programme, and Bacher has no doubt that, apart from Tshwete's great role, it was this that overcame the hostility of Mackerdhuj and his colleagues. 'The development programme sucked Mackerdhuj in. He had no money, no expertise, he wanted to develop cricket for his own people. We had a well structured programme which was not window dressing.' But even now the problems were not over and there would be (as Mackerdhuj puts it) an attempt at 'power play' by the white body before unity could be formalized.

In other sports things were also moving, although here the leading player was Sam Ramsamy. Having spent almost two decades being Mr No, the man who stopped contact with white sporting South Africa, he was now being seen as the man who could give it tickets to the Games – the Olympic Games. In February, soon after Mandela's release, Juan Antonio Samaranch, President of the International Olympic Committee, had called a meeting of the Apartheid and Olympics Commission, which he had set up two years previously and whose special advisor was Ramsamy. At its meeting in Kuwait the Commission asked the African National Olympic Committees Association (ANOCA) to take charge of when and how South Africa could come back to the international fold. As Samaranch would later say, 'A solution to the problem of apartheid must originate within Africa.' The same month, with the blessing of Samaranch, Ramsamy met with Johan du Plessis, President of the white National Olympic

Committee, as a result of which Ramsamy made a quite favourable report on South Africa.

Soon after that, however, things appeared likely to be derailed when du Plessis, on his return to South Africa, enlisted Elijah Barayi, the black President of the Congress of South African Trade Unions, to help him campaign for a return of the country to Olympic sport. This campaign, entitled 'Sport for All Youth', adopted as its maxim 'Love Thy Neighbour'. In a letter to Krish Naidoo urging talks, du Plessis referred to Mahatma Gandhi and quoted verses from an obscure Indian saint, urging that they should 'decide on a suitable date to set the wheels of fate in motion'. There was no point, du Plessis insisted, in he and Barayi spending time in 'sackcloth and ashes disecting [sic] past injustices, real or imaginary, arguing about who belongs and who does not'.

In principle, such sentiments may have been laudable, but in the prevailing climate of South Africa they were inexcusably naive and inflammatory. Twenty years previously du Plessis's predecessor had spoken the language of white supremacy: now, it seemed, his successor had turned into a woolly-minded mystic.

Ramsamy quickly slapped du Plessis down and then set about charting his own path. By this time he had distanced himself from SACOS. At its executive meeting in Cape Town on 13 and 14 January, there had been a long list of complaints against Ramsamy, including the fact that he didn't get on with Brutus, and the SACOS executive then recommended that the organization's affiliates instruct that Ramsamy's 'patronage be revoked immediately'. SACOS and NSC were now as fiercely opposed as the white and black bodies had ever been, and Ramsamy had thrown in his lot with NSC and its very different sporting outlook.

That outlook had still not been spelled out in any great detail to the outside world, which continued to see South Africa's sporting return as possible only after the enactment of one man, one vote and the complete abolition of apartheid. This impression was strengthened when it was announced that Ramsamy would be visiting South Africa in August 1990 as a representative of ANOCA to examine the changes that had taken place.

Immediately his visit was announced *The Times* of London published an editorial denouncing it. Entitled 'Sport in the Bearpit', it warned that this was not a magnanimous gesture in response to de Klerk's repudiation of apartheid. 'By appointing him, the arbiters of participation in the Olympic Games are signalling that they have no intention of readmitting South Africa until black majority rule is established. The Gleneagles Accord remains in force. There is little prospect of cricket authorities – terrified of losing lucrative tours to non-white countries – lifting their boycott. South Africa retains a seat on rugby's ruling body, but only in the sense that Banquo had a seat at Macbeth's table.'

'The Thunderer' had often been wrong on the South Africa question, but seldom can it have revealed so starkly its blindness to what was actually happening in the country. To make matters worse, the leader writer evidently thought Ramsamy was going on behalf of the IOC when, if he had read his own sports writer's report, he would have learnt that ANOCA was unrelated to the IOC. Africa had engineered white South Africa's exclusion from the Olympic Games: Africa would welcome it back. Both Ramsamy and Samaranch were insistent on that.

The Times was on firmer ground when it said that the sporting boycott had affected whites, had been effective in breaking down barriers, and was supported even by those who did not like sanctions. Then, quite unwittingly, it came to the nub of the problem: 'As long as Nelson Mandela and other black leaders wish the rest of the world to continue to isolate South African sport the ban will remain.' What *The Times* had failed to discover, or at least to understand, were the moves ANC had been making in the direction of lifting the ban. However, lifting the ban was not just a simple question of readmitting South Africa. It immediately raised a host of questions, such as which sports body should be readmitted: the old discredited white body or the non-racial body that had been struggling against apartheid?

In interviews before he left London Ramsamy stressed that he would be going with an open mind and he wanted South Africa to come back to international sport and the Olympic Games. The journalists in London reporting this may have been sceptical, but the administrators in South Africa took him at his word and the man who had left South Africa in 1972 one step ahead of the Special Branch now returned as something of a hero. Days before his arrival newspapers devoted hundreds of column inches speculating on what he might do; and once he arrived they charted his progress around the country as if it was some sporting royal visit.

At the airport to welcome him was the South African National Olympic Committee, the organization that Brutus had helped ban from the Olympics and which Ramsamy's SANROC virtually supplanted as the voice of Olympic sport. Now they and the NSC were joint hosts for the visit and surprised Ramsamy by the warmth of their reception. Soon he was on first-name terms, being called Sam as if he was an old friend, not an old foe. 'It was surprising that I was received most warmly by a group which I had opposed for many years. They saw in me a saviour for South African sport and one who was going to lead them out of the wilderness.' By the time he boarded the plane for Brazzaville (Congo), du Plessis was hailing him as a 'hero' who had 'given South Africans a new vision of the road ahead'.

Ramsamy could have had no illusions of the problems that lay ahead. On paper there were four well-matched multi-sport organizations in South Africa: the predominantly white Confederation of South African Sport (COSAS) and the South African National Olympic Committee (SANOC), and the non-racial or black bodies of the NSC and SACOS. But while the black bodies knew something about the white officials, the whites were mostly ignorant about their black counterparts.

Ramsamy found Willie Basson, President of COSAS, 'progressive and genuine' but not in complete control of the 108 affiliates (one of them, the athletics body, was still organizing rebel tours). Also when COSAS said it accepted a moratorium on international tours, it meant no rebel tours – but it was keen on official tours, such as the ones rugby had organized until the mid–1980s. SANOC, which in the past had inflicted Reg Honey and Frank Braun on the world of sport, now had some good affiliates, but 'others displayed paternalistic and racial attitudes and arrogantly felt that their approach was correct'. SACOS did not merely want apartheid eradicated: it insisted that there should be 'no international sports exchange until all historical racial imbalances have been rectified'. For Ramsamy this meeting with his old friends in SACOS could not have been easy. Their president, Joe Ebrahim, had said one meeting could not 'sort out the bad blood that has developed'; and when Ramsamy met Dannie Craven's rugby body SACOS held demonstrations outside Ramsamy's hotel, condemning him for speaking to such 'racist' bodies. Craven proved as irascible as ever. Before he met Ramsamy he told reporters that he would not be telling him what his rugby board had done to normalize sport because 'he [Ramsamy] should know'. As far as he was concerned, de Klerk's reforms meant that everything Ramsamy had asked for had been done.

Despite this and other difficulties, Ramsamy's report was optimistic, echoing the NSC's position. It did not say how or when South Africa should be readmitted but there were hints that Ramsamy was beginning to think that it was time to rethink the sports boycott.

From Johannesburg, Ramsamy flew to Brazzaville to meet Jean Claude Ganga, the supremo of African sport. Ramsamy's next stop, in early September, was the fourth International Conference Against Apartheid in Stockholm. Muleleki George and Mthobi Tyamzashe were there and, of course, Juan Antonio Samaranch. There were hints in George's and Samaranch's speeches of the compromise that might come, and Ramsamy emphasized that South Africa's readmission to the international fold was a question of when, not whether, it would happen. However, the best that could be hoped for seemed to be that South Africa would compete in the 1996 Olympics.

Indeed, the conference tried its best to dampen speculation of immediate success. The London *Daily Telegraph* headlined its report of the conference, 'Time not yet ripe to reward S. Africa'. The Stockholm Statement Against Apartheid Sport urged all countries to 'tighten the boycott against apartheid sports' until the people of South Africa gave the call. And there were arguments, such as those presented in the *Telegraph* by John Lawrence, which urged that for that to happen, 'apartheid must be wholly abolished, and be seen and proved to be abolished, before South African sport can be readmitted to world sport. Like a cancerous growth, if apartheid is not completely eradicated from all aspects of South African life, then like cancer itself, it will once again grow, and destroy. For one cannot cure cancer by cutting out only the more visible parts of it.'

At this time of course, nothing fundamental had changed in South Africa. Mandela had been released and the ANC unbanned but this was no more than a return to the situation just before the massacre at Sharpeville: the laws that under-pinned apartheid were still in force. De Klerk had promised to abolish them but had not yet done so, and as far as the sports world, conditioned by the slogan 'no normal sport in an abnormal society', was concerned, abolition of apartheid meant not only removal of such laws but the enactment of one man, one vote. But is this what Tshwete had in mind when he spoke of the abolition of apartheid in his keynote address at the launch of the NSC? Or Ramsamy?

The first indication that sports administrators were not linking their demand so directly to a political change came when Ganga called a meeting on South Africa at Harare on 3 and 4 November. Back in August, on the evening of his arrival at Johannesburg, Ramsamy had chaired a meeting between the executive committees of SANOC and NSC which led to the setting up of a five-man committee to examine future problems. Ganga's November conference in Harare was a more elaborate, formal version of this. It was, if you like, the sports equivalent of the national convention that the ANC had been demanding for many years to solve the country's political problems. For the first time all the main South African sports bodies were there: SACOS, NSC, COSAS, SANOC and, of course, SANROC. Each brought one representative of their affiliated Olympic code. It was the first time that sports leaders from all the white and black bodies had met in this fashion, and the first time they all acknowledged that the road forward lay through continental Africa.

At the suggestion of the black Africans a co-ordinating committee made up of two representatives from each of the five organizations was set up – 'an unholy alliance' Ramsamy called it, but a necessary one: 'we had to start somewhere.' That decision recognized that it would not be possible for the IOC, or any other international sports body, merely to readmit the white body that had been suspended or expelled, as some whites fondly hoped: in each case a new body representing the 'new' South Africa would have to be formed.

In January 1991 Ramsamy ended his 18-year-exile in England and returned to Johannesburg. He did it in style, taking up temporary residence in the prestigious Carlton Hotel in the centre of town. One of the first to contact him was Ali Bacher. Now abandoning the gospel of rebel tours and preaching unity and development, Bacher invited Ramsamy to lunch at the Wanderers. 'It was an historic lunch. It was historic in that I was coming back to South Africa and that it was the first time I had been to the Wanderers Club. We were both aware of the fact that not much earlier blacks would not have been allowed in as members of the club. I began to realize that Ali and I had a lot of things in common, although we were representing two different constituencies.'

In a sense both needed each other. For Bacher, Ramsamy

as an ally meant he was reaching out to the man who had symbolized the sports boycott to the international community. For Ramsamy, aware that to the enemies he already had on the right he was also adding some new ones on the left, Bacher represented a bridge to the progressive whites in the sporting community he needed to reach. The two men quickly established a personal rapport.

'After I set up offices at the Carlton it was getting rather expensive sending faxes, telephones, etc, and Ali was extraordinarily generous. He said, "Sam, come and work here." He gave me one of his secretaries and I used Ali's main office for the two days of the week when Ali worked from home. I had the use of his duplicator, the typist, the fax machine, the lot – and he never charged me a single penny. So in many ways Ali played a part in the formation of the National Olympic Committee of South Africa, and I don't think NOCSA will ever forget it.'

On 12 January 1991 the President of the Zimbabwe Olympic Committee, an executive member of the African Sports Group, called a meeting of the co-ordinating committee that had been formed in Harare by Ganga. Ramsamy was unanimously elected its President, and South Africa was launched on the road to the Olympics. On 9 March Ramsamy and his committee flew to Gaborone in Botswana to meet with Ganga and his colleagues. Here it was that all the five sports bodies agreed to form a single national Olympic sports body, and it was announced that, once the apartheid laws were abolished, South Africa could apply for readmission to the Olympic games. The co-ordinating committee was given a new name: the Interim National Olympic Committee of South Africa (INOCSA).

There were still problems. The white-controlled COSAS, which had its own idea of what the sports moratorium should be, said its affiliates were autonomous and could not be told when and whom to play at international level. For a time it seemed there would be yet another split but eventually COSAS toed the line. Three weeks after the Botswana meeting, Ramsamy, as President of INOCSA, played host to the first IOC delegation to visit South Africa since the one led by Lord Killanin in 1967. The 1991 delegation was headed by a Senegalese judge, Keba Mbaye, Vice-President of the IOC and Chairman of the Apartheid and Olympics Commission. Also present were Ganga, Major-General Henry Edmund Olufeni Adefope and the great American hurdler Edwin Moses. The only IOC member who had no connection with Africa was Kevan Gosper, the delegate from Australia.

Mbaye's commission laid down the steps by which South Africa could return to the Olympic movement. It declared that 'recognition be granted to INOCSA on condition that apartheid be abolished and that INOCSA be speedily formed into a permanent, democratically elected body complying in its structure and actions with the Olympic Charter, having as members unified non-racial codes of Olympic sports'. In other words, the moratorium still applied, but if everything went well, if de Klerk abolished the laws of apartheid as he had promised he would, South Africa might even be back for the 1992 Olympics. Ten days after the commission left South Africa, Roger Heywood of the London *Daily Telegraph*, in a quite gushing piece on Ramsamy, reckoned that he had six months in which to prove to the IOC 'that South Africa deserves a place in the Olympic Games in Barcelona next year'.

Few even in South Africa could keep up with the pace of change. It was barely six months since Ramsamy's first visit in August 1990 but already the time span of South Africa's return had shortened by four years. Then Ramsamy's talk of a return by 1996 had sounded hopeful, if over-optimistic; now even 1992 did not seem soon enough. Ramsamy admits 'things moved very quickly' and praises the foresight of Ganga, Samaranch and Mbaye:

'They said, "Look, we have to be one step ahead of the rest of the world. We know what's coming. Sport can play a very important role. It can be the catalyst for developing non-racialism. It can be the catalyst for developing an amicable political settlement, and most importantly we have to start in sport now because we need a development programme to address the inequities of the past." ' Samaranch's desire to have South Africa back in time for the 1992 Olympics was also intensified by the fact that the Games were being held in his home town of Barcelona. It would mean the Olympic family would be complete for the first time.

But the spur for such speed was the fact that Ramsamy, Samaranch and everyone else in sports were feeling the hot breath of the politicians. In the past, as we have seen, politicians had been only reluctantly drawn by anti-apartheid activists to support the sports boycott. Following de Klerk's speech, John Major and Bob Hawke started making noises suggesting that in order to 'reward' de Klerk the sports boycott should be lifted. They feared a white backlash to the proposed changes and thought this could be neutralized by removing the sports boycott. That would make the whites, famous for their love of sports, feel that it was worth reforming the political system. In urging such action, these politicians showed their love of sport to be sentimental and politically expedient and their grasp of South African realities to be feeble. With a fight going on between 'now-ers' and 'not quite-yetters' there was, warned the *Guardian*'s Matthew Engel, the danger of 'John Major and Bob Hawke encouraging white sports officials to break out of the talks with their black counterparts and start organizing boycott-busting tours on their own . . . the best thing other Prime Ministers can do right now is to shut up.'

As the politicians fretted, Ramsamy and his colleagues had been thinking up their own compromise – one that would satisfy the whites yet make it acceptable to the blacks. In the discussions that had begun the previous August and continued ever since, Ramsamy and his allies in the NSC wrestled with what became known as the Zimbabwe syndrome. Interestingly it was also the example Chris Day, Bacher's friend, had cited to me in 1989. This was that, despite the fact that Zimbabwe had been free for over 10 years, its sports structure had hardly changed since the days of Ian Smith's racist regime. 'We didn't want that to happen in South Africa. We knew what we wanted, we knew what the white South Africans wanted. They wanted international competition. The blacks wanted a development programme which would provide them opportunities and facilities to come up to where the whites are. If we wait for a political settlement, what happens? Once a settlement comes, white South Africa will get international competition. In the new South Africa with one man, one vote, everyone is equal – so there is not going to be a development programme. In other words, once you get a political settlement, how are you going to persuade the white sportsmen to have a development programme? In Zimbabwe, with the exception of boxing, athletics, soccer and a little bit of cricket, there is hardly any integration in sports. In Namibia, with the odd exception it is an all-white set-up.

'We didn't want that. We wanted an integrated set-up and we wanted to force parity. I believe this is the time to force integration, to effect development. In the new South Africa the Government will have new priorities of social welfare: they are going to worry about education, housing, social status, not about building sports facilities. So we decided there should be a compromise: the blacks would let the whites have international competition and the whites would provide facilities and opportunities for black development in sport. It is this compromise that is working its way through South African sports.'

In a sense Ramsamy and his friends in the NSC and the ANC had taken the carrots and stick argument which had so long been favoured by many white South Africans and devised their own version. Long before de Klerk's speech, whites had been insisting that they had learnt from the boycott and isolation and that it was time the carrot of international competition should be given to them. Ramsamy's version of the carrot metaphor was shrewder and more equitable.

Cricket should have provided the best example of this approach. But while on the surface the unity talks were proceeding well, there was still some tension and one big unresolved problem. This exploded during the talks held on 20 April at the Holiday Inn, near Johannesburg airport. This had been billed as a formal talk with the various committees and provincial representatives gathered to report back on how unity was proceeding at the local level. The date for unity, June 1991, had been set and Bacher was preparing an elaborate banquet at which the guest speakers would include E. W. Swanton, Sir Gary Sobers and Richie Benaud. But just as the delegates were breaking for lunch there was a hiccough. Dakin told Mackerdhuj that his side felt the proposed new united body's executive should be a merger of the existing executives of the two bodies, with Dakin acting as the first President. Since Dakin's executive had 10 members and Mackerdhuj's seven this would have given the old white body an automatic majority. Mackerdhuj saw it as 'a power play' and for the next four hours, while the provincial representatives kicked their heels in the conference room, the two executives met in an upstairs suite and argued.

Mackerdhuj's cricket body wanted the new executive to have an equal number of representatives from the two old organizations, and since Dakin could not see how he could drop three of his members, a compromise was worked out which enabled Mackerdhuj to increase his executive to 10 members. Mackerdhuj had no objection to becoming Dakin's Vice-President, but he proposed that in the second year their positions should be reversed with Mackerdhuj becoming president and Dakin Vice-President.

As these internal problems were being solved the bigger problem was that, unlike the Olympic Games, there was no formal pathway laid down for South African cricket to come back into the fold. There was no Samaranch heading the ICC, and the early indications were not favourable. In March 1991 Colin Cowdrey had rung Bacher and told him the best he could offer was that the ICC would meet the united cricket board informally after its annual meeting in July, have a chat and get to know Bacher and his people. 'No way,' replied an angry Bacher. 'We are not coming for a cup of tea at Lord's. We are going for a full application.'

After all that was happening in South Africa, Cowdrey's tea and sympathy would take him no further forward then in the days of isolation. Cowdrey's call was made from Barbados, where he was consulting with Clyde Walcott, head of the West Indies Board. The West Indies, along with Indian and Pakistan, had been firm opponents of white South Africa and the call made Bacher realize he had to launch his own diplomatic offensive to enlist support. It was now that he became aware of the ANC's power.

That same month Bacher travelled to Harare with Steve Tshwete to meet the High Commissioners of India and Pakistan to establish some initial contact. Bacher returned very hopeful with both the High Commissioners polite and courteous. Bacher had also been in regular touch with David Richards, chief executive of the Australian board. Richards was then negotiating with India over India's proposed tour to Australia in the winter of 1991, and he put Bacher in touch with Jagmohan Dalmiya, Secretary of the Indian board. Bacher, who can use the phone like an extension of his own self, rang an astonished Dalmiya in Calcutta. Dalmiya's first words were, 'I didn't know you could ring India from South Africa.' But the two struck up an instant rapport. Between that first call in April and the ICC meeting in July, Bacher made about 40 calls to Dalmiya, so by the time they met in London in July they both felt they knew each other intimately.

In April Bacher had also met Thabo Mbeki, now back in South Africa and living in Johannesburg's once-white enclave of Mayfair, which was fast becoming a haven for well-off, well-connected non-whites. Also at the meeting were Gerald Mogise, a high official in the ANC's military wing, and Essot Pahad, a key member of the Communist party. 'They said,' recalls Bacher, 'I should go with Steve to London, and gave me a letter to take with me.' The letter said South Africa should be readmitted to international cricket and that the ANC backed such readmission.

Cowdrey, however, was still obdurate. Technically, it was too late to have South Africa's readmission placed on the ICC agenda as the time limit for the inclusion of the item had long gone. Bacher had consulted lawyers about this and they advised him that legally the chances were not good. But where the law could not reach, the ANC could, as Bacher was to discover. Nelson Mandela, in one of his chats with John Major, had raised the question of cricket. De Klerk had also spoken to Major, and Bacher now urged the South African Foreign Ministry to try to move things. A day later he got a call to say it had been done. The South African Government had spoken to Major who, in turn, rang Cowdrey to suggest that perhaps the item could, somehow, be considered by the ICC even if it was not on the agenda. Cowdrey accepted the plan. So just as South Africa's expulsion had never involved a formal ICC process, its readmission would, in a way, be through the back door.

Bacher was now in London doing the rounds of the cricket and diplomatic world with Tshwete. It was this visit that was to cement their relationship and prove the power of the ANC. In one two-hour drive to Birmingham he told Bacher about his solitary confinement. 'His first 24 hours took an hour to narrate. When we got to Edgbaston I felt sick.' Having met the Indians and Pakistanis in Harare, Bacher and Tshwete now concentrated in London on the ambassadors from New Zealand, Sri Lanka and the West Indies. 'For those five days Steve went from pillar to post speaking softly and trying to persuade these High Commissioners. I shall never forget going to see the High Commissioner of Guyana. As we entered, I saw a photographs of Fidel Castro. I thought, "Shit, we've got no bloody price here." But that meeting made me realize the power of the ANC. When I had met Thabo I had asked him about the views of the PAC [Pan-African Congress] and the other organizations. In

London, not even the Guyanese asked about them. The High Commissioner said, "Look, you asked us to boycott South Africa and we did. Now you are asking us to go and play with it. Do you mean to say things have changed?" Steve said, very softly, "Yes" – and that was it.'

Finally, there was a little local difficulty with Lord Griffiths, then President of the MCC. Tshwete had accompanied Bacher to Lord's, probably the first time an ANC military figure had entered the hallowed portals. After Tshwete had explained why the ANC and Mandela were supporting the South African application, Lord Griffiths said: 'Look, all this sounds very good. But I really think, to help your case even further, a letter from Buthelezi would really complete the whole presentation.' To hear from someone like Griffiths the name of the man who was the great enemy of the ANC and whose armed gangs were continuing a campaign of indiscriminate killings in the townships was too much for Tshwete. He nearly went through the roof, and after a few minutes Lord Griffiths turned to Cowdrey and said, 'Mr Chairman, in retrospect I don't think it was such a good suggestion.'

By June everything in the cricket garden seemed lovely. Nothing illustrated this better than that when Sunil Gavaskar flew into Jan Smuts for the unity banquet he was met at the airport by Bacher and Ramsamy, who then chaired a joint airport press conference to welcome the great cricketer in a symbolic moment of reconciliation. Just as significant was the presence at the unification dinner of Walter Sisulu and his wife Albertina, a prominent leader of the ANC women's wing. Just before the dinner Bacher had taken Gary Sobers and Gavaskar to Soweto, where, as they played with the black kids, Bacher was hailed as 'Comrade Ali'. Mandela invited Sobers and Gavaskar to his plush Soweto home, where he reminisced about his days watching cricket from behind the cages and expressed warm appreciation of the township programme.

The ICC was to meet at Lord's on 10 July to vote on a

resolution proposing South Africa's readmission to international cricket. And such was Bacher's friendship with Dalmiya that India, the most resolute enemy of apartheid sport, had agreed to propose the motion of readmission. But just as Bacher arrived in London for the meeting, things suddenly started to go wrong. Personally Bacher was at a low ebb, his mother Rose having died a few days earlier. With the ICC meetings on a Wednesday, Bacher had arrived in London the previous Friday hoping for some good news. Instead, the next day Dalmiya rang from the apartment he had hired in London for the duration of the meeting to tell him that news from India was, quite unexpectedly, bad. Many in India, Dalmiya told Bacher, were questioning his strategy of proposing South Africa for membership – it was too sudden a switch from their hitherto staunchest opposition to South Africa. 'They are saying, what the hell are you doing proposing them?'

Dalmiya added that he was also under pressure from the West Indies and Pakistan. The West Indies did not like the idea of a resolution being proposed after the agenda had been decided. In June Mandela had visited the Caribbean and had endorsed the proposal of South Africa's return at the meeting of the West Indies leaders held in Jamaica. Presided over by Michael Manley, the Jamaican Prime Minister, the Caribbean leaders were not entirely convinced but nobody dared question Mandela. However, recalls Sir 'Sonny' Ramphal, Secretary-General of the Commonwealth, who was present, their ambivalence was reflected in the fact that the West Indies decided to sit on the fence. Pakistan, partly irked by India's sponsorship, was very lukewarm. All this left Dalmiya exposed. 'Ali,' he pleaded, 'you've got to do something. You'd better get somebody to talk to Scindia' (Mahadav Rao Scindia, President of the Indian board, who had not come to London).

That somebody would have to be Tshwete. But he was still busy with the first-ever formal gathering of the ANC in Durban, which was bringing together the exiles and the internal members in a historic meeting. He could get to London only on the Monday morning, and even that involved some tricky travel arrangements. No sooner had Tshwete arrived than Bacher rang Scindia in India. 'I did not know Scindia, although Cowdrey had mentioned his name. I introduced myself. I spoke to him for about 20 minutes, explaining who I was. Then I said I had got somebody from the ANC to talk to him, and gave the phone to Steve.'

Tshwete spoke for about 15 minutes, and it was one of the most nerve-racking 15 minutes Bacher had ever spent. Then he put the phone down and, coming over to Bacher, put his arms on his shoulders and said: 'Don't worry about it. It has been done.' Half an hour later Bacher's phone rang. It was Dalmiya who said: 'Well done! Scindia has instructed me to propose South Africa.'

There was still opposition from Pakistan, who in a meeting with Tshwete kept saying that his statements were contradicted by others. An exasperated Tshwete finally said, 'We are the best doctors in the South African situation.' Sam Ramsamy was also at hand to lend assistance. He was on his way to Lausanne, where the IOC was meeting on 9 July to consider South Africa's application to rejoin the Olympic movement. He met several of the Caribbean High Commissioners, as well as Ramphal, in London, assuring them that he and Bacher were speaking with one voice.

At the meeting in Switzerland the IOC admitted INOSCA, which immediately dropped the 'I' and became the National Olympic Committee of South Africa. The break with SACOS was now complete, that organization having withdrawn from INOCSA and refusing to go to Lausanne.

The next day, 10 July, there was a slight hitch at the ICC. Chaotic as ever, the organization had managed to lose its copies of the constitution of the new South African united cricket board. Fresh copies had to be faxed from Johannesburg on the morning of the meeting. In the end it all came right, with India proposing and Australia seconding the resolution. Clyde Walcott expressed reservations about voting on a resolution that was not on the agenda, but Cowdrey ruled it was in order. Walcott did not formally oppose it but abstained, reflecting the doubts felt in the Caribbean at the speed of the whole thing and evidently not happy with the way Cowdrey had handled it. Mackerdhuj, Dakin, Bacher and Tshwete linked arms and posed at Lord's, and at a celebration dinner Ramsamy joined them as an honoured guest.

Even now it did not follow that South Africa would immediately be back in international competition. Cowdrey, partly in order to placate the West Indies, had ruled out South African participation in the 1992 World Cup. But Australia were very keen, and then quite by chance Nelson Mandela intervened. In August Clive Lloyd visited South Africa, mainly to have a look at the township programme. Bacher took him to meet Mandela at the ANC's headquarters at Shell House in central Johannesburg. A Swedish delegation was also due to see Mandela and the international media had gathered for that. When they saw Lloyd with Mandela they sensed a good story, and one journalist asked Mandela: 'What about the World Cup? Should South Africa be playing in it?' Mandela replied, 'The World Cup? Yes, South Africa should be in the World Cup, why not?'

That made the headlines. Then the Sri Lankan minister Tyroon Fernando got into the act. After a phone conversation with Bacher he proposed a special ICC meeting in Sharjah (UAE) in October to discuss the issue. Cowdrey agreed, but declined to take the ICC Secretary Lt-Col John Stephenson along on the interesting grounds that the ICC could not afford two air fares. Dalmiya was by now out of power in Indian cricket and Bacher had to deal with Scindia, who was much more cautious, more of a politician. South Africa in the World Cup was, he felt, going too fast, too soon. Derek Murray represented the West Indies and came with a mandate not to support the motion. But, urged on by World Cup hosts Australia, who wanted South Africa for the money it would bring, the ICC agreed and even Murray ended up backing South Africa's participation.

As we have seen, it was following this decision that Bacher and company went to India and found themselves suddenly, quite magically, returning to international sport. By this time everybody was welcoming South Africa. In October, the week before the ICC meeting in Sharjah, the Commonwealth Prime Ministers' Conference took place at Harare and agreed that the boycott should be lifted on a sport by sport basis. On 6 November, as the cricketers prepared to leave for India, the National Sports and Olympic Congress announced that it had decided to accept the IOC invitation to participate in the 1992 Olympic Games.

It was not an easy decision. The NSC had held a special general meeting in Johannesburg on 26 October, then another on 2 November, before announcing the decision. There was not merely the question of the sports boycott, although that was tricky enough. South Africa still had a white minority Government, apartheid was still in operation, and the Olympic Games were an occasion for flag waving. But what flag should South African sportsmen carry in Barcelona. And what anthem would be sung if they won a gold medal?

The NSC could hardly accept the flag of a white Government whose repression of non-whites was so painfully evident. The South African flag – an amalgam of the Union Jack and the Boer republic flags – is meant to represent the Dutch and English races: blacks and browns have no place on it. Similarly, 'Die Stem', the national anthem, was also very much an Afrikaner anthem. It was decided that the flag would be a specially designed one of blue, red and green with a grey diamond-shaped background representing the country's wealth and the other colours representing the sea, the land and the crops. Should South Africa win a gold medal then Beethoven's 'Ode to Joy', from the last movement of the Choral Symphony, which was also the Olympic hymn, would be played. The decision provoked a storm of protest from the Government, with de Klerk personally castigating Ramsamy.

Even today many whites do not understand why the flag and the anthem should be rejected, and such feelings were to become even more pronounced when, in the summer of 1992, an official All Blacks team played a Test in Johannesburg. It showed that, for all the talk of the new South Africa, the old one was not that easily eradicated. It required another IOC delegation to visit the country before Barcelona could be negotiated. But by this time Ramsamy had led South Africa back, marching under the flag he had designed and the new sporting South Africa was well and truly born. It demonstrated that here was a country in which the ANC, having no political power and whose members did not even have the basic rights of citizenship, were the effective arbiters of its sporting destiny. South Africa had indeed had a remarkable metamorphosis.

In the process South Africans, blacks and whites, have been discovering each other as never before. This had been vividly brought home on that hurriedly arranged trip to India in November 1991. The last time we saw them they were waiting at Gate 5, Jan Smuts airport, for the plane to Calcutta.

As the plane touched down at Calcutta airport, Hoosen looked out of the window and felt a sense of dread. All he could see was milling throngs of people. 'Oh, no,' he thought, 'not another protest against South Africa.' In fact this was a welcome party, perhaps the largest and grandest welcome any cricket team has ever received. And this from hosts who had never played them, had never even seen them before.

Calcutta is a city of *hujuk*, a Bengali word which means sudden enthusiasm, a city of contradictions where, amidst much-photographed poverty and degradation, there is perhaps the cleanest and best-kept underground railway in the world. That day the city opened its heart to the South Africans: women in saris applied *tilak*, a red mark, to the foreheads of the South Africans, each of whom was garlanded with flowers and had petals thrown at them. Then the visitors

were escorted to the city in a cavalcade accompanied by
more than 100 motorcyclists. At almost every step of the
15-mile journey huge, cheering crowds held up banners of
welcome; twice the motorcade stopped for speeches from
Bacher, Dalmiya and others. By the time the South Africans
arrived in the centre of Calcutta they were quite overwhelmed.

Ewie Cronje had boarded the plane never having met any
Indians socially. He had become friendly with Alvin Kallicharran when the Guyanan played cricket for Orange Free
State, and there had been the odd Indian ball boys he had
come across when playing tennis in Durban. Now he was
just overwhelmed by the reception. 'That will be a lasting
impression, the highlight of my life. We were treated like
kings.' At the end of the tour Richard Snell, one of the white
players, had turned to Hoosen and said, 'Eek man, it took
me to go to India to realize how warm the Indians were.'
He needed only to have driven a few miles out of the white
northern suburbs of Johannesburg to Lenasia to have discovered that quality in his own countrymen.

For the South Africans of Indian origins on that trip the
experiences were just as profound but different. The poverty
in the streets of Calcutta had reduced Hoosen to tears. As
an official of the South African board he wanted South Africa
to win, but he also wanted the Indians to show they could
play cricket. The Indians of South Africa, long derided as
collies, desperately needed their compatriots to do well.
Watching the Indian cricketers in the nets Hoosen could not
see how these brown, frail-looking figures could compete
against the heavy, muscular white South African. To him the
Indian team looked like school kids. He turned to Jimmy
Cook, one of the South African opening batsmen, and said,
'This looks like a team from Lenasia. You will beat them
easily.' The next day it was the Indians who beat the South
Africans easily, deflating much of the arrogance with which
the white South Africans had entered the fray.

In the two and half years since that Calcutta trip South

African cricket and sport has come a long way. In the South African summer of 1992, when they entertained the Indians, the South African officials kept apologizing that their hospitality could not match that shown to them in India. In fact, it was on a grand scale. The Indians suffered no racial harassment on the tour, and at least one of their officials compared the cricket situation in South Africa favourably with that in Zimbabwe, a country that had been free for over 10 years, yet whose sports organizations were much more racist than that of the 'new' South Africans.

This is not to underestimate the problems that remain. On the day the South African cricket team, having reached the semi-finals of the World Cup, returned to a glittering reception in Johannesburg. Hoosen was among the many officials to receive them. Afterwards, when he got back to his car, he was approached by two Afrikaner bully boys. Seeing his pro-West Indian T-shirt the Afrikaners asked him who he supported. When he replied West Indies, they set on him, and the next day he arrived in the office with a black eye.

Yet the very same World Cup had shown the part sports could play in the new South Africa. De Klerk, under pressure form the white right, to whom he had lost a couple of parliamentary by-elections, decided to hold a referendum amongst the white electorate as to whether to continue with the reform process. The voting coincided with South African participation in the cricket World Cup and de Klerk and his supporters shrewdly exploited this to get a 'yes' vote. One of the advertisements used during the campaign showed a deserted and overgrown cricket field with broken wickets, contrasting that with a picture of the South African cricketers celebrating their victory over Australia at the start of the competition. The advertisement read: 'Without reform South Africa hasn't got a sporting chance. Vote yes on March 17 and keep South Africa in the sporting game.'

The message, as Adrian Guelke says, was that a 'no' vote would mean the return to sporting isolation, while 'yes' would mean that the reward the whites had got for starting

the reform process would continue. The whites voted over-
whelmingly for reform, with a very high turnout of English
voters.

It was perhaps fortunate that the referendum coincided
with a cricket World Cup and not a rugby one. The rugby
authorities have still not fully put their house in order. By
contrast, Bacher has so shrewdly arranged the South African
cricket calendar that this summer her players tour England
– having already played Tests with India, West Indies and
Sri Lanka – countries white South Africa had shunned during
the long reign of white supremacy.

The progress of South African sport has been such that
this summer they were admitted to the Commonwealth
Games, to be held in Victoria, Canada. South Africa last
played in the Games in 1958. The readmission indicated the
acceptance of South African sport, despite the fact that there
is still no definite indication that the political nation will
rejoin the Commonwealth. Sport, having once been a symbol
of opposition to South Africa, was now leading it places it
had rarely been before.

The magnitude of the part played by the sporting boycott
in the dismantling of apartheid is debatable. Even at the
height of the boycott white South Africans continued to
compete at international levels in many sports, notably golf,
tennis, motor racing and professional boxing. There can be
no doubt, however, that the boycott made many whites,
particularly the more politically aware young ones, feel like
pariahs. And while the sport boycott may not have unravel-
led apartheid – the economic sanctions enforced mainly by
the Americans from 1986 undoubtedly played a greater part
– the sports boycott brought revolutionary changes to the
organization of sport in South Africa. Some of the most
obdurate white supremacists among the sports administrators were obliged to amend their racist image or be forced
from office. And overall, of course, the campaign reminded
not only white sportsmen and officials but also the politicians
of every persuasion that the ANC could exercise overwhelm-

ing political power even without resorting to force. It remains to be seen whether the political and cultural transformations crucial to South Africa's erratic passage to democracy and justice for all can be carried through with as little turmoil.

Index

245